"With his characteristic mastery of th   erly
compelling conclusions, Paul Barnet   trials of Jesus in their historical context   ical,
religious, and social elements that underpin the Gospels' portrayals of these
pivotal moments in human history. I highly recommend it as a book deserving
of careful study and reflection."

—**Constantine R. Campbell**
professor of biblical studies
Sydney College of Divinity

"Respected senior scholar Paul Barnett sets Jesus's trials in an informatively
wider sociopolitical context than is typical in other discussions. The book is
eminently readable and finds cohesiveness in the ancient evidence."

—**Craig S. Keener**
F. M. and Ada Thompson Professor of Biblical Studies
Asbury Theological Seminary

"Paul Barnett's detailed study of the historical and cultural background and
the individual characters of the trial narratives is both fascinating and enlight-
ening. The information provided by the trials serves as a window into the
meaning and historical significance of the crucifixion, relating it not only to
the history preceding it, but also to the history that follows it, in the birth
of the church. I know of no other book that provides such a brilliant and
helpful synthesis."

—**Donald A. Hagner**
George Eldon Ladd Professor Emeritus of New Testament
Fuller Theological Seminary

"Paul Barnett is a serious and experienced scholar and ancient historian. The
latter training comes to the fore in this book, which sheds clear light on the
historical background to the life, trial, and death of Jesus."

—**Alanna Nobbs**
professor emerita
Macquarie University

"This volume provides a sweeping backdrop to the context of Jesus's ministry,
arrest, and trials. Deeply informative, accessible, and fascinating, Barnett tells

the story not just about Jesus, but about all of Israel's history leading to the climactic finale of the messiah's death."

—**Gary M. Burge**
adjunct professor of New Testament
Calvin Theological Seminary

"Informed by a deep grasp of the history, cultural forces, and major players (political and religious) leading up to Jesus's public appearance in the late AD 20s, this book is a gamechanger for making sense of many New Testament complexities and crosscurrents. Best of all, it accounts for how 'a culture of hatred of Jesus' (Barnett's words) saw his death kick-start what became the largest religion in the world today. This is the best short book on the subject from this angle that I have ever read."

—**Robert W. Yarbrough**
professor of New Testament
Covenant Theological Seminary

"Here we have another 'classic Barnett': a historical investigation combined with theological considerations, a consistent focus on the biblical and relevant extrabiblical texts, and a refreshing refusal to engage with (and drown in) secondary literature. The general reader will benefit immensely from reading Barnett's latest study of Jesus and the early church."

—**Eckhard J. Schnabel**
Mary F. Rockefeller Distinguished Professor of New Testament
Gordon-Conwell Theological Seminary

THE
TRIALS
OF
JESUS

Evidence, Conclusions,
and Aftermath

PAUL BARNETT

WILLIAM B. EERDMANS PUBLISHING COMPANY
GRAND RAPIDS, MICHIGAN

Wm. B. Eerdmans Publishing Co.
4035 Park East Court SE, Grand Rapids, Michigan 49546
www.eerdmans.com

Book design by Lydia Hall

Printed in the United States of America

30 29 28 27 26 25 24   1 2 3 4 5 6 7

ISBN 978-0-8028-8433-6

Library of Congress Cataloging-in-Publication Data

A catalog record for this book is available from the Library of Congress.

For Justice Ken Handley AO, KC

CONTENTS

THE NIGHT HE "WAS BETRAYED"

The world's oldest Christian liturgy was created by Jesus "on the night he was betrayed" but reformulated as a third-person narrative by his disciples soon after the first Easter. Jesus's remembrance meal of bread and wine became the central rite from the beginning of earliest Christianity.

The Eucharist memorialized the last night of Jesus. It was a night like no other. The young prophet was betrayed by one of his disciples, denied by their spokesman, and deserted by the rest. Arrested, he was brought to Annas, the senior high priest, who interrogated him and had him beaten. Next, he was sent to the incumbent high priest, Caiaphas, for trial by "all the chief priests and the elders and the scribes," at the conclusion of which he was again beaten, this time severely. The Gospels then record Jesus being interrogated twice by Pilate, being "scourged" after the first and "flogged" after the second.

The Gospels offer bare accounts of what happened but offer no commentary on Jesus's emotions or physical reaction to the extremity of suffering of that night. Worse was to follow, crucifixion.

The Night of the Trials of Jesus: 14/15 Nissan (April) 33

About midnight	The arrest of Jesus	Mark 14:43–50
		John 18:1–12
Midnight to daybreak	Jesus before Annas	John 18:13, 19–24
	Jesus before Caiaphas	John 18:24, 28

	Trial before Caiaphas and Sanhedrin	Mark 14:53–65
Daybreak (6 a.m.)	After consultation involving chief priests, elders, and scribes, they deliver Jesus to Pilate	Mark 15:1
Sunrise	Trial before Pilate	Mark 15:2–15
	Inquiry by Herod Antipas	Luke 23:6–16
	Trial before Pilate	John 18:28–19:16
9 a.m.–noon	Procession to Golgotha and crucifixion	Mark 15:20–39
3 p.m.	The death of Jesus	

By all accounts, the events of that night are complex and call for explanation. Why, for example, was it necessary for interrogations by *two* high priests, and what was their relationship? If Jesus was condemned by the supreme Jewish council, why must Jesus also appear before the Roman governor, and why twice? Why did the tetrarch of Galilee also interrogate Jesus? How can we explain the Jewish authority's capacity to dictate the outcome of the trial that was led by the all-powerful Roman governor?

Answers to these questions will emerge as we reflect on the remote and immediate settings for the Gospels.

THE REMOTE BACKGROUND TO THESE EVENTS

Some might think turning the last page of Old Testament history to the first page of New Testament history entails reading one continuous story. In fact, several hundred years separated the history of the last kings of Israel and the narratives about Jesus, including his arrest, trials, and death.

The remote background to the narratives about Jesus is critically important. Aramaic, one of the two major languages spoken by Jesus, was introduced to the Jews in the Persian era following the Jews' return to their homeland.[1] The other, Koine Greek, entered the Jewish world following Alexander's conquests in the fourth century, as Israel became a vassal state, first of the Ptolemies of Alexandria, then of the Seleucids of Antioch. By Jesus's time, Greek appears to have been more widely spoken and written than Aramaic.

1. The Jews' return from Babylon to Yehud (Judea) occurred 520–515 BC.

In 165 BC the outbreak of law-based "zeal" delivered the Jews from the power of aggressive Greek religious culture of the Antioch-based Seleucids. Under the Maccabean dynasties (165–37 BC) the Jews managed to preserve their law-based integrity, while also reconnecting Galilee, Samaria, and Idumea with Judea as one political entity ruled by their kings. The inclusion of Idumea, however, provided the intrusive pathway to power in Judea, first by Antipater, and then by his son Herod the "Great." The Roman Pompey's invasion in 63 BC presaged the inevitable Roman political control of the entire Levant. The united forces of Romans led by Mark Antony and Herod in 40 BC overwhelmed the last of the Maccabean dynasts and paved the way for the beginning of Herod's uncontested reign from 37 to 4 BC.

Herod ruled a united realm surrounded by compliant city-states. Although outwardly "Jewish," as signaled by the vast temple in Jerusalem, Herod's world was politically Roman and culturally and linguistically Greek. Jesus of Nazareth was born in Bethlehem in the last several years of Herod's life. Despite writing no fewer than seven wills, Herod was unable to identify a son able to rule an undivided kingdom. In 4 BC, following Herod's death, Caesar Augustus endorsed a tripartite division of the kingdom.

THE IMMEDIATE SETTING

Herod's passing marked the beginning of the immediate setting for the advent of Jesus, his trials and death, and the birth of the church. Herod's son Archelaus failed as ruler (*ethnarch*) of Judea and was exiled in AD 6 by Caesar Augustus, who took the momentous step of making Judea a Roman province, now to be ruled by a military governor (called a "prefect"). Worse from the viewpoint of the Judeans was the introduction of a personal tax to be paid to the Roman Caesar. The census beforehand and the imposition of the tax provoked a serious uprising led by Judas the Galilean (a.k.a. Gaulanite) and Saddok, a Pharisee. According to Josephus, this insurrection was the spark that lit the numerous outbreaks of civil disturbance during the next six decades, issuing in Vespasian's invasion of the Holy Land in 66, which ended four years later with the destruction of the Holy City and the holy place.

In AD 6 the Romans relocated the capital of Judea from Jerusalem to Caesarea Maritima. Among other consequences of this act, the Sanhedrin and high priest became more directly powerful in the administration of the Holy City. The high priest was now, in effect, a "client" ruler, governing the city and beyond on behalf of the Roman prefect. Critically, however, only Caesar's appointed prefect had the *ius gladii*, "the right of the sword," the *imperium* bestowed by Caesar to execute capital punishment.

Shortly after the creation of the province, the Romans appointed Annas high priest. Following his lengthy tenure, he was succeeded by his son-in-law Caiaphas, who also ruled Jerusalem for many years. Several of the five sons of Annas also held the office of high priest during the following years. Significant for our study was the stranglehold of Annas (high priest AD 6–15) and Caiaphas (high priest 18–36) that overarched the appearance of Jesus, his trials and execution, and the birth of the church. Our argument will be that Jesus represented a critical threat to the Annas-Caiaphas joint pontificate. However, it was not in their interests to be held responsible for the death of Jesus, a popular prophet. Far better, they appeared to have reasoned, for the hated Roman occupiers to be blamed.

Critical to the unfolding of events in Judea was the moving of the tectonic plates in Rome. Tiberius succeeded Augustus in 14, but by 26 he had wearied of the constant demands of the imperial office and instead took up residence on the island of Capri, offshore from Naples, from which he did not return to Rome. He had appointed Sejanus as Praetorian prefect in 14, whom he now tasked with administering both Rome and the empire. In 26 Sejanus appointed Pontius Pilate as prefect of Judea, whereupon he took up residence in Caesarea Maritima.

Soon after his appointment, Pilate would have become aware of the popular prophet John the Baptist, who was active in Perea, the territory on the eastern side of the Jordan that belonged to the tetrarchy of Galilee. Herod Antipas secured the arrest of John, his imprisonment in the fortress Machaerus,[2] and later his execution. Beforehand, an even more popular prophet arose in Galilee, Jesus of Nazareth. Pilate would have known of his exploits and his practice of making pilgrim journeys to Jerusalem.

Jewish writers Philo and Josephus are severely critical of Pilate for his treatment of the people of Judea, and later of the Samaritans. In the year 31 Tiberius secured the execution of Sejanus and, moreover, wrote to his governors advising positive policies toward his Jewish subjects. Pilate's position in Judea

---

2. Machaerus (Greek *machaira*), meaning sword, was constructed by Herod near the east side of the Dead Sea, opposite Masada. Under Herod Antipas it served as a frontier bastion against the Nabateans as well as a prison. Its remote location removed the popular prophet John from the public eye.

was now less secure, which the high priests Annas and Caiaphas understood and exploited during Pilate's trials of Jesus.

THE TRIALS OF JESUS AND THE GOSPEL OF LUKE

Earlier, at a critical point in his narrative, Luke locates the beginning of John the Baptist's preaching to "the fifteenth year of Tiberius's rule" (i.e., 28/29) when Pontius Pilate was governor of Judea, when Herod (Antipas) was tetrarch of Galilee, during the high priesthood of Annas and Caiaphas. Jesus's baptism, which marked the beginning of his ministry, probably occurred within two years of John's preaching.[3]

There were three jurisdictions in which Jesus had become active: Galilee (ruled by Herod the tetrarch), Jerusalem (ruled by the high priest Annas and his son-in-law Caiaphas), and Judea (ruled by the Roman governor, Pontius Pilate).

It appears that Luke "framed" the ministry of Jesus between two poles, commencing with the named leaders in those three jurisdictions and concluding with interrogations by these "judges" on that fateful night—*Annas* the high priest, *Caiaphas* the high priest, *Herod* the tetrarch, and *Pontius Pilate* the Roman governor. The greater part of Luke's narrative of Jesus falls between Luke 3:1–2 and 22:66–23:16.

This book is focused on these four men—Annas, Caiaphas, Herod the tetrarch, and Pontius Pilate—and the one they "judged," Jesus of Nazareth.

THE JEWISH AND ROMAN TRIALS

Trials occupy an important place in modern democratic societies. Most people are aware of "the presumption of innocence" for the accused, that the "burden of proof" rests with the state through an independent judiciary, and that the verdict must be "beyond reasonable doubt." In short, the justice system in criminal cases provides strong protection for the accused individual.

The Gospels record a Jewish trial and two Roman trials, likely connected. It is clear from these texts that the accused man, Jesus, did not enjoy the protection and rights expected in liberal democracies.

---

3. Jesus's public ministry proper began after John's imprisonment and occupied several annual visits to feasts in Jerusalem, dating the Passover of death to AD 33.

The Sanhedrin Trial

The Sanhedrin trial, however, did reveal the necessity for the evidence of at least two witnesses, based on Deuteronomy 19:15: "A single witness shall not suffice against a person for any crime or for any wrong in connection with any offense that he has committed. Only on the evidence of two witnesses or of three witnesses shall a charge be established."[4] While the trial of Jesus was in keeping with Deuteronomy, the application was flawed; the witnesses were dishonest and did not agree.[5]

Authorities suggest that the Sanhedrin trial was hurried and did not follow the requirements set out in the Mishnah tractate Sanhedrin. Nevertheless, some of its requirements in capital cases should be noted; it is unlikely that the major articles of Sanhedrin procedure would have been overturned in the trial of Jesus.

The trial of a false prophet or the high priest must be conducted by the court of one and seventy;[6] we note that the high priest was not above the law.[7] A verdict of acquittal could be reached by a majority of one, whereas a verdict of condemnation required a majority of two.[8] The tractate names those ineligible to be witnesses: kinsmen of the accused, friends or enemies of the accused, and those who pursued dishonest trades.[9] If the trial found the accused guilty, his sentence was to be held over to the following day,[10] a provision ignored in the Sanhedrin trial of Jesus.

The high priests Annas and Caiaphas were determined to be rid of Jesus quickly, and by the hands of the Romans.[11]

---

4. Unless otherwise indicated, all Scripture references come from the English Standard Version. The Deuteronomy provision reappears in the New Testament regarding trials within churches (Matt. 18:16; John 7:51; 8:17; 2 Cor. 13:1; 1 Tim. 5:19; Heb. 10:28) and later became a pillar in the justice systems within democracies.

5. According to m. Sanhedrin 5.2, if witnesses contradict one another, whether during the inquiries or the cross-examination, their evidence becomes invalid. Witnesses were proved by questioning: In what week of the year? In what month? On what date of the month? On what day? In what hour? In what place?

6. m. Sanhedrin 1.5.

7. m. Sanhedrin 2.1.

8. m. Sanhedrin 1.6.

9. m. Sanhedrin 2.3, 4.

10. m. Sanhedrin 5.5.

11. The Jews said to Pilate, "It is not lawful for us to put anyone to death"

The Roman Trial

The procedures of the Roman trial were different. Pilate, acting in his role as judge, jury, and executioner, began by asking the temple authorities, "What accusation (*katēgoria*) do you bring against this man?" (John 18:29), to which the chief priests charged that Jesus claimed to be "King of the Jews" (18:33). After detailed inquiry, Pilate declared, "I find no guilt (*aitia*) in him" (19:6).

Pilate took Jesus's silence to be disrespectful: "You will not speak to me? Do you not know that I have authority (*exousia*, Latin *imperium*) to release you and authority to crucify (*staurōsai*) you?" (19:10). The prefect declared his verdict from the "judgement seat" (*bēma*) (19:13).[12] The accused was either released or punished, depending on the prefect's decision.

Josephus provides some details of a trial conducted by the Roman procurator Gessius Florus (64–66) in Jerusalem.[13] "Florus lodged at [Herod's] Palace, and on the following day had a tribunal (*bēma*) placed in front of the building and took his seat; the chief priests, the nobles and the most eminent citizens then presented themselves before the tribunal. [These] implored a pardon for the individuals who had acted disrespectfully."[14] In this case, Florus's rejection of the pleas for acquittal issued in a major disturbance, with many being killed.

This brief narrative mentions the "tribunal" on which the procurator/judge was seated and those who, in this incident, argued for the pardon of the accused.

The "separation of powers" is fundamental to democratic government. This, however, was foreign to Roman administration. The Caesar imparted full authority for capital punishment (the *ius gladii*, the "right of the sword") to the governor. This was the extension of Caesar's all-powerful rule to his provincial appointee.[15]

(John 18:31). This is consistent with Josephus's observation that only a prefect appointed by Caesar had *ius gladii*, "the right of the sword."

12. See also Acts 18:12; cf. 2 Cor. 5:10.

13. See Acts 18:12 for Gallio's trial of Paul in Corinth.

14. Josephus, *Jewish War* 2.301–304.

15. Josephus, *Jewish War* 2.117; *Jewish Antiquities* 18.2.

The Two Trials

The gospel accounts recognize the differences between the Sanhedrin trial and the Roman trial. The former was executed on behalf of the Sanhedrin, with particular emphasis on the veracity of at least two independent witnesses. The Roman trial was conducted by the single figure of the prefect (on behalf of the Caesar), who heard the accusation and then canvassed negative and positive evidence against the accused before reaching his verdict.

It is difficult to escape the conclusion that Pilate found Jesus to be innocent of the charge and sought to release him. Critical to Pilate's judgment was that Jesus was not supported by an army; he was no pretender-king. Pilate judged Jesus to be innocent but succumbed to the pressure of the high priest to declare Jesus guilty and order his crucifixion.

On the other hand, however, the high priest was determined that Pilate indict Jesus come what may. Caiaphas's was the greater guilt.

The Mishnah tractate Sanhedrin identified numerous laws for a just trial, but these were mostly ignored. Both Caiaphas and Pilate were guilty of the mistrial of Jesus, but Caiaphas's culpability was the greater.

THE MYSTERY OF THE BIRTH OF THE CHURCH

It comes as a surprise that immediately following the death of their teacher the disciples began remembering him weekly in the simple but evocative rite, the Lord's Supper (Acts 2:42). We might have expected the disciples to have begun memorializing him months, even years, after the events of that night.

Consistent with this, but no less surprising, was the immediate birth of the church and the faith it held to and proclaimed. As early as circa AD 34, a mere year following the fateful Passover, Paul, now a believer, recorded his earlier attempt to destroy the church of God and its faith (Gal. 1:13, 23).

Furthermore, the book of Acts records numerous and extended accounts of the apostles' message as delivered in the Holy City. The mystery is how these men, in the days and weeks immediately following the death of their teacher, were able to proclaim the extended message about him so soon, and with such assurance.

It is worth noting that religious and political movements in the provinces tended to dissipate once the Romans had killed their leaders. During the Roman occupation of Judea, from AD 6 to 66, numerous minor uprisings led by rebel leaders and prophets spawned movements that disappeared with the deaths of their various leaders.[16] One exception was the birth of Christianity and its rapid subsequent growth, first in Palestine and then within the wider empire.

We are correct in thinking that the judges of Jesus—Annas, Caiaphas, Herod Antipas, and Pontius Pilate—assumed that the removal of the prophet from Galilee would spell the end of his movement, an oddball collection of fishermen, peasants, a "zealot," and a toll collector.

The radical earliness of the birth of the church is a matter of record and must have surprised the political leadership of those times.

The explanation for the earliness of the apostles' preaching is to be found three years earlier. Each gospel makes it clear that soon after his baptism Jesus "called" twelve men to be "with" him, to become his disciples (Mark 3:14). For them this involved hearing their master, like a prophet, publicly proclaiming the advent of the kingdom of God and disputing with the Pharisees over the application of the law. In private with them, however, like a rabbi, he explained the meaning of his public discourses. It is useful to distinguish the exoteric and esoteric teachings of Jesus.

Jesus's extended didactic setting explains how the disciples readily and *immediately* were able to proclaim Jesus's message in the Holy City, and beyond. It means, in effect, that the disciples' formulation of their message and the birth of the church were coterminous, and historically early.

Despite expectations, the trials and execution of Jesus by crucifixion did not spell the end of his influence, but, on the contrary, they explained its continuation and growth. Critical, however, was the disciples' conviction that their tried and crucified leader had been raised alive from the dead.

CONCLUSION

On that night Jesus was denied repeatedly by Peter, subjected to harrowing interrogation and terrible repeated beatings prior to the horrors of crucifixion. Between them, the four Gospels describe what happened but say little about the emotional or physical pain that the young prophet endured that night and the next day. It fell to Paul, although not a witness, to speak of "the sufferings of Christ" (2 Cor. 1:5; Phil. 3:10; Col. 1:24).

16. The dynasty of Ezekias in Galilee is another important, if mystifying, exception (see p. 71).

The various interrogations and trials of that night call for explanations. Why were Annas, Caiaphas, Pontius Pilate, and Herod Antipas involved? If Jesus was guilty of blasphemy, as the high priests believed, why didn't they seek Pilate's permission to have the culprit stoned to death? Pilate, a cruel man by all accounts, was unconvinced that Jesus was a pretender-king. He was unwilling to convict Jesus for crucifixion, but why did he allow himself to be bullied by the priests to execute Jesus that way?

These and other questions will be the subject of inquiry in the following pages.

Part 1

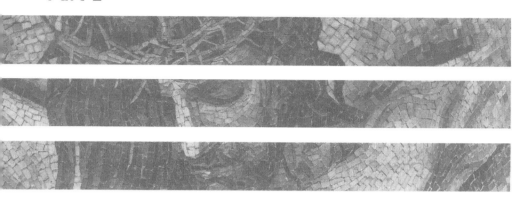

THE DYNASTIC
BACKGROUND

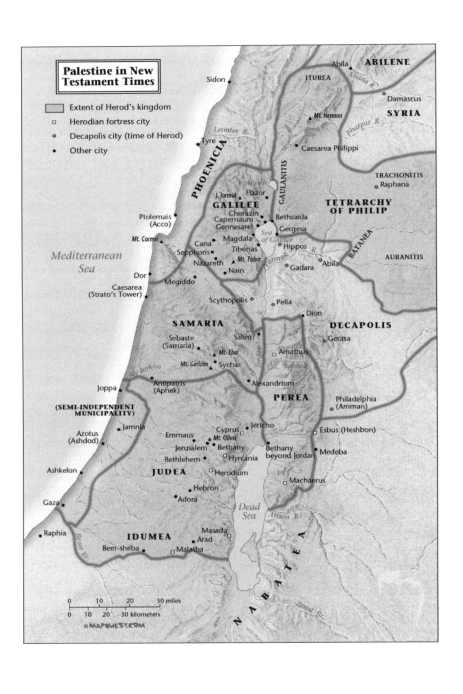

Palestine in New Testament Times

Extent of Herod's kingdom
□ Herodian fortress city
○ Decapolis city (time of Herod)
• Other city

ABILENE
Abila
ITUREA
Sidon
Damascus
Mt. Hermon
SYRIA
Leontes R.
Pharpar R.
Tyre
Caesarea Philippi
PHOENICIA
TRACHONITIS
Raphana
GAULANITIS
Huleh
J. Jarmuk Hazor
GALILEE
Chorazin
Bethsaida
TETRARCHY
OF PHILIP
Ptolemais
(Acco)
Capernaum
Gennesaret
Gergesa
Sea of Galilee
Mt. Carmel
Cana Magdala
Hippos
BATANEA
Sepphoris
Tiberias
AURANITIS
Kishon
Nazareth Mt. Tabor
Yarmuk R.
Abila
Nain
Gadara
Dor
Megiddo
Caesarea
(Strato's Tower)
Scythopolis
Pella
Dion
Mediterranean
Sea
SAMARIA
DECAPOLIS
Sebaste
(Samaria)
Salim?
Gerasa
Mt. Ebal
Amathus
Jordan R.
Jabbok
Mt. Gerizim Sychar
R. Jarkon
Alexandrium
Joppa
Antipatris
(Aphek)
PEREA
Philadelphia
(Amman)
(SEMI-INDEPENDENT
MUNICIPALITY)
Cyprus Jericho
Esbus (Heshbon)
Jamnia
Emmaus Mt. Olivet
Azotus
(Ashdod)
Jerusalem Bethany
Bethany
beyond Jordan
Medeba
Bethlehem Hyrcania
Ashkelon
JUDEA
Herodium
Machaerus
Hebron
Gaza
Adora
Dead
Sea
Arnon R.
Raphia
IDUMEA
Masada
Beer-sheba
Arad
Malatha
NABATEA
Besor Br.
Zered Br.

0   10   20   30 miles
0   10   20   30 kilometers
©MAPQUEST.COM

THE PERSIANS

(539–331 BC)

In 587 BC the invading Babylonians destroyed the temple in Jerusalem and deported the most prominent Jews to exile in Babylon.

The misery of the exiles can still be heard in this lament.

> By the waters of Babylon,
>   there we sat down and wept,
>   when we remembered Zion.
> On the willows there
>   we hung up our lyres.
> For there our captors
>   required of us songs,
> and our tormentors, mirth, saying,
>   "Sing us one of the songs of Zion!"
> How shall we sing the LORD's song
>   in a foreign land?
> If I forget you, O Jerusalem,
>   let my right hand forget its skill!
> Let my tongue stick to the roof of my mouth,
>   if I do not remember you,
>   if I do not set Jerusalem
>   above my highest joy! (Ps. 137:1–6)

The sense of loss and heartache comes down through the centuries in these words.

RETURN TO JERUSALEM BECOMES A REALITY

However, thanks to the rise of a new empire in 539 BC, their longing for a return to Jerusalem became a reality after seventy years. In that year Cyrus the Great invaded parts of a divided Babylonian Empire and declared himself king. The new Persian Empire, the greatest ever up to that time, continued until 331 BC. Included within that empire was the tiny province of Judah, homeland of the exiled Jews, now to be known as *Yahud*.

The significance for God's covenant people was remarkable. If the exile in Babylon had continued indefinitely, it is almost certain that the deportees would have been eventually assimilated into Babylonian religion and culture. Furthermore, those Judeans who remained in the Southern Kingdom would have progressively intermarried with local Arabs and Samaritans. A continuing Babylonian Empire would have spelled the end of Jewish religious and cultural identity.

The advent of the Persian Empire was the instrument of Israel's survival.

The Persian epoch deserves to be better known. It extended for two centuries, and its leaders took a more permissive attitude to the Lord's people than had the Babylonians or the Assyrians before them. Our historical sources for the Persians are numerous. They include biblical texts (Esther, Ezra, Nehemiah, Haggai, Zechariah, [Deutero-] Isaiah, Joel, Malachi, the books of Chronicles), references by Herodotus in the *Histories* and by Xenophon in the *Anabasis*, and archaeological artifacts like the justly famous Cyrus cylinder.

The Cyrus cylinder was created after Cyrus's conquest of the neo-Babylonian empire and its incorporation into the new Persian Empire. Crafted in clay and couched in the language of political propaganda, the cylinder denounced the defeated Nabonidus, asserted Cyrus's choice by the god Marduk, and celebrated the king's generosity in repatriating captive peoples.

However, the cylinder makes no reference to the Jews or Judah. Nevertheless, the words of Ezra the scribe leave no doubt about Cyrus's concerns for the repatriation of the exiled people back to their homeland, Judah. These are Ezra's first words, recording as they do Cyrus's decision that the temple of the Lord in Jerusalem be rebuilt and that Jews be allowed to return to their land.

In the first year of Cyrus king of Persia, that the word of the Lord by the mouth of Jeremiah might be fulfilled, the Lord stirred up the spirit of Cyrus king of Persia, so that he made a proclamation throughout all his kingdom and also put it in writing: "Thus says Cyrus king of Persia: The Lord, the God of heaven, has given me all the kingdoms of the earth, and he has charged me to build him a house at Jerusalem, which is in Judah. Whoever is among you of all his people, may his God be with him, and let him go up to Jerusalem, which is in Judah, and rebuild the house of the Lord, the God of Israel—he is the God who is in Jerusalem." (Ezra 1:1–3)

The prophet Isaiah makes remarkable reference by name to Cyrus, the Lord's "messiah."

> Thus says the Lord to his *anointed*, to Cyrus,
>   whose right hand I have grasped,
> to subdue nations before him
>   and to loose the belts of kings,
> to open doors before him
>   that gates may not be closed. (Isa. 45:1; see also 44:26, 28)

Ezra reported that, led by Zerubbabel, many exiles returned to Jerusalem and Judah, each to his own town (Ezra 2:1). There were 42,360 such people gathered from the towns and villages of Babylon. Those who returned to Jerusalem built an altar and offered the sacrifices to the Lord. However, the foundations of the temple had not yet been laid. Under the leadership of Zerubbabel, the faithful people commenced construction of the foundations of the house of the Lord. But such was the local opposition that King Artaxerxes ordered the work to cease (Ezra 4:23).

Once the first group left Babylon, Ezra set about researching lineages and compiling detailed family lists of his people. By the time Ezra departed from Babylon for Jerusalem some years later, he had established the genealogy of every Jewish family in Babylon.

Only with the advent of a new ruler, Darius, whose servants retrieved a copy of Cyrus's original decree, did work on the temple recommence (Ezra 4:24). The prophets Haggai and Zechariah directed the people to resume the construction of the temple. The temple was duly rebuilt and dedicated in the sixth year of the reign of Darius.

EZRA'S DISTURBING DISCOVERY

It was in the reign of Darius's successor Artaxerxes I that Ezra the scribe was sent to Jerusalem. Ezra was leader of a second wave returning to the Holy Land. There were only 1,500 people in all. During his sojourn in Jerusalem Ezra made a disturbing discovery: "Officials approached me and said, 'The people of Israel and the priests and the Levites have not separated themselves from the peoples of the lands with their abominations, from the Canaanites, the Hittites, the Perizzites, the Jebusites, the Ammonites, the Moabites, the Egyptians, and the Amorites. For they have taken some of their daughters to be wives for themselves and for their sons, so that the holy race has mixed itself with the peoples of the lands. And in this faithlessness the hand of the officials and chief men has been foremost'" (Ezra 9:1–2).

The people assembled by Ezra confessed their sins, which included marrying non-Jews. Ezra publicly called on Jewish men who had taken foreign wives to divorce them; those who failed to do so would forfeit their property and be banned from attending the sacred assembly. The book of Ezra ends with the list of men who had married foreign women but makes no reference to those who divorced such women.

In 465 BC Nehemiah, cupbearer to Artaxerxes, received a message that "the wall of Jerusalem is broken down, and its gates are destroyed by fire" (Neh. 1:3). Nehemiah, upon requesting permission of the king, set out from Susa for Jerusalem with the mission to rebuild the walls of Jerusalem and thereby provide security for the Lord's people, who were exposed to the depredations of hostile Samaritans, Ammonites, Arabs, and Philistines. Nehemiah arrived in Jerusalem about twenty years after Ezra's final visit. He served as Artaxerxes's governor in Judah for twelve years, quickly rebuilding the walls of the city and then repopulating it with residents of pure Jewish stock by demanding that the men divorce their foreign wives.

Given the hostility of other kingdoms to the Lord's elect people, it is a mystery why successive Persian kings viewed them so favorably. Why did later Persian kings Darius and his son Xerxes repeatedly attack mainland Greeks whereas earlier Persian rulers displayed practical mercy to the people of Judah and their cult center, Jerusalem? The prophet Isaiah and the Jewish leaders Ezra and Nehemiah were in no doubt. The Lord had moved the Persian leaders to do his will.

A clue may be found in Herodotus's observation that the Persians did not sacrifice to graven images of the gods but offered their sacrifices directly to the sky above.[1] Did the Persians believe that their nonsacrificial worship of gods somehow made the aniconic Jews their cousins?

For at least four reasons, the Persian era was critical to the formation of the Judaism that was the religious and social setting for the trials of Jesus of Nazareth. First, Ezra and Nehemiah restored the centrality of the law of Moses in the public life of the people. The great prophets had repeatedly recalled the people to the law. Under Ezra and Nehemiah, the law was codified in a new, deeper, and permanent way.

The decisive leadership of Ezra the scribe became a pattern for others in the years to come. During the Hasmonean years there evolved law-based leaders known as Hasideans ("holy ones") who became active supporters of Mattathias, founder of a new dynasty: "Then there were gathered unto them [Mattathias and fellow Hasmonean leaders] a company of the Chasidim, mighty men of Israel, who willingly offered themselves to the Law" (1 Macc. 2:42).

There is an absence of evidence between the Persian era and the outbreak of the Hasmonean (a.k.a. Maccabean) revolt against the Seleucids of Syria in 165 BC. It is likely, however, that the Hasidim belonged to the tradition begun by Ezra the scribe. At the same time, it is likely that the Hasidim formed a bridge to the scribes and Pharisees who are so important in the era of Jesus and his trials.

The second reason the Persian era was so critical to the formation of the Judaism of Jesus's day is that the systematic and decisive actions of Ezra and Nehemiah recovered the racial purity of the descendants of Abraham. The genealogies recorded by the Gospels of Matthew and Luke indicate that biological descent from the patriarchs was of critical importance at the time of Jesus. The genealogies in Matthew and Luke may have depended on the labors of Ezra centuries earlier.

Third, the concerns of Cyrus and successive Persian kings that Jerusalem and its sacred place be restored were critically important for the consolidation of the religious identity of the people. True, Zerubbabel's temple was unimpressive. Yet its very existence was a necessary precursor for the magnificent cult center begun by Herod the "Great" circa 20 BC and which had been substantially completed by the time of Jesus's ministry.

Fourth, the Persians facilitated the dissemination of Aramaic as the common tongue of the Jews in Palestine. The origin of the language is attributed to Arameans, an ancient people from Mesopotamia. Although Aramaic was

---

1. Herodotus, *The Histories* 1.132 (translation Tom Holland).

but one of the languages of the Persian Empire, it became the language of the Jewish people in their homeland.

This is strikingly confirmed by the appearance of Aramaic words in the Gospel of Mark—place-names (e.g., *Akeldama, Bethzatha, Gabbatha, Golgotha*), surnames (e.g., *Cephas, Boanerges*), words in common use (e.g., *korban, messias, cananaean, hosanna, pascha, rabbi, satanas*), and words spoken by Jesus during his ministry (e.g., *amēn, mammōn, raka, talitha cumi, ephthatha, abba*). Most significant of all was Jesus's poignant quotation of Psalm 22 spoken from the cross just a few hours after his death sentence by Pilate, *Eloi Eloi lema sabachthani*. These were not the Hebrew words of that psalm but an Aramaic version, the language bestowed on the Jews by the Persians.

These Aramaisms embedded in the Greek Gospel of Mark support the view that under the Persians Aramaic became widely used in Galilee and Judea in the time of Jesus. Mark, and his mentor, Peter, were evidently familiar with the Aramaic language.

Josephus, a propagandist and apologist writing in the early 70s, confirmed that Aramaic was "the language of our country" (Judea). He sent his *Jewish War*, written in Aramaic, to people of "Parthia, Babylonia, and Arabia and the Jewish Dispersion in Mesopotamia and the inhabitants of Adiabene," that is, to dispersed Arameans in what had been the Persian Empire.[2]

In Rome, Josephus determined to translate the Aramaic text of his *Jewish War* into the Greek tongue "for the sake of such as live under the government of the Romans."[3] Josephus's Greek text of the *Jewish War* has survived, but its precursor, the Aramaic version, has not.

The pre-Damascus Paul, a Pharisee, referred to his "former life in Judaism" in which he said he was "advancing . . . beyond many" of his own age (Gal. 1:13–14). By this he meant such study of and commitment to the law of Moses that would be expressed in violent action toward those he deemed to have departed from its pathways.

The violent, law-based "Judaism" referred to by Paul had its origins in Persia several centuries earlier through the law-based activism of Ezra and Nehemiah. They were the antecedents of the Pharisee movement that played such a critical part in the opposition to Jesus. The pharisaic mission to impose the law of God on everybody in the Holy Land exposed the nonconformity of

2. Josephus, *Jewish War* 1.6.
3. Josephus, *Jewish War* 1.3.

those whom the Pharisees called "sinners," a despised underclass who lived by "despised" trades, notably tax collectors and prostitutes. Jesus's "friendship" with these "outsiders" predefined him negatively as he faced Caiaphas and the members of the Sanhedrin.

That hostility created a culture of hatred of Jesus that provided the setting for his arrest, trials, and crucifixion.

3

HELLENISM

In the fourth century BC, in a series of brilliant military victories, Alexander the Great, king of Macedonia, conquered the vast Persian Empire. In the years following Alexander's death in 323 BC, the generals, his so-called successors (the *diadochoi*), repeatedly fought over and divided up the former Persian Empire. Israel was under direct Greek rule from 301 to 165 BC.

Throughout those many years Israel was surrounded by and ruled by Hellenism and permeated and penetrated by Hellenism. Roman power—when it arrived in 63 BC—was imposed from above, but Hellenism also seeped in from all sides, potentially corrupting the people and their leaders from within. Although Christianity was born in the era of Roman hegemony, the language and cultural background against which the new movement is most helpfully understood are not Roman but Greek.

THE PTOLEMAIC CENTURY (301–200 BC)

Little Israel lay between the most powerful of these new kingdoms, Egypt to the south and Syria to the north. From 301 to 200 Israel was subject to the control of the Ptolemies in Egypt (whose capital was Alexandria), and, broadly speaking, from 200 until 165 she lay within the realm of the Seleucid dynasty in Syria (capital, Antioch).

334–323 BC	Alexander conquers the Persian Empire
323–301 BC	Wars between Alexander's "successors"
301–200 BC	Ptolemaic dynasty controls Israel
200–165 BC	Seleucid dynasty controls Israel

The Ptolemies were a dynasty based on the intermarriage of the Egyptian pharaohs and the conquering Greeks. They were a Greco-Egyptian empire based in Alexandria. The first new ruler was Ptolemy, who gave his name to the kingdom and empire he founded. Palestine was geographically and administratively part of that empire, becoming an administrative extension of Egypt.

In Palestine, as in Egypt proper, the Ptolemies created major administrative units that they called *hyparchies*. The hyparchies Gaulanitis, Galilaia, Samaraia, Judaia, Peraia, and Idumaia continued under those names into New Testament times. Each hyparchy was presided over by a *hyparch*, "underruler." The hyparchies were further subdivided into toparchies, each led by a *toparch*, "ruler of a place." Within the toparchies were the *kōmai*, "towns," each subject to a *kōmarch*, "town ruler."

The Ptolemies created a vast bureaucratic structure covering the lands of their empire. Although after a century Palestine passed out of Ptolemaic control, many of the administrative units remained in place during the subsequent centuries, even after the Romans arrived in 63 BC. The larger units became subject to differing regimes, some under the Romans (Judea, Samaria, Idumea), others under Herodian rulers (Galilee and Perea).

The gospel writers do not mention toparchies, but their contemporary Josephus names thirteen in Judea and more generally refers to them in the territories of Gamala, Gaulanitis, Batanea, and Trachonitis.[1] In the course of their travels, Jesus and his disciples would have crossed the many boundaries of the toparchies in Galilee, Samaria, and Judea.

The Ptolemies recognized the political power of high priests, whether in Jerusalem or Mount Gerizim (in Samaria). To provide a counterbalance to the potential political influence of high priests, the Ptolemies created a Senate (*Gerousia*), a "council of elders," for each principality. We may have thought that the Sanhedrin, as it came to be called, developed within the covenantal history of Israel. The body that passed judgment on Jesus on "the night he was handed over" was not of Jewish origin but was created by the Hellenistic

1. Josephus, *Jewish War* 3.53–56. Also, Pliny, *Natural History* 5.70.

Greco-Egyptian rulers in Alexandria. Their *Gerousia* was a critical expression of Hellenism at the heart of Judaism.

The Macedonian newcomers were quickly influenced by the divinely sanctioned king-centered culture of Egypt. Following the practice of the pharaohs, the Ptolemaic rulers claimed ownership of most of the land, which was worked by locals on a rental basis. This was a radical break from earlier covenantal practices that allowed ordinary Israelites to own land and pass it on to their heirs.

Many plantations newly established on the king's lands were devoted to cultivating crops like grains, papyrus, dyes, and balsam for international export trade. The Greco-Egyptian king had state monopolies on the production of oil, various cloths, metals, salt, and spices.

The conquering Greeks brought with them various technologies like the waterwheel for irrigation, the treadmill for grinding grain, the iron plow, the oil press, and the winepress. Hellenism changed patterns of land ownership, farming, and trade, effecting nothing less than an agricultural revolution in Israel during the Ptolemaic period.

The Ptolemies tended to administer their subjects through wealthy and aristocratic Jews such as the members of the *Gerousia*, senior bureaucrats, large-estate owners, businessmen, and tax contractors. By the time of Jesus and his trials, the agricultural and economic worlds of Galilee and Judea had changed for the worse for the covenantal people. The rich became richer and the poor poorer.

Each of the four judges of Jesus was a man of power, whether Caiaphas, the high priest and head of the Sanhedrin; his father-in-law, Annas; Herod Antipas, the ruler of Galilee-Perea; or Pontius Pilate, the military governor of Judea. Jesus of Nazareth stood before each of them in turn as a poor, powerless, friendless, betrayed man.

Of great significance was the introduction of the Greek language to the Holy Land during the century of Ptolemaic rule. It was a simplified form of Greek known as Koine ("common") Greek, which was becoming the *lingua franca* of the eastern Mediterranean. In the new cities of the East, various academies and schools arose, teaching Greek philosophy, history, mathematics, literature, and science—all in Koine.

The Ptolemaic epoch witnessed the beginning of the hellenization of Israel, a process that continued and grew through the next three centuries. By the time of Jesus, we are confident that Greek was even more widespread than

Aramaic. The Greek in which the four Gospels are written implies that Jesus taught extensively in Greek. It is all but certain that the judges of Jesus—Annas, Caiaphas, Antipas, Pilate—interviewed Jesus in Koine Greek.

Ambitious Jews who looked to Alexandria for acquiring greater wealth and power had no alternative but to learn this language. Jews of the upper echelons not only loved Koine but they also came to love things Greek, including Greek religion and philosophy.

Herondas, a Jew of the period, referred in rapturous terms to Ptolemaic Egypt.

> For all there is and will be, can be found in Egypt,
> Riches, stadiums, power, fine weather,
> Reputation, theatres, philosophers, gold, young men,
> The sanctuary of the kindred gods, the king,
> A just one, the museum, wine, every good thing,
> Whatever you want, and women.[2]

Indeed, only those Jews who learned and loved the language and culture of Greece had any future, economically and politically speaking. Those who lacked the skills of Hellenism were conscious of their disadvantage. A voice from the period complained about promised wages withheld by his masters: "They have seen that I am a barbarian . . . [and] that I do not know how to live like a Greek [*hellenizein*]."[3] It was a clear disadvantage not to know Koine or the ways of Greek thinking.

THE "EXTREME OF HELLENIZATION"

The century of Ptolemaic rule ended in defeat in 200 BC at the Battle of Paneion, the cult center of the god Pan, later renamed Caesarea Philippi. Under the Seleucid victor Antiochus III, life in Israel continued much the same as it had in the previous century when the Ptolemies ruled.

This was to change dramatically with the advent of his son Antiochus IV in 175 BC. Upon taking office, Antiochus was confronted with repayment of crushing debts owed to the Romans that had been incurred by his father. This was

2. Quoted in Martin Hengel, *Judaism and Hellenism*, 2 vols. (London: SCM, 1973), 1:37.
3. Quoted in Hengel, *Judaism and Hellenism*, 1:39.

made worse by the loss of tribute-paying territories in the north and east of the Seleucid empire. Antiochus was forced to take desperate measures to find money wherever he could. He turned his attention to the treasures located in various temples within his realm, including the temple of the Lord in Jerusalem.

In 174 BC Antiochus removed the conservative high priest Onias III and replaced him with his hellenizing brother, Jason. Under Jason the treasures of the temple were pillaged for the king and overtly Greek practices introduced. Young Jewish men began wearing distinctively Greek clothing. Greek-style male athletic competitions began to be held in Jerusalem. As in the worlds of the Greeks, the competitors (males) were naked, and efforts were made to obscure their circumcision. "There was such an extreme of Hellenization and increase in the adoption of foreign ways because of the surpassing wickedness of Jason, who was ungodly and no high priest" (2 Macc. 4:13).

Things came to a head after 168 BC when Antiochus was ignominiously defeated in Egypt. He was angered to find some people of Israel who remained loyal to the Ptolemies, their previous masters. Events swiftly took their course. Antiochus IV abolished Jerusalem as a city-state and renamed it New Antioch.

During the years 168–167 BC Antiochus began demolishing the walls of the city. He appointed yet another high priest, Menelaus, a convinced hellenizer, who had outbribed Jason for the office, and who was the first high priest not to have descended from Zadok the priest. Under Menelaus services in the temple were discontinued and copies of the Sacred Scriptures destroyed. Circumcision was forbidden and covenantal food laws abolished. In climax an altar to Zeus was installed in the temple and unclean animals (pigs) sacrificed upon it. Altars to Greco-Syrian deities were set up throughout Israel and local people were required to offer sacrifice. It would now be a capital offense to circumcise a son, possess a scroll of scripture, or refuse to eat swine sacrificed on a local altar.

> Behold our holy place, our beauty
> and our glory have been laid waste;
> the Gentiles have profaned it. (1 Macc. 2:12)

It is likely that these hellenizing actions were not solely religious in intent but motivated by political concerns to break the spirit of the Jewish people and make them compliant members of the Seleucid kingdom.

This proved to be an unsuccessful policy. As we shall see, the Jews staged a revolt and managed to establish a discrete Jewish kingdom based on the Hasmonean (Maccabean) dynasty. However, the influence of Hellenism that began in 301 BC was unstoppable. The members of the Hasmonean family proved to be affected by Hellenism in its many forms.

Of great importance was the continuing expansion of interest in the Greek language. The Hasmoneans employed Greek in the administration of their kingdom. High priests, bureaucrats, merchants, and traders were Greek speaking. The two books 1 and 2 Maccabees, which chronicled the Hasmonean revolt, were written in Greek.

The Aramaic language bequeathed to Israel from the Persians was now progressively overlaid by Koine Greek.[4] Both languages were current in the era of Jesus, although there was probably an uneven presence of one over the other. Furthermore, the less well educated may have been limited to speaking but not writing these languages.

By the era of the New Testament, both Aramaic and Greek were spoken in the land of Israel. Jesus taught in both languages, depending on the local circumstances. Greek, however, became the more prominent. Jesus taught primarily in Greek, and his teachings were recorded in the Greek of the Gospels.

4. Martin Hengel, *The "Hellenization" of Judaea in the First Century after Christ* (London: SCM, 1989), 7–8.

"ZEAL" FOR THE LORD

(165 BC)

The great majority of the Jewish people were passively appalled by the assaults on their religious heritage and their freedom to worship whom they chose. There were, however, two groups who opposed the gentiles' attempt to compromise their faith.

"ZEAL" IN THE TIME OF ANTIOCHUS

One such group were the Hasideans ("holy ones"), who probably arose in the time of the Persians. They opposed Antiochus's attack on the law of God and were cut down because they would not fight on the Sabbath: "For they said, 'Let us all die in our innocence; heaven and earth testify for us that you are killing us unjustly.' So they attacked them on the sabbath, and they died, with their wives" (1 Macc. 1:38–39).

If passive acceptance of death in preference to breaking God's covenant was the way of the Hasideans, it was not to be the way of the members of the Hashmon family. Their senior member, Mattathias of Modein, was a poor priest who had five sons. When Antiochus's edicts came to be obeyed outside Jerusalem, Mattathias struck down and killed a Jew in the act of offering a pagan sacrifice. "When Mattathias saw it, he burned with *zeal* . . . he ran and killed him on the altar" (1 Macc. 2:24).

Mattathias led his sons and supporters in tearing down the altars, and forcibly circumcising all the uncircumcised boys they found. On his deathbed Mattathias spoke these words:

Now, my children, show *zeal* for the law,
and give your lives for the covenant of our ancestors. (1 Macc. 2:50)

Reference to "zeal" by the patriarch of the Hasmoneans was to have profound influence in the coming years, including during the era of Jesus. The word "zeal" was applied to those whose loyalty to the Lord and the law was greater than their claim to life.

The ideology of "zeal" as expressed by Mattathias was inspired by an incident recorded in Numbers 25. In Shittim the Israelites began to "whore with the daughters of Moab" and to bow down to "Baal of Peor." A plague had fallen upon the people on account of their worship of Baal of Peor. When Zimri, a Hebrew man, brazenly and publicly brought Cosbi, a Midianite woman, to his family, Phinehas, son of Eleazar, son of Aaron the priest, ran a spear through the man and the woman. Soon afterward the plague ceased.

The words of the Lord to Moses about the actions of Phinehas are important: "Phinehas son of Eleazar, son of Aaron the priest, has turned back My wrath from the Israelites because he was *zealous* among them with My *zeal*, so that I did not destroy the Israelites in My *zeal*. Therefore declare: I grant him My covenant of peace. It will be a covenant of perpetual priesthood for him and his descendants because he was *zealous* for his God and made atonement for the Israelites" (Num. 25:11–13, Holman Christian Standard Bible). The reference to Mattathias's "zeal" in 1 Maccabees 2:50 almost certainly picks up the Lord's approval of the "zeal" of Phinehas recorded in Numbers 25:11–13. In its turn, the "zeal" of the Hasmonean patriarch became an inspiration in the following years, including in the time of Herod and into the decades following.

"ZEAL" DURING THE REIGN OF HEROD

Earnest Jews felt deep resentment against their king, Herod. Although circumcised, he was not a blood descendant of Abraham. He was loyal to his gentile masters, the hated Romans.

Furthermore, he was, at heart, a dedicated Hellenist who built a theater and an amphitheater in Jerusalem.[1] In place of sacred religious observations, the people of the Holy City were confronted with spectacles that recalled the aggressive Hellenism of Antiochus IV.

---

1. Josephus, *Jewish Antiquities* 15.267.

To counter criticism Herod forbade unauthorized public assembly, forced the population to take oaths of loyalty, the first to him alone, but the second to him and the Roman Caesar, Augustus.[2] Under the influence of the Pharisees, many refused to take those loyalty oaths.

Herod was feared for his brutality against anyone known to criticize him. In addition to his known network of spies, the king himself mingled incognito in public places. Many who raised their voices against him simply disappeared into his newly built network of fortress-prisons.[3]

However, the spirit of Maccabean "zeal" revived under Herod's cruelty, although Josephus doesn't apply that vocabulary in his narrative. Nevertheless, the refusal of many to take oaths of loyalty was "zeal" by another name.

In the last days of Herod, forty student rabbis tore down the effigy of an eagle that the king had secured to the gates of the temple.[4] Their teachers pointed out that such a symbol was contrary to the law. Herod was attempting to appease Augustus by this display of the much-loved symbol of the Romans. Their "zeal" cost them their lives and is rightly understood as a "zealous" act.

2. Josephus, *Jewish Antiquities* 15.366, 368; 17.42.
3. Josephus, *Jewish Antiquities* 15.366.
4. Josephus, *Jewish Antiquities* 17.151.

5

THE MACCABEAN DYNASTY

(165–37 BC)

Mattathias's oldest son, Judas, assumed the leadership of the Jews against the Seleucids. His nickname "hammer," translated "Maccabeus," became the alternative way of referring to their more formal former name, "Hasmonean." Judas Maccabeus successfully gained partial autonomy from the Antioch-based Seleucids.

Judas the victor over the Seleucids was succeeded in turn by his four brothers and their descendants.[1]

165–160	Judas
160–142	Jonathan
142–134	Simon
134–104	John Hyrcanus
103–76	Alexander Jannaeus
76–67	Alexandra
67–37	Civil War

Ironically, despite their victory over intrusive Hellenism, the Maccabean leaders adopted many of the features of their Greek overlords, the Antioch-based Seleucids. The Maccabean kingship models were deeply influenced by the rulers in Antioch.

---

1. For the early years of Maccabean rule, we are dependent on 1 Maccabees (written ca. 135–104 BC) and 2 Maccabees (written between ca. 150 and 120 BC).

KINGS WHO WERE HIGH PRIESTS

As a family of priestly lineage, the various kings from Jonathan onward took to themselves the position of high priest, reinforcing their authority. As priest-kings who succumbed to ungodly behavior, they lost the support of former allies, the Hasideans. An anonymous apocalyptist late in the era of the New Testament was to reflect critically about them. "Then there shall be raised up among them kings bearing rule, and they shall call themselves priests of the Most-High God: they shall assuredly work iniquity in the holy of holies" (As. Mos. 6). The Maccabean politicizing of the high priesthood established a precedent that was followed by the appointments of Herod and Archelaus. Once Judea became a Roman province (in AD 6), the high priesthood became increasingly politically powerful.

HASIDEANS, PHARISEES, AND ESSENES

Meanwhile the ranks of the Hasideans, whose roots go back to the Persian era, became divided between those who remained in the towns and villages and those who withdrew into separatist communities. In time the former evolved into the Pharisees, who established teaching academies in Jerusalem and synagogues everywhere as meeting places for the Sabbath-day reading of the Law and the Prophets and for social gatherings.

The latter became known as the Essenes, who established the settlement near the eastern shore of the Dead Sea, whose beliefs and practices were revealed in the Dead Sea Scrolls discovered in 1947. While the Dead Sea Essenes were celibate, other Essenes who lived on edges of the towns were allowed to marry. The Gate of the Essenes in Jerusalem is evidence of an Essene community in the era of early Christianity that may have been quite close to the Upper Room community.[2]

KOINE GREEK

The Koine Greek language flourished among the Jews, as witnessed by the two books of Maccabees, both written in Greek.[3] Because of the surrounding

2. Josephus, *Jewish War* 5.145.
3. Martin Hengel, *The "Hellenization" of Judaea in the First Century after Christ* (London: SCM, 1989), 7–18.

culture of Hellenism, Koine flourished among the Jews in Palestine, soon rivaling Aramaic as the common language.

Despite an impression of compromise with things Greek, the Maccabean rulers were regarded as heroic, and many Jewish boys were given the names Judas, Jonathan, Simon, and John, several of which appear in the pages of the Gospels.

MACCABEAN CONQUESTS

The Maccabean rulers became progressively independent of the superpower in the north. At the same time, these rulers aggressively expanded their borders. John Hyrcanus (134–104 BC) captured Idumea, Samaria, and part of Galilee, all of which he incorporated in his kingdom. His sons Aristobulus I (104–103 BC) and Alexander Jannaeus (103–76 BC) consolidated their father's conquests, enlarging the kingdom from the Mediterranean coast to east of the Jordan.

The acquisition of these territories was to have important consequences. Herod the king was an Idumean; Jesus of Nazareth was a Galilean. Despite consolidation of various territories, Jews avoided contact with Samaritans. Jesus visited Samaria, and a famous parable featured a Samaritan who was "good."

GALILEE, NAZARETH, AND THE NAZARENE

Richly fertile Galilee was a key location in the Northern Kingdom, Israel, which was captured by the Assyrians in 732 BC, years before the Southern Kingdom fell to the Babylonians. The Assyrians deported many Jews from Galilee while also importing non-Jews into the region, which perhaps explains the epithet "Galilee of the nations" (Isa. 9:1–2). The prophet Isaiah predicted that the people of the nations who lived in and around Galilee were to see "a great light," a promise of the advent of the Messiah.

As noted, John Hyrcanus overran this region, making it the northern frontier of his expanding kingdom.

When the holy family returned from Egypt, they took up residence in Nazareth, a small village in lower Galilee. According to Matthew 2:23, this was to fulfill prophecy that the Messiah would be "called a Nazarene," which is curious since the Old Testament doesn't mention Nazareth and there is no prophecy, "He shall be called a Nazarene." The likely explanation is that the word "Nazarene" is a wordplay on the Hebrew word *netzer*, meaning a shoot from a tree. Matthew was almost certainly alluding to Isaiah 11:1—

> There shall come forth a shoot from the stump of Jesse,
>   and from his roots a sprout (Hebrew *netzer*) will blossom.
>
>   (author's translation)

Jesse was the father of David, so that Isaiah was prophesying the coming of a new David.

This prophecy must have been widely known. When the blind beggar Bartimaeus heard that Jesus the Nazorean was passing by, he exclaimed, "Jesus, *son of David*, have mercy on me!" (Mark 10:47).

This choice of name for Nazareth may have been in recognition of a village whose predominant inhabitants were descendants of David, from whom was to come God's anointed king, the Messiah. The message of the genealogy found in the first chapter of the Gospel of Matthew is that Jesus was a descendant first of Abraham and second of David.

LATTER DAYS OF THE MACCABEES

Hellenism had threatened to engulf the Jews and destroy their religious identity. The Maccabean rulers, despite their many failures, exploited the growing weakness of the Antioch-based kingdom, making Israel and her faith relatively secure in an island of Hellenism.

The lowest point of the Maccabean rulers occurred under Alexander Jannaeus (103–76 BC). Not content to consolidate his realm, he willfully attacked and destroyed surrounding Hellenistic cities. He combined his role as king with high priest, thereby degrading both offices.

He was succeeded by his widow, Alexandra (76–67 BC), who appointed her inept son Hyrcanus II as high priest. Her younger son was the ambitious Aristobulus II. When Alexandra died, the supporters of her two sons engaged in a civil war.

The death of Alexandra coincided with the entry into Judean politics of the scheming Idumean politician Antipater, father of Herod the "Great." For his part, Antipater recognized the importance of Roman power, which, led by the redoubtable Roman general Pompey "Magnus," had reduced the Seleucid kingdom in Syria to a Roman province.

Pompey arrived in Judea in 63 BC, taking the side of Hyrcanus against his brother Aristobulus. The Roman legions occupied Judea and successfully besieged the temple. The year 63 BC effectively marked the end of Jewish rule of the Holy Land.

From that time the Maccabean kingdom was to be ruled by the Idumean Antipater, his son Herod, and his sons Archelaus, Antipas, and Philip, each one ruling as a dependent client of the Romans.

6

THE ROMANS

Judea had been subject to foreign powers from the era of the Babylonians, who were followed by the Persians, the Ptolemies, and the Seleucids. The Jews, led by the Maccabean dynasts, secured their independent domestic rule with the added conquests of Idumea and Galilee.

Then, in 63 BC the Romans arrived, led by Pompey. Although the Jews continued to rule, inevitably each passing decade brought the Jewish territories closer to direct Roman rule through the creation of a province that included Judea, Idumea, and Samaria.

The Roman encroachment eastward meant the progressive collapse of the Hellenistic empires, first the Seleucids in 64 BC and then the Ptolemies in 31 BC. Inevitably Israel came under Roman rule.

In AD 6 Augustus made Judea a Roman province, with Caesarea Maritima the new capital. In that year Jewish opposition to the Roman census and imposition of direct personal taxation marked the beginning of steadily deteriorating relationships between the Roman occupiers and the Jewish people. In 66 the Roman legions led by Vespasian invaded Galilee, and in 70 his son Titus oversaw the capture of Jerusalem and the destruction of the great temple. Yet another Roman-Jewish war erupted in 132–135, in which the Jews were again defeated. After that Jews were banished from their ancestral homeland. Jerusalem became in turn Roman, Byzantine, Islamic, and until the twentieth century, Turkish.

Of the nations that occupied Israel—Persia, Greece, Rome—the Greeks presented the greatest challenge to her cultural and religious identity. Notwithstanding the military might of Rome, which twice overwhelmed her, it was the more subtle influence of Greek culture, "Hellenism,"[1] during the three centuries before the Roman provincialization of Judea in 6 that most threatened Israel's covenantal loyalty to the Lord, her God, and his law.

Throughout those many years Israel was surrounded by Hellenism and was indeed permeated and penetrated by Hellenism. Roman power was imposed from above, but Hellenism crept in from all sides, potentially corrupting the people and their leaders from within. Although Christianity was born in the era of Roman hegemony, the language, and the cultural background against which the new movement is most helpfully understood, was not Roman but Greek.

POMPEY MAGNUS

Born in 106 BC, Gnaeus Pompeius Magnus (the "great") was one of a small group of Roman aristocrats and a onetime triumvir with Julius Caesar and Crassus who competed politically and militarily for control of the Roman world.

In the late Roman Republic, there was a well-defined career path for aspiring politicians, the so-called *cursus honorum*: the quaestorship at thirty, the praetorship at thirty-nine, and the consulship at forty-three. The expectation was that military service and governorships would be interspersed between these magistracies.

Pompey was a precocious figure. At age twenty-three, based on family wealth, he recruited a private army of three legions. In the years to come he moved between military leadership and political appointments independently of traditional expectations. For instance, in his early years he declined to take the role of provincial governor. Later he accepted the appointment as proconsul of Spain but governed the region from Rome via a proxy.

As a soldier Pompey had the nickname "teenage butcher." Pompey is chiefly famous for his destruction of piracy in the Mediterranean and for the eventual defeat of anti-Roman forces in Asia Minor. In 89 BC Mithridates VI (120–63 BC), the young king of Pontus, had allied himself with Tigranes the Great, king of Armenia, against the Romans. In 88 BC their armies overran Cappadocia and Bithynia and successfully resisted Roman attempts to defeat these forces. Eventually, however, in 66 BC Pompey's legions brutally defeated Mithridates's armies and gained control of Asia Minor.

---

1. Jews of the Maccabean era employed the term "Hellenism" (2 Macc. 4:13).

Roman military prowess struck fear into the hearts of those who resisted them. Mithridates commented: "The Romans have from of old known but one ground for waging war with all nations, peoples and kings—inveterate lust of empire and wealth . . . they leave nothing that they do not lay their hands on—homes, wives, land, power—they are a gang of men with no fatherland or ancestry of their own, swept together of old to be a plague to the whole world . . . they treat as their enemies all men . . . that refuse to serve them as slaves."[2]

In 66 BC Cicero, the famous jurist, echoed similar sentiments against his fellow Romans' military campaigns in Asia, led by Pompey. "It is difficult to convey to you . . . the bitter hatred felt for us among foreign nations because of the unbridled and outrageous behaviour of the men whom we have sent to govern them during the past years. . . . They actually look around for wealthy and flourishing cities in order to find an occasion of waging war against them and thus gratify their lust for plunder."[3] Tacitus quoted the diatribe of the British leader Calagus:

> Robbers of the world, having by their universal plunder exhausted the land, they rifle the sheep. If the enemy is rich, they are rapacious; if he is poor, they lust for dominion; neither the east nor the west has been able to satisfy them. Alone among men they covet with equal eagerness poverty and riches. To robbery, slaughter, plunder, they give the lying name of empire; they make a wasteland and call it peace. . . . Our goods and fortunes they collect for their tribute, our harvest for their granaries. Our very hands and bodies, under the lash and in the midst of insult, are worn down by the toil of clearing forests and morasses.[4]

The brutal, all-conquering Pompey led his legions into Syria and in 64 BC made the power base of the Seleucids into a Roman province, establishing the capital in Antioch.

The following year Pompey led his legions into the Holy Land. Some years later a religious poet remembered the brutality of the Romans: "The lawless

---

2. Quoted in F. F. Bruce, *New Testament History* (Bristol, UK: Oliphants, 1971), 9 (citing Sallust, *Historical Fragment* 4.69.1–23).

3. Quoted in Bruce, *New Testament History*, 10 (citing Cicero, *Pro Lege manilia* 65–66).

4. Tacitus, *Agricola* 31, 32.

one laid waste our land so that none inhabited it. They destroyed young and old and their children together" (Pss. Sol. 17:13–15).[5]

Most offensive of Pompey's deeds was his desecration of the temple of the Lord. Twelve thousand defenders were slaughtered. The inner space, the "holy of holies," could be entered only by the high priest, only once a year on the Day of Atonement. Into this sacred place the godless Pompey entered, thereby profaning it (although not pillaging its sacred vessels).

Another religious poem gives this commentary:

> Arrogantly the sinner broke down the strong walls
> with a battering ram and you did not interfere.
> Gentile foreigners went up to your place of sacrifice;
> they arrogantly trampled it with their sandals. (Pss. Sol. 2:1–6)

A decade and a half later, when Pompey fled from Julius Caesar to find refuge in Egypt, he was murdered on arrival. Pompey's sacrilege was not forgotten. Once again, a religious poem offers its interpretation:

> I had not long to wait before God showed me the insolent one
> slain on the mountains of Egypt,
> Esteemed least of the least, on land and sea,
> His body tossed this way and that on the billows with
>   much insolence
> with none to bury him, since he had rejected God with dishonour.
>
> (Pss. Sol. 2:26–27)

POMPEY IN PALESTINE

Pompey's conquest of Palestine in 63 BC dramatically changed the course of history. Palestine now came under Roman rule, which, however, was indirect and imposed gradually. At first Pompey sided with Hyrcanus II against his brother Aristobulus II, thus resolving the civil war between the last members of the Maccabean dynasty. Hyrcanus was given the title "ethnarch" ("ruler of people") and supported by the emerging power of Antipater, the Idumean,

---

5. The Psalms of Solomon were written as protest in the era of Pompey. They are an example of pseudepigraphy.

and father of Herod. Aristobulus II, his sons, and his daughters were sent as captives to Rome to march in Pompey's victory parade along with many captive Jews who were made slaves.

Pompey diminished the power of the Jews by separating the Hellenic coastal cities from Raphia to Dora from Judea and the ten Hellenic inland autonomous cities of the Decapolis ("ten cities"). Thanks to Pompey, the Jewish territory was now ringed by Greek-speaking coastal city-states and those cities of the Decapolis most closely adjacent to Galilee and Judea—Scythopolis, Hippos, Gadara, Pella, Gerasa, and Philadelphia. The cities of the Decapolis, while independent of each other, were together answerable to the governor of Syria.

Judea and Galilee were now surrounded by Greek-speaking settlements, inevitably further spreading the use of Koine Greek among the Jewish people in Judea and Galilee, including within Jerusalem.

Pompey also confirmed Samaria's geographical independence from Judea. This meant that Judea and Galilee became geographically separated. After the exile of Archelaus in 6, Augustus attached Samaria to Judea as part of the Roman province.

Circa 34, the newly appointed "apostle" Paul left Damascus for two or more years in "Arabia," that is, the kingdom of the Nabateans then ruled by Aretas IV (2 Cor. 11:32–33). In his journey he would have passed through the eastern-most regions of the Decapolis, which were Greek speaking. Aramaic was the common tongue of the Nabateans. Paul, however, was fluent in both languages.

It is not possible to overestimate the importance of Pompey's conquest of Palestine. His support of Hyrcanus II and liaison with Antipater effectively paved the way for the Roman appointment of Herod as king.

After Herod's death there was no suitable successor to his throne. Augustus realigned Herod's will, dividing his realm into three regions, each ruled by a son—Judea (Archelaus), Galilee (Antipas), Gaulanitis (Philip)—each of whom was a client puppet of the Caesar. Then, due to the failure of Archelaus's rule in Judea, in the year 6 that region was made a Roman province.

In Judea the momentous census and application of a poll tax to Rome in 6 was the precursor to numerous acts of insurgency that necessitated the Roman invasion of 66, the climax of which was the destruction of Jerusalem and the temple in 70. When Philip died in 34 and Antipas was exiled in 39, both of those tetrarchies were made subject to direct Roman provincial rule.

AFTER POMPEY

The so-called First Triumvirate (60–53 BC) was a private agreement between three wealthy and powerful leaders—Julius Caesar, Pompey, and Crassus—who used their wealth and military support to bypass the Roman Senate to pursue their own ambitions. The deal was sealed by intermarriage: Pompey married Caesar's daughter, Julia; Caesar was married to Calpurnia, whose father was Piso, the friend of Crassus.

The deaths of Crassus and Julia contributed to the collapse of the First Triumvirate, leaving the military giants Caesar and Pompey vying for sole power. In 49 BC Julius Caesar, returning from victories in Gaul, refused to repatriate his legions and against convention marched them across the Rubicon River into the Eternal City. Caesar now ruled Rome as dictator.

War between the former triumvirs Julius Caesar and Pompey followed, issuing in Caesar's victory at Pharsalus (Greece) in 48 BC. Pompey fled to Egypt, where he was assassinated on arrival by a servant of Ptolemy XII, a client of Caesar.

On "the ides of March" in 44 BC, Caesar, now self-styled as dictator and sole ruler for life, himself fell to the swords of the Roman senators.

MARK ANTONY (83–30 BC)

Mark Antony became very important in the eastern Roman Empire following the murder of Julius Caesar in 44 BC. Antony was a relative of Caesar's and his supporter. After Caesar, he was the most powerful general and politician in the empire.

Antony joined Octavian (Caesar's distant relative and his adopted "son") and Lepidus (a lesser figure) in the creation of the so-called second triumvirate. Antony and Octavian joined forces to defeat Caesar's assassins in the Battle of Philippi in 42 BC.

In 41 BC Antony compelled Cleopatra VII Philopator to meet him in Tarsus to explain why her forces did not support Antony at Philippi. An alliance was forged in Tarsus. Antony made Egypt his base and moved in with Cleopatra, with whom he had two sons, despite his marriage to Fulvia back in Rome. After Fulvia died, Antony married Octavian's sister Octavia, despite his engagement with Cleopatra. In 37 BC Antony sent Octavia back to Rome, formally divorcing her in 32 BC.

The two leaders divided Rome's dominion into the western and eastern provinces, allocating the west to Octavian and the east to Mark Antony. For Antony this meant making his base in the strategic client kingdom of Egypt, then ruled by the Ptolemaic Cleopatra. Not least, to be the supremo in the East provided Antony access to its riches and thereby the capacity to recruit and pay for an enlarged army.

Now located in the East, Antony faced greater challenges than Octavian did in the West. The western provinces had been subdued by Caesar and others (including Antony, whose legions occupied Germany), whereas the East was threatened by the formidable and hostile Parthian Empire. In 53 BC the legions of Crassus had been defeated by Parthia in the Battle of Carrhae, a humiliation Rome was never to forget.

From that time the eastern provinces and client kingdoms became urgently important to Roman interests. This was significantly true of Judea, whose geographical location was a buffer to a Parthian invasion of Egypt, a major food supplier to Rome.

The eastern empire now subject to Antony's rule was composed of provinces (Macedonia, Asia, Bithynia, Cilicia, Cyprus) and client kingdoms (Galatia, Pontus, Cappadocia, Armenia, Judea, Commagene, Nabatea, and Ptolemaic Egypt). The disparate nature of these differing jurisdictions proved to be challenging to Mark Antony. Antony had a direct line of authority through the provinces, whereas his relationship with the client kingdoms was uneven and indirect.

As well, in 34 BC Antony was forced to cede to Cleopatra the so-called Alexandrian Donations, the client kingdoms Cyprus, Libya, Syria, and Cilicia, over whom she appointed her sons. She became known as "queen of kings."

Antipater, Herod's father, had saved Julius Caesar in the Battle of the Nile, in 48 BC. As a reward Caesar conferred Roman citizenship on Antipater and later appointed him as the first procurator of Judea.

Antony was also aware of the strategic importance of Judea to Roman interests in the East. By 42 BC he had come to appreciate the value of the Idumean Antipater and his sons, Herod and Phasael. He appointed the young men as tetrarchs, now responsible for stability of the Holy Land.

In 40 BC the Parthians reached Syria and invaded Judea. Herod fled to Egypt, then to Rome, where, sponsored by Octavian and Antony, the Senate appointed him king of Judea. On his return to the East, Herod, allied with

Mark Antony, successfully subdued his enemies in 40–37 BC. In 37 BC, Herod assumed unchallenged control of his kingdom.

In 36 Antony led a huge army against the Parthians but was humiliated in defeat, losing eighty thousand legionaries. In that year Octavian accused Mark Antony of "going native," that is, adopting non-Roman values and practices. Antony formally renounced his alliance with Octavian. War was now inevitable. In 32 BC the Roman Senate declared war on Cleopatra.

The final event in this remarkable saga was the sea battle between the forces of Octavian and Antony and Cleopatra in 31 BC at Actium, in western Greece. Defeated, Antony and his consort returned to Alexandria, where they committed suicide. The prospect of being brought back to Rome as trophies of war, marched through the streets, was unbearable.

In the following year (30 BC) Egypt was made a Roman province.

Mark Antony had recognized the strategic importance of Judea. Along with other Roman leaders, he identified the Idumean Antipater and his son Herod as men capable of ruling Judea for them. For their part, the two men were adroit in their capacity to reassure their Roman masters of their ability to do so.

As a client king serving under Mark Antony, what was Herod to do following the death of his patron in 31 BC? In tribute to their respective diplomatic wisdoms, Octavian and Herod embraced one another. He became a "friend" of Caesar and an "ally" of Rome.

In the following years Herod consolidated his kingdom and successfully fulfilled the strategic defense of Judea against the Parthians.

The long and stable rule of Octavian, later known as Augustus, ended decades of civil war. Augustus introduced a family-connected autocracy, the Julio-Claudian dynasty, who governed the empire from the victory of Augustus in 31 BC to the death of Nero in AD 68.

7

THE INTRUDING IDUMEANS

The Idumeans were descendants of the Edomites, a desert people who had occupied the region between the Gulf of Aqaba and the Dead Sea. In the time of the exodus, they had blocked the route of the Hebrews to the promised land. The Edomites were descendants of Esau, the rejected child of the patriarch Isaac, who married Canaanite wives and was the sworn enemy of the Jewish people. Ironically, one of their number was destined to become king of the Jews.

By the latter part of the Hellenistic era, the Idumeans had migrated from south of the Dead Sea to occupy the tract of land from the Dead Sea to the coastal plain and from Bethlehem almost to Beersheba. They became wealthy as traders and farmers.

During the rule of the Hasmonean John Hyrcanus (134–104 BC), the Jews conquered the Idumeans and, in effect, colonized them. This was to have remarkable and unexpected consequences in the coming years. Of most importance is that the Idumeans began to adopt Jewish religion and practice. Previously they had been influenced by Hellenistic deities, but then—whether by force or by more gradual means—the people of Idumea adopted Judaism, though with varying degrees of understanding.

ANTIPAS, ANTIPATER, AND HEROD

Herod's grandfather Antipas and his father, Antipater, became wealthy and powerful, borne up by Idumea's rising prosperity. It is likely that this powerful family lived at Marissa, the capital.

Herod himself was very wealthy, apart from the riches he accrued later as king of the Jews. Although Antipas and Antipater, like Herod, had been assimilated to a degree to Judaism, each displayed considerable interest in the wider world of the Greeks. Hellenism probably permeated Idumea to a greater degree than Judea, where the Pharisees and the Essenes staunchly opposed it. Even their names—Antipas, Antipater, and Herod—were Greek.

Both Antipater and Herod in turn proved to be ambitious for power within their neighbor, Judea. Both were shrewd and ruthless politicians exploiting the power vacuum in the last days of the Hasmonean era. Both men showed canny opportunism as each in turn courted successive Roman generals whose campaigns brought them to the eastern Mediterranean.

For the next twenty-five years Antipater adroitly wooed other great Roman leaders who came to the East—Julius Caesar, Cassius, and Mark Antony. By these relationships Antipater acquired Roman citizenship and immunity from taxation. In effect, Antipater became a "client" of these notable Romans, looking out for their interests in that part of the East and enjoying the benefits of their patronage in return. Antipater's grip on power in the Jewish homeland and his strongly established network of friendships with leading Romans and with powerful leaders in adjoining countries laid the foundation for Herod's ultimate emergence as "king of the Jews."

THE END OF THE MACCABEES

Initially Antipater became governor of Idumea. From that base he involved himself in Jewish affairs, taking sides in the struggle for power in Israel between Aristobulus and Hyrcanus, sons of Alexandra. The weak and ineffectual Hyrcanus found himself overshadowed by Antipater, who won the support of Pompey against Aristobulus.

Through Pompey's intervention (63 BC) Hyrcanus became ruler of the Jews in name, but Antipater was the real power in the land. Josephus knew this. He wrote, "[Hyrcanus] seems to have been mild and moderate in all things and to have ruled by leaving most things to his administrators to do, since he was not interested in general affairs nor clever enough to govern a kingdom. That Antipater and Herod advanced so far was due to his mildness."[1]

Aristobulus claimed victory over Hyrcanus but surrendered to Pompey in 63 BC. When Pompey captured Jerusalem and entered the holy place, it

1. Josephus, *Jewish Antiquities* 15.182.

spelled the end of Aristobulus's reign and effectively the end of the independence of Judea as a Jewish state.

In 61 BC Aristobulus was forced to march in front of Pompey in a victory parade in Rome. This was not the end of his remarkable story. In 56 BC he escaped from prison in Rome and returned to Judea, where he was captured and taken once more to Rome. In 49 BC, however, he was set free by Julius Caesar and sent with a strong military force against his enemy Pompey in Syria. He did not die in battle, however, but beforehand, poisoned by an ally of Pompey.

IDUMEANS AND NABATEANS

Another tribal group that became prosperous during the same general period, and with whom there were close family and financial connections, was the Nabateans, the Idumeans' eastern neighbors, whose capital was Petra. The wealth of the Nabateans was due to their skills in water management and their taxation of traders who passed through their territory.

The Idumean Antipater was married to Cypros, from an aristocratic Nabatean family in Petra. Herod, then, was part Idumean, part Nabatean, with no Jewish blood in his veins.

There were to be ongoing relationships between Herod and the Nabateans. Herod's sister Salome sought marriage with Syllaeus, a Nabatean. Herod refused the request because Syllaeus was uncircumcised. Herod's son, Antipas, the tetrarch of Galilee-Perea (ca. 3 BC–AD 39), was initially married to Phasaelis, the daughter of Aretas IV, the greatest king of the Nabateans (9 BC–AD 40). Due to Antipas's divorce of Phasaelis and his marriage to Herodias, Aretas invaded the tetrarch's territories in the late thirties, inflicting a humiliating defeat, and thus hastening Antipas's ultimate downfall.

ANTIPATER AND HEROD

Antipater, the wily and ruthless Idumean, created the political setting that his son Herod was not slow to exploit. It is important to recognize the role of Antipater making the way for his son, Herod, who would prove to be the most powerful king in a thousand years of Jewish history.

In 47 BC the Romans appointed Herod,[2] who was twenty-six, as gover-

2. By Sextus Caesar, governor of Syria?

nor of Galilee. His chief mission was to capture and execute the local warlord Hezekiah, the father of a dynasty of rebels against the Romans.

- Hezekiah was the father of Judas, who captured Galilee in 4 BC after the death of Herod.
- In AD 6, this Judas, with the Pharisee Saddok, led the rebellion against the Romans at the time of the census and the poll tax when Judea became a Roman province.
- In AD 46 Judas's sons, James and Simon, were executed by the procurator Tiberius Alexander.
- In AD 66 the Romans executed Menahem, another descendant of Hezekiah (most likely a grandson).
- Hezekiah began what was in effect a dynasty of anti-Rome insurgents.

Herod's military success in Galilee displayed his personal athleticism and military skills. These, together with immovable loyalty to Rome, marked him as a future king who could bring stability to the volatile and unstable world of Judea, Samaria, and Galilee.

The young man's experience in Galilee gave him firsthand experience of the natural wealth of the region that surrounded a vast freshwater lake and was blessed by good rainfall. Furthermore, Galilee was bordered by Hellenistic city-states through which numerous traders and travelers passed. Herod would have understood wealthy Galilee's tax-harvesting potential.

Seventy-seven years later Jesus, a young rabbi, emerged from the obscurity of Nazareth. Through the Gospels we see him walking in the hills and valleys of Galilee and hear him announcing the imminent dawning of the kingdom of God and telling many parables, including about a shepherd, a sower, a harvester, a thankless son, a damaging windstorm, and the unexpected kindness of a Samaritan. He was destined to become the founder of the world's greatest religious movement.

8

ALLIANCE OF ANTONY AND HEROD

(40–37 BC)

Herod was as adept in securing the confidence of the leading Roman generals as had been his father, Antipater. First, he won the patronage of Mark Antony, who used his influence in Rome by the vote of the Senate in 40 BC to have Herod appointed king of Judea, Galilee, and Perea. Later, after the death of Antony (by suicide in 30 BC, following his defeat at Actium in 31), Herod swiftly switched his loyalty to Octavian.

His father, Antipater, had proved to be loyal to Roman leadership. Evidently the Romans saw in Herod, son of Antipater, a reliable leader capable of overcoming the chaos in Israel. The civil war between sons of Alexandra, Hyrcanus II and Aristobulus II, continued, despite the eventual death of Aristobulus. Maccabean hopes now rested on his son, Antigonus.

There was another problem the Romans faced, which reflected their own chaotic situation at Rome and in the East. The strong man Julius Caesar had been assassinated in 44 BC; Octavian and Mark Antony defeated the assassins Brutus and Cassius in Philippi in 42 BC. Mark Antony's entanglement with Cleopatra allowed the rise of Parthian strength on the empire's eastern frontier.

Meanwhile the Parthians, who were formidable fighters, secured their own leadership and invaded Judea. They formed an alliance with Antigonus, son of the now-deceased Aristobulus, whom they crowned king of Judea.

Rome depended on Egypt for its supply of grain, which was given to the people of the city. The mobile Parthians were a threat to Egypt, which in turn made Israel important to the Romans. This explains the interest of the great Romans in the political stability of the land.

In Roman eyes, Herod was the man, most likely the only man, who could bring an end to the civil war between the last sons of the Maccabean dynasty. Equally important was their confidence that he was the right person to assume the leadership and to unify the sorely divided nation.

Their time-honored policy was to appoint trusted locals as "client" kings as the first step toward imposing direct provincial rule. The Romans would have regarded Herod as an ideal first step in that process. They may not, however, have estimated just how capable Herod would prove to be, nor the remarkable length of his reign.

In 40 BC the Parthians invaded Judea; appointed Antigonus (son of Aristobulus II) king; captured and deported his uncle, Hyrcanus; and occupied Jerusalem. Herod, however, displeased the surviving Maccabeans by not appointing one of their number high priest. Instead, Herod nominated a Babylonian Jew, Ananel, as high priest.

This was a momentous event. From now on high priests were appointed at the will of political leaders, whether Herod or the Roman governors. Gone forever was the tradition that high priests were appointed from among the descendants of Aaron.

Herod escaped from besieged Jerusalem and traveled to Rome via Masada, Alexandria, and Rhodes. In the Senate Mark Antony proposed that Herod should be appointed king based on his proven loyalty to Rome and his capacity to defeat Antigonus and the Parthians. The Senate unanimously endorsed this proposal. Antony with Herod, led by the consuls and other leaders, proceeded to the temple of Jupiter to offer sacrifices and to lay up the decree in the Capitol.[1] The Senate named Herod king of Judea, Galilee, and Perea. To those regions Idumea and Samaria were added later.

In 39 BC Herod returned to the East, landing in Ptolemais, and progressively captured the lands that had fallen into the hands of the Parthians and their puppet king, Antigonus. In 38 Herod returned to Galilee to finalize the campaigns against local insurgents. The next year he recaptured Jerusalem. Later that year Mark Antony captured and executed Antigonus.

The way was now clear for Herod to exercise his royal power, which he did under the patronage of Antony and Cleopatra.

---

1. Josephus, *Jewish War* 1.285.

Part 2

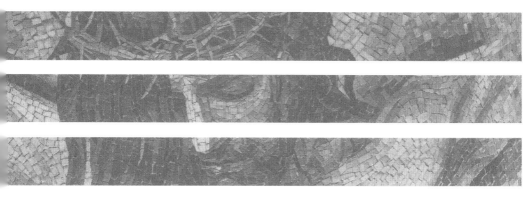

KINGS,
HIGH PRIESTS,
AND OTHER
OFFICIALS

9

HEROD THE "GREAT"

(37–4 BC)

More than any ruler who preceded him, Herod left his stamp on the homeland of the Jews. There were his remarkable buildings (the great temple), his network of fortresses (e.g., Masada, Herodium, Sebaste), and the great artificial harbor at Caesarea. Each of these, and many others, was fully on view in the time of Jesus a few decades after Herod's death. Also, thanks to Herod, the diffusion of the Greek language begun in the era of Alexander's "successors" continued under a king who was a dedicated Hellenist. These and many other engineering and cultural achievements were the marks of his long and ambitious reign that created the environment in which Jesus of Nazareth lived and was eventually tried and executed.

HEROD AND THE ROMANS

During the years 40–31 BC Herod attended to the affairs of his kingdom under the patronage of Mark Antony and his consort Cleopatra. The defeat of Antony and Cleopatra in 31 at the Battle of Actium, however, left Herod vulnerable. At great risk he journeyed to Rhodes to meet the new master of the now-undivided Roman world, Augustus. Remarkably, Herod left Rhodes stronger than ever; Augustus and Herod became firm allies.

Thus, the Jews were not destined to have a righteous king of the line of David, as hoped for in the Psalms of Solomon, but an Idumean, a descendant of Israel's hated enemy, the Edomites, a people descended from Esau, the apostate brother of Jacob. The Jews were to suffer grievous oppression under Herod's rule for almost four decades.

Himself a child of Hellenism (his name means "hero"—as of Greek gods and heroes), Herod was to be a father of Hellenism among his people. Moreover, Herod's sons, his grandson, and his great-grandson were to rule sections of Israel for a century after his death. The fortunes of the Jewish people in Palestine were inextricably linked to the Herodian dynasty for approximately one and a half centuries, that is, from the arrival of Pompey in Jerusalem in 63 BC.

Roman Rule by Herod, King of the Jews

BC

65	Beginning of era of influence of Antipater, the Idumean
63	Pompey invades Judea, captures Jerusalem, enters temple
40	In Rome: Herod is appointed "king" by Roman Senate
40–37	War in Israel: Herod + Romans vs. Antigonus + Parthians
	Herod "client" of Mark Antony
37	Herod undisputed ruler of Israel
31	Battle of Actium: Augustus sole Roman leader
	Herod removes Hyrcanus
	In Rhodes: Augustus embraces Herod as "client" ruler
29	Murder of Herod's wife Mariamne
20	Oath of loyalty by the nation to Herod
12	Herod's border disputes with Nabateans
	Herod loses Augustus's confidence
7	Oath of loyalty by Jewish nation to Augustus and Herod
	Herod executes his sons Alexander and Aristobulus
5?	Birth of Jesus of Nazareth
4	Golden eagle incident at the temple; martyrdom of Pharisees
	Herod executes his son Antipater
	Death of Herod

HEROD REMOVES RIVALS

Herod's doorway to power was his father, Antipater. Like his father, Herod flattered those above him, while crushing the opposition beneath him. Further, Herod was a prodigious warrior and hunter, as well as a resourceful and determined military leader. He decisively seized the opportunity provided him through his father's position.

Once in power, a new king customarily removed his dynastic rivals. Nevertheless, the ruthlessness and thoroughness of Herod's purges attracted notice in the historical sources. Surviving members of the ousted Hasmonean dynasty were his targets. First, Herod defeated and then executed his military foe Antigonus in 37 BC, and his son the high priest Aristobulus in 36. Hyrcanus II, a former high priest, despite his alliance with Herod's father, suffered the same fate in 30. Mariamne I, Herod's wife, who was Hyrcanus's granddaughter, was murdered in 29. Her mother, Alexandra, fell before Herod in 28. The king's jealousy extended beyond the Maccabees. In 27 he removed Costobar, governor of Idumea, who was married to his sister, Salome.

Herod's latter years saw fierce competition for the succession between the sons of various of his nine wives. Among these were Mariamne's sons Alexander and Aristobulus, whose popularity he measured against his own unpopularity and whose possible vengeance for their mother's death he had reason to fear. Herod executed Alexander and Aristobulus in 7 BC. Competing with them and also with the now-aged king was Antipater, a son of his first wife, Doris. In 4 BC, five days before he died, Herod executed Antipater. The chief survivors of these final bloody years, who themselves were also fierce rivals, were the sons of the Samaritan Malthake, Archelaus and Antipas. The immediate future was to lie with them, not with the descendants of the Maccabees. However, Aristobulus's son, Agrippa I, was to become king of Trachonitis in AD 37, then of Galilee-Perea in 39, and finally of a united Israel in 41.

The Roman emperor, no stranger to interdynastic bloodletting, was struck by Herod's ferocity toward his own sons. "When [Augustus] heard that Herod king of the Jews had . . . put to death . . . the king's son . . . , he said, 'I'd rather be Herod's pig than Herod's son.'"[1]

Josephus, too, was critical of Herod's behavior toward potential rivals, including from within his own family.

> [Herod] died on the fifth day after having his son Antipater killed. He had reigned for thirty-four years from the time when he had put Antigonus to death, and for thirty-seven years from the time when he had been ap-

---

1. Macrobius, *Saturnalia* 2.4.11.

pointed king by the Romans. He was a man who was cruel to all alike and one who easily gave in to anger and was contemptuous of justice.

As for the affairs of his household and his relationship with his sons, he had in his own opinion at least, enjoyed very good fortune since he had not failed to get the better of those whom he had considered his enemies, but in my opinion he was very unfortunate indeed.[2]

HEROD, "CLIENT" RULER FOR AUGUSTUS

The Roman policy was to install a "client" king over a conquered people as a first step toward more direct rule in a Roman province under the administration of a Roman governor. This policy made good sense. The Romans shrewdly recognized that an indigenous appointee could more likely control his people than the Romans themselves, provided, of course, that this local ruler was absolutely loyal to his Roman masters. Herod was a "client" king to rule the Jews for the Romans.

Initially the Roman potentate Herod served, from 40 BC, was Mark Antony, who was based in Alexandria with the Greco-Egyptian princess Cleopatra, his coregent. It was customary for a "client" ruler to name important buildings after the one he served. Herod named his new fortress in Jerusalem after Antony, as Josephus notes. "The fortress he restored at a lavish cost in a style no way inferior to that of a palace, and called it Antonia in honour of Antony."[3] According to Josephus, "the fortress . . . called Antonia" was used as a garrison for Roman soldiers to supervise the temple area. The vast gatherings of Jews at the great feasts always presented the possibility of serious disturbances. Jesus may have been taken for trial to the Antonia by the governor, Pontius Pilate, though it is more likely that this took place in the precincts of Herod's former palace (now the Praetorium), some distance away in the upper city.

During Paul's final visit to Jerusalem in AD 58, he was rescued from an angry mob in the temple precincts by a cohort of Roman soldiers who were most likely posted in the Antonia Fortress and to which Paul would have been taken (Acts 21:34, 37).

In 31 BC, however, Antony and Cleopatra's control of the eastern Mediterranean region ended. Their forces were defeated by Augustus at the sea battle

2. Josephus, *Jewish Antiquities* 17.191.
3. Josephus, *Jewish War* 5.224.

of Actium off the western coast of Greece. Augustus now ruled the entire empire—east and west—unopposed. Herod promptly redirected his loyalty to a new master, Augustus, who extended Herod's position and prestige beyond that enjoyed under Antony. Herod indeed became "friend and ally of the Romans."

The Romans had clear expectations of such a "friend and ally," including the provision of auxiliary troops to support the legions, if need arose. Above all, he was to secure his borders against invasion from the east. Egypt, a prime source of grain supplies for Rome, was vulnerable to invasion from Parthia.

There were also limitations. A client king could not enter alliances with other kings. Moreover, client monarchies were not hereditary; the Roman Caesar must agree to the succession. However, beyond those expectations and limitations, Herod seems to have enjoyed a free hand within his kingdom and beyond. Nor does he appear to have been required to pay tribute to the Romans, allowing him to amass even greater wealth during his lifetime.

Herod also formed a close attachment to Augustus's son-in-law Agrippa, the second-most powerful Roman. These, too, were to have significant buildings named after them, as Josephus, a Jerusalemite, knew well. "But what Herod valued more than all these privileges was that in Caesar's affection he stood next after Agrippa, and in Agrippa's next after Caesar. His own palace, which he erected in the upper city, comprised two most spacious and beautiful buildings, with which the Temple itself bore no comparison; these he named after his friends, the one Caesareum, the other Agrippeum."[4]

Thus, Herod's reign falls into two broad but unequal subdivisions. In the first, 40–31 BC, Herod struggled to secure his place under the oversight of Antony and Cleopatra. During these years Herod set about eliminating rivals and opponents from the Maccabean dynasty that he and his father before him had overturned.

In the second broad era, 31–4 BC, Herod was subject to the new master of the world, Augustus, whose greater confidence he came to enjoy. Herod was now secure both externally and internally. Consistent with the Romans' expectations of a client king ruling a volatile people whose frontiers were exposed, Herod extended his boundaries, built up his military strength, established a ring of defensive buffer colonies, created defensive fortresses in Jerusalem and throughout his realm and an extensive network of spies. It was during this

4. Josephus, *Jewish War* 1.400–402.

latter period that Herod applied himself to his remarkable building program, both inside and outside Israel.

HEROD, A HELLENISTIC MONARCH

The hellenization of Palestine began in the aftermath of Alexander's conquests through the kingdoms, respectively, of Egypt and Syria. Despite their initial "zeal" for the Lord and his covenant, the Maccabees succumbed to the enticements of Hellenism. Hellenization continued and accelerated through Israel's most powerful king since Solomon, Herod the "Great."

Whereas under the Maccabees this hellenization was unexpected and opposed, in Herod's case it was intentionally embraced. The expectation of Herod's Roman masters was that their "friend and ally" would promote Greco-Roman culture to prepare a subject people for their ultimate assimilation as a province under direct Roman rule. There is every reason to believe that Herod pursued this program freely and with enthusiasm.

He carefully modeled the upper echelons—his court, bureaucracy, and army—along the lines of the kingdoms of the Ptolemies and the Seleucids. Effectively all positions of authority within these structures were occupied by Greeks or hellenized Jews. Attending Herod were a cluster of men with Greek names—Nicolaus the historian, Ptolemy the administrator of finance, Andromachus and Gemellus the advisors, and Irenaeus the rhetorician. These offices were typical of a Hellenistic monarchy. Greek was the language of Herod's court, and of his inscriptions and coins; Maccabean coins, by contrast, were mostly in Hebrew.

The focus of power, to which ambitious people gravitated upward, was not Jewish but, to generalize, Greek. Herod's conciliar advice came not from the Sanhedrin of the Jews, of which we hear little during the years of his reign, but from his own "gentlemen," his courtiers. Herod killed most of the existing members of the Sanhedrin when he came to power.

The ever-suspicious Herod surrounded himself with military units that were drawn not from Jewish but from non-Jewish sources—Germans, Thracians, and Gauls. Early in his reign he appointed Boethus, an Alexandrian, as high priest as a means of marrying his beautiful daughter Mariamne (II), thus also controlling the office of high priest. Herod's policies made statements about foreigners and foreigners' values that were plain for all to see and that in time must have brought to bear their own influence among the people.

This was evident also in cultural matters. Soon after he came under Augustus's patronage (that is, after 31 BC), Herod built a theater, an amphitheater, and a hippodrome in Jerusalem. He attempted to introduce quadrennial, Greek-style athletic and music contests, as well as Roman-style chariot and horse races and fights between gladiators.

Of greatest offense to his people, however, were the iconic trophies for the victors that Herod displayed in Jerusalem. Such was the protest about these images that Herod was forced to remove them. Nevertheless, the games and spectacles continued and contributed to the weakening of inherited values among the covenant people of the Lord. The corrupting influences of Antiochus IV were being revisited upon the Jews in the persona of their own king. Josephus knew this well. "Herod . . . gradually corrupted the ancient way of life, which had hitherto been inviolable. As a result, we suffered considerable harm at a later time as well, because those things were neglected which had formerly induced piety in the masses."[5]

Herod created a seaside palace in Caesarea where he established a theater and racetrack for runners and chariots. A section of the racetrack could be reshaped as a gladiatorial arena.

Building and town planning played their part in changing cultural values. The architectural styles Herod employed in his imposing structures in Jerusalem and Caesarea, but also in Jericho and Samaria, were not local but foreign, whether Greek or Roman. The presentation of these structures, though mute, was eloquent; the future lay not with Israel's covenantal past but with the gentiles, their buildings, technology, values, and practices.

Herod saw himself as "benefactor" in the style of a Hellenistic monarch. In regard to such rulers, Luke commented, "Those in authority over them are called benefactors" (Luke 22:25). Herod expressed his "benefactions" in his construction of monumental buildings inside and outside Israel and his provision of famine relief, again, both inside and outside his kingdom. Although Herod's generosity beyond Israel was chiefly directed toward gentiles, he did secure protection for Jews of the diaspora from local oppression.

Nevertheless, Herod was far from unfettered in his programs and policies. Conservative values were powerfully upheld by the Pharisees as the moral and theological watchdogs of the broad mass of the people. These could find sharp expression in acts of "zeal," as in the violent opposition to the introduction of

---

5. Josephus, *Jewish Antiquities* 15.257.

images at the athletic games, in their opposition to the loyalty oath to Augustus and Herod, and in the golden eagle incident discussed below.[6]

This innate stubborn resistance against Hellenism may explain Herod's caution in several areas. He avoided portraiture in his coins and human and animal representations in decorations in his palaces. He refused permission for his sister to marry Syllaeus unless the Nabatean was circumcised. He is believed to have abstained from eating pork. These, however, were probably token gestures, designed to mollify his subjects. Of greatest significance, however, was his erection of the massive temple for the Lord. To avoid offense Herod employed a thousand priests specially trained as masons and carpenters for work on the sacred precincts. But the architectural style of that great structure was not Jewish but Greco-Roman.

Notwithstanding these concessions to traditional scruples, the overall impact of his reign, which was doubtless intentional, was to move his people in the direction of Greco-Roman values and standards. Herod would have realized better than anybody that his success in this must accelerate the Romanization of his realm and its ultimate loss from his family to the emperor's provincial prefects. Perhaps, though, he knew that his obstinate subjects would not be ready for such drastic change for many years and that his sons could look forward to inheriting his kingdom.

HEROD, BUILDER IN JERUSALEM

Herod was a prodigious builder, including in Jerusalem. His most famous structure was his great temple dedicated to the worship of the Lord. To provide a level base for the temple in the steep ravines of Jerusalem, it was necessary for Herod's engineers to erect a marble platform 912 feet (south) by 1,536 feet (east) by 1,035 feet (north) by 1,590 feet (west), an area approximating fifteen football fields! The platform was supported by massive walls of carefully chiseled masonry, some stones being 40 feet in length. This great marble podium was enclosed on all sides by roofed porticoes. Within this enclosed space and occupying less than one-quarter of the whole was the temple itself. The open space on the platform between the porticoes and the temple was called

---

6. Significantly and surprisingly, Josephus doesn't use the language of "zeal" for righteous reaction against Herod's actions.

the Court of the Gentiles, where hundreds of thousands of pilgrims could assemble for the great feasts. Many people remarked on its size and beauty.

It was a structure more noteworthy than any under the sun.[7]

He who has not seen Herod's temple has not seen beauty.[8]

The buildings . . . are of most exceeding beauty and magnificence so as to be universal objects of admiration.[9]

Josephus was struck with wonder at the size of the complex and the speed of its erection—it was officially opened only one and a half years after work had begun. He gave credence to the popular belief that no rain fell by day during this initial construction period, a sign that it was "a manifestation of the power of God." Jesus, however, prophesied the destruction of the temple, following his purging of the vendors. As an eyewitness, Josephus graphically described those terrible events in August-September AD 70.

Another great structure erected by Herod, as mentioned above, was "[his] own palace . . . in the upper city." This comprised two buildings (named after his patrons Augustus and Agrippa) and was located to the south of the present Jaffa Gate of Jerusalem. These buildings were commandeered by the Romans after Judea was made a province in AD 6 as the military barracks and residence for the prefect when he visited Jerusalem. This complex of structures was most likely the Praetorium mentioned in the Gospel of John where the Roman trial of Jesus occurred.

The Praetorium was built with two internal open spaces. The Roman trial occurred in an open space (where Jesus was accused, later flogged, and condemned) and also a space inside its structure (where Pilate interrogated Jesus in private). The population of Jerusalem would have been restricted to the street outside.

Josephus describes a trial scene thirty years later under Florus, the Roman procurator. The procurator was seeking to punish a number of malefactors

---

7. Josephus, *Jewish Antiquities* 15.411.
8. b. Bava Batra 4a.
9. Philo, *Special Laws* 1.73.

involved in recent disturbances in Jerusalem. While the circumstances are different from those associated with Jesus, Josephus's account gives some idea of the details of Jesus's trial. "Florus lodged at [Herod's] palace and on the following day had a tribunal (*bēma*) placed in front of the building and took his seat. The chief priests, the nobles and the most eminent citizens then presented themselves before the tribunal."[10]

From this passage we note that (1) on arrival in Jerusalem from Caesarea, the governor lodged at the former palace of Herod (as, doubtless, Pilate also did); (2) the judgment tribunal was in front of the building (as, probably, Pilate's bench also was); and (3) the leaders of the people were present to make the accusation, which, in this case, however, they declined to do. Jesus's accusers were limited to the temple hierarchy, whereas the above account also includes "nobles" and "eminent citizens."

HEROD, BUILDER OF A GREAT SEAPORT

Herod's vision extended far beyond the boundaries of his realm. A major problem for Herod was the lack of any safe harbor on his coastland. Ships from Rome, Greece, Egypt, or Syria were forced to anchor in the open sea, leaving them vulnerable to onshore winds. Many ships were dashed to pieces on an inhospitable shoreline.

Herod conceived the idea of an artificial harbor at an ancient though run-down settlement called Strato's Tower. This he renamed Caesarea after his patron Caesar Augustus. It is referred to as Caesarea Maritima to distinguish it from other cities named after the emperor. In circa 23 BC Herod's builders began to rebuild the city with magnificent public buildings constructed of white marble. Water was brought for the large population of the new city by aqueducts, whose remains are still to be seen today. Most significant of all, however, was Herod's great harbor, which exceeded the Piraeus, the port of Athens.

Herod's motives in the building of Caesarea were twofold. A great port for his kingdom was fundamental to the expansion of trade into, as well as out of, Israel. But Caesarea was also Herod's bridge to the world's stage on which, so it appears, he desired to be a significant player. Herod was no passive client king, content to be in the obscurity of remote Israel. Caesarea was Herod's statement to the world outside, perhaps his most important symbol. Caesarea

---

10. Josephus, *Jewish War* 2.301.

provided a magnificent entry to his kingdom, as well as a majestic point from which to step out to the western world. Again, Josephus is our witness.

> Notwithstanding the totally recalcitrant nature of the site, [Herod] grappled with the difficulties so successfully, that the solidity of the masonry defied the sea, while its beauty was such as if no obstacle had existed. Having determined upon the comparative size of the harbour as we have stated, he had blocks of stone let down into twenty fathoms of water, most of them measuring fifty feet in length, some even larger. Upon the submarine foundation thus laid he constructed above the surface a mole two hundred feet broad; of which one hundred were built out to break the surge, whence this portion was called the breakwater, while the remainder supported a stone wall encircling the harbour. From this wall arose, at intervals, massive towers, the loftiest and most magnificent of which was called Drusion after the stepson of Caesar.
>
> Numerous inlets in the wall provided landing places for mariners putting into the harbour, while the whole circular terrace fronting these channels served as a broad promenade for disembarking passengers.[11]

In AD 6 Herod's patron Augustus took the momentous step of annexing Judea as a Roman province. Archelaus, Herod's son, had proved to be an inadequate ruler. Disgruntled Jewish aristocrats who had earlier lobbied for autonomy under the Romans were now successful in their requests. Caesarea came into its own as the capital of the new province. Successive Roman prefects and procurators made their home in Herod's new city, from which they administered the province, making periodic visits to Jerusalem, the previous capital.

While there is no evidence that Jesus visited Caesarea, the great seaport was to become important in the history of early Christianity. In circa 34 Caesarea became the home and center of operations of Philip "the evangelist." Soon afterward Peter was drawn to the city, where he preached the gospel to those assembled in the house of the Roman centurion Cornelius. It is probable that Christianity spread from Caesarea to the cities of Phoenicia—Tyre, Sidon, Ptolemais—through the ministry of Philip the evangelist.

In 41 Judea reverted to its former status as a kingdom ruled by a Jewish king. Herod Agrippa I, the grandson of Herod, upon his accession, attempted to de-

---

11. Josephus, *Jewish War* 1.408–413.

stroy the leadership of the church in Jerusalem (Acts 12:1–3). Agrippa had James Zebedee killed and imprisoned Peter with the same intention.[12] However, Peter escaped. After Agrippa took up residence in Caesarea, he met his death following a ceremony in the amphitheater when the people venerated him as a "god." Caesarea was a city of mixed population. Gentiles probably predominated over Jews. Racial conflict between Jews and gentiles in 66 was to be the spark that lit the great war between Jews and Romans that blazed throughout 66–74.

The apostle Paul was no stranger to Caesarea. A recent convert but now in danger in Judea, he embarked from Caesarea to Tarsus circa 36. After his missionary tour through Greece circa 49–52, Paul disembarked in Caesarea for Jerusalem, reembarking later for his journey north to Antioch. Circa 57 Paul returned briefly to Caesarea as the houseguest of Philip the evangelist. Some weeks later Paul was brought back under guard from Jerusalem to the capital, where he remained the prisoner of successive procurators Felix and Festus for more than two years. Finally, Paul sailed from Caesarea under escort for trial before Caesar in Rome. In the centuries to come, Caesarea became a great world center of Christian scholarship, especially through the work of Origen.

HEROD, BENEFACTOR OF FOREIGN CITIES

Herod, king of the Jews, in addition to his formidable program of building within Israel, was also a generous "benefactor" of Hellenistic cities and institutions.

By his patronage to the cities and states of the eastern Mediterranean, Herod was to bring himself and his kingdom into international prominence, but as a Hellenophile, a lover of things Greek. No longer could Herod's nation be regarded as a narrow theocratic Jewish enclave.

Many cities benefited from the king's largesse, whether Ascalon in the south; Tripolis, Ptolemais, Berytus, Tyre, Sidon in Phoenicia; Laodicea and Antioch in Syria; or the inland cities Panias and Damascus. Here the king donated a colonnade, there a temple, there an aqueduct, there a gymnasium. During the thirties and forties, these hellenized cities were visited by Christian preachers like Philip the evangelist, or others whose names have not survived.

---

12. It is likely that High Priest Matthias, son of Annas, assisted Agrippa's attempt to destroy Christianity. See chap. 24, "The Annas Vendetta."

The benefactions of Herod, lover of things Greek, extended even to the Greek world proper, to cities of Achaea (Athens, Sparta, Elis), to Epirus (Nicopolis), to the Greek islands of the Aegean (Cos, Rhodes, Samos), and to Lycia and Pergamum on the western coast of the Aegean. Herod's thorough love of Hellenism is seen in his endowment of the Olympic games, which he revived after years of neglect, and over which he served as president (*agonothētes*). From Nicolaus of Damascus, Herod's court historian, Josephus paints this impressive picture.

> His bounty to the people of Elis, on the other hand, was a gift not only to Hellas at large but to the whole world, wherever the fame of the Olympic games penetrates. For observing that these were declining for want of funds and that this solitary relic of ancient Greece was sinking into decay, he not only accepted the post of president for the quadrennial celebration which coincided with his visit on his voyage to Rome, but he endowed them for all time with revenues, which should preserve an unfading memory of his term as president.[13]

Herod's gifts to Hellenistic cities and festivals would inevitably have involved him in the worship and sacrifices of the deities of Greece and possibly also of the mystery cults. Among the Jews, Herod their king presented himself as an observant Jew, but his real sympathies lay with the gentiles. Josephus observed that Herod "was on more friendly terms with Greeks than with Jews."

As it happens during the next century after Herod, Paul, the Jew, chosen to be the Apostle to the Gentiles, was to bring a quite different message to many of the regions that benefited from the patronage of Herod, the benefactor. Paul was to proclaim a new world ruler, Jesus, the crucified and resurrected Son of David.

HEROD'S REPRESSIVE REGIME

Herod financed his massive building program and maintained an expensive court by repressive taxation of the people at large and, more particularly, by pillaging the property of the wealthy aristocrats who stood outside the circle of

---

13. Josephus, *Jewish War* 1.427.

his supporters. At his death there were public protests pleading a reduction in taxation. A delegation of nobles went to Rome seeking local "autonomy" under direct Roman rule. Even that was preferred to further oppression from a son of Herod. Nevertheless, those who complained loudest were the wealthy; the king had acted generously by gifts to the poor in the famine of 25 BC and had relieved their taxes in the famines of 20 BC (by a third) and 14 BC (by a quarter).

Aware that he was hated by the Jews, Herod imported many foreign mercenaries to bolster local security. Having secured Jerusalem for himself by the construction of the Antonia and his own fortified palace, Herod created a number of fortresses throughout his kingdom. The nine fortresses he established—among them Masada, Herodium, and Machaerus, which were also royal palaces—served as a counterbalance against possible Jewish opposition as well as providing dungeons for any who dared express a criticism that might be overheard by Herod's extensive network of spies. Knowing the people feared he was seeking to dissolve their religion, the king forbade any public assembly or meeting. He himself would mingle with the crowds in disguise to spy on the people.

Some decades later an apocalyptist was to comment negatively about Herod.

And an insolent king shall succeed [the Hasmoneans], who shall not be of the race of the priests, a man bold and shameless, and he shall judge them as they shall deserve. And he shall cut off their chief men with the sword, and shall destroy them in secret places, so that no one may know where their bodies are. He shall slay the old and the young, and he shall not spare. Then the fear of him will be bitter unto them in their land. And he shall execute judgements on them as the Egyptians executed upon them, during thirty and four years, and he shall punish them. (Ass. Mos. 6)

HEROD AND AUGUSTUS: THE GOLDEN EAGLE INCIDENT

In the latter part of Herod's reign, his relationship with his imperial patron soured. Herod's pursuit of military action in 12 BC against his eastern neighbors, the Nabateans, is known to have displeased Augustus, who reduced his status from "friend" to "subject."

In 7 BC, in what appears to have been an attempt to shore up his reputation with Augustus, the king decreed that his subjects swear an oath of allegiance to himself and the Roman Caesar. In 20 BC Herod had secured an oath of loyalty from the people, but it was directed only to him. The stringent terms of such oaths in other places are known through surviving records, though no details of Herod's oath formulae have come down to us.

Herod's double-oath requirement in 7 BC was acceded to by the entire nation. The Pharisees, however, refused to comply and were punished by a fine. At the beginning of his reign, Herod had enjoyed a measure of support from the leading Pharisees Samaias and Pollion. From 7 BC until his death in 4 BC, however, relationships between the king and the Pharisees deteriorated significantly. Herod's pro-Greek, pro-Roman policies led to a conservative backlash.

In a rash, final attempt to regain the support and confidence of Augustus, the king, now aged seventy, had a large effigy of an eagle, colored gold, attached to the exterior of the great door of the temple of the Lord in Jerusalem. Most probably Herod was acknowledging the power of Rome by this action; the eagle was a symbol for Rome, sitting on top of their military standards. This was in contempt of the law of God, which forbade the creation of any representation of the Lord by any living creature. The two leading Pharisees, Judas and Matthias, inflamed their young disciples, who lowered themselves from ropes to hack down the golden eagle. The idolatrous symbol of gentile power had no place on the temple of the Lord! "This it was which these doctors now exhorted their disciples to cut down, telling them that, even if the action proved hazardous, it was a noble deed to die for the law of one's country; for the souls of those who came to an end attained immortality and an eternally abiding sense of felicity; it was only the ignoble, uninitiated in their philosophy, who clung in their ignorance to life and preferred death on a sick-bed to that of a hero."[14]

As noted, Josephus didn't apply the specific vocabulary of "zeal" to religious activists, including these rabbis and their disciples, whose life-or-death commitment to the laws of God resemble Mattathias and his sons a century and a half earlier.

For their part Judas and Matthias and their fellow martyrs anticipated by a decade the zealous rabbi Saddok, who joined Judas the Galilean in leading the uprising over the Roman census that prepared the way for the imposition of the Roman direct tax on individuals in 6. Their battle cry was "No master, except God." Only the Lord was fit to number his people. To allow the gentile to do that was as much a sellout to gentile power as the golden eagle on the tem-

---

14. Josephus, *Jewish War* 1.650.

ple had been. A rising tide of "zeal" for the honor of Yahweh, therefore, marks the latter days of Herod the king, during which Jesus of Nazareth was born.

A PARANOID KING: THE ARREST OF THE NOTABLES AND THE SLAUGHTER OF THE INNOCENTS

Near death, racked with disease and plagued with anxiety, Herod devised a scheme to ensure an appropriate level of grief at his passing, which he discerned was imminent. Knowing of universal hatred toward him, he ordered a decree that respected citizens from every village should be rounded up and held in the hippodrome in Jerusalem. He ordered that, at his death, these eminent persons were to be executed. There would be mourning throughout the land, if not for him, then for these men. They were duly arrested and imprisoned in the hippodrome. Herod's death followed quickly, but his orders were overruled by his sister Salome and the notables released. The king is quoted by Josephus as follows: "I know that the Jews will celebrate my death by a festival; yet I can obtain a vicarious mourning and a magnificent funeral, if you consent to follow my instructions. You know these men here in custody; the moment I expire have them surrounded by the soldiers and massacred; so that all Judaea and every household weep for me, whether they will or no."[15]

The killing of the baby boys of Bethlehem at Herod's order, according to Matthew 2:16, is questioned by many scholars and is uncorroborated by Josephus. However, such a massacre may have only involved a relatively small number of children in a village as small as Bethlehem. In any case, it is consistent with the character of Herod in his plan to kill the notables, as described above by Josephus. Macrobius, a fourth-century author, refers to Herod's slaughter of all the boys under two years of age in Syria. While there is no evidence of a Syria-wide assault on baby boys, Macrobius's words may echo an earlier source, now lost, corroborating Matthew's account of the king's evil designs on the boys from the village of Bethlehem.

HEROD'S REIGN AS BACKGROUND TO THE BIRTH OF JESUS

In all probability Joseph and Mary were quite young when they were married, as was customary. At the time of the king's death in 4 BC, Jesus was a child.

15. Josephus, *Jewish War* 1.659–666.

Thus, we assume that Joseph and Mary were born in and lived through the latter half of Herod's reign, that is, during the era of Augustus's patronage from 31 BC.

Joseph was a descendant of the royal house of David, from whose line God's anointed king ("Messiah") was expected to come. It has been suggested that Joseph's Davidic forebears had been exiled in Babylon but had subsequently settled upon their return in obscurity and relative poverty in Nazareth in Galilee. Joseph may have been secure from the danger represented by Herod in the isolation and relative inaccessibility of Nazareth.

Mary, too, was from Nazareth. She was related to Elizabeth, who, with her husband, Zechariah, was of priestly descent, and who lived in the hill country of Judea; Zechariah and Elizabeth were the parents of John the Baptist. It is not known whether Mary had been brought up in Judea, near Elizabeth, or in Nazareth in Galilee.

The tenor of the early chapters of the Gospel of Luke suggests that Joseph and Mary belonged to a devout but poor sector of Jewish society, which was relatively untouched by the wealth and corruption of the cities that were the centers of power in Herodian Israel. Each had lived through the middle and later years of Herod's reign but, whether by choice or by accident, had been isolated from it. Pious folk these, whose life centered on the Torah in the home, the synagogue, and the temple. Jesus's parents belonged to a devout, conservative culture of the covenant of the Lord in which the Pharisees, and a prophet like John the Baptist, found support. They were remote in every sense from the Hellenistic world of Herod, king of the Jews, in Jerusalem.

The reign of Herod was the immediate background to the birth of Jesus of Nazareth, descendant of David, Messiah of Israel. Herod's great buildings and Hellenistic culture continued after his passing in 4 BC, initially during the rule of Archelaus in Judea, but also when Augustus made Judea a province in AD 6. Jerusalem was "Herodian" in streetscape and culture during the years of Jesus's ministry, 29–33, notably so at the time of Jesus's arrest, trials, and crucifixion.

HEROD'S WILLS AND THE PROBLEM OF SUCCESSION

Under Augustus, Herod consolidated and expanded his territories, but he must have, at the same time, been preoccupied with the question of who was to succeed him. That issue was complicated by several factors. One was the presence of his nine wives, who lived together, several of them maneuvering to have their sons succeed Herod as king. Mariamne I, the Hasmonean princess, sought to have either or both of her charismatic sons Alexander and Aristobulus succeed Herod. Doris, his first wife, lobbied for her capable son Antipater to fulfill that role. Malthake, the Samaritan wife, doubtless harbored hopes for her young sons, Archelaus and Antipas.

Was Herod's successor to have Jewish blood, Hasmonean blood, or Samaritan blood?

Complicating matters further, whoever Herod nominated must be approved by Augustus. The wives and their sons were no strangers to Rome and the corridors of power. Both mothers and sons traveled to Rome to promote their own interests with the Caesar and his household.

It is no surprise, therefore, that Herod wrote as many as seven wills, beginning in 23 BC and continuing to 4 BC, a few weeks before his death.

Initially Herod nominated as his successor Alexander, son of Mariamne I, who was nineteen at the time. However, when Alexander fell out of favor in 14 BC, the king named the twenty-six-year-old Antipater as the future king. Antipater was the son of the king's first wife, Doris, who had come back into favor. Antipater traveled to Rome with the will for Augustus to endorse. He dressed regally as "a friend of Caesar."

Herod wrote a third will in 12 BC, in which he named Antipater king, with Alexander and Aristobulus as "subordinate kings."

However, by 7 BC the sons of Mariamne fell out of favor and were executed. The new will (the fourth!) named Antipater as king, to be succeeded by the teenaged Herod Philip I. Significantly, Herod bypassed Malthake's sons, Archelaus and Antipas.

In 5 BC Herod removed Herod Philip I as successor to Antipater. Herod executed Antipater and looked to Archelaus and Antipas, the sons of the Samaritan Malthake, to succeed him. However, the king disliked Archelaus, so he named (in his fifth will) as his successor the seventeen-year-old Antipas. Finally, in 4 BC (in the seventh will) he named Archelaus as king and Antipas and Herod Philip II as tetrarchs. Archelaus was to rule half the kingdom (Judea, Idumea, Samaria), Antipas a quarter (Galilee and Perea), and Philip a quarter (Gaulanitis).

Augustus basically approved the final will except that Archelaus was not to be "king" but to hold the lesser title "ethnarch." Antipas and Philip were to be titled "tetrarch" (ruler of a quarter).

Augustus's preference was for Herod to be succeeded by one ruler, as nominated by him. The endless struggles within the palace, however, disposed of the best prospects, Alexander, Aristobulus, and Antipater. When the king died in 4 BC, his realm was divided into an ethnarchy and two tetrarchies, the latter to be led by teenagers.

Inevitably two consequences followed: the immediate division of the kingdom into three separate jurisdictions led to their inevitable absorption later into the Roman provincial system.

Herod the "Great" was succeeded in Judea and Samaria by Archelaus, a failed leader, whose territories became Roman colonies in AD 6. In 33, Jesus from Nazareth in Galilee was arrested; subjected to interrogation, a Jewish trial, and a Roman trial; and found guilty and crucified as "king of the Jews." In effect, this cluster of events occurred in a political and religious setting that had been established by the lengthy rule of Herod (40–4 BC).

10

ARCHELAUS, ETHNARCH OF JUDEA, IDUMEA, AND SAMARIA

(4 BC–AD 6)

After the public mourning for Herod (March 4 BC), his son Archelaus immediately identified himself as heir to the throne. He went to the temple dressed in white and addressed people from a golden throne. But he asserted that he and the people must await Augustus's decision on the successor to Herod the king. Many, however, immediately demanded reduction of taxes; others the abolition of duty; and others the release of prisoners. Archelaus readily agreed to these requests.

Had matters rested there, the transition of power to Archelaus might have passed without difficulty. However, the memory of Herod's brutality toward the men who removed the golden eagle from the gate of the temple burned deeply within the chief protesters, the Pharisees and their supporters.[1] Public protest had been forbidden by Herod.[2] The agitators demanded the sacking of Herod's favored officials, including the high priest, Joazar.

Archelaus sent a senior military officer to the crowds to urge patience, but the disaffected showered him with stones. When the Passover season approached, the protesters occupied the temple. A small cohort of soldiers failed to resolve the problem, so Archelaus unleashed the whole army on the

---

1. The Pharisees related well to Herod at first, but relationships deteriorated thereafter, reaching their negative climax with the killing of the younger Pharisees who removed the golden eagle from the gate of the temple.

2. Josephus, *Antiquities* 15.369.

protesters—his infantry and cavalry. Three thousand were slain, the others ordered back to their homes.

Soon afterward Archelaus, his supporters, and his opponents set out by sea for Rome to meet with Caesar Augustus (early May). Beforehand in Caesarea Maritima they were met by Sabinus, procurator of Syria, who had come "to take charge of Herod's estate." Archelaus had anticipated Sabinus's intentions and arranged for Varus, legate of Syria, to come and block Sabinus's plans.

It is unclear why two senior officials in Antioch, Varus the legate and Sabinus the procurator, were pitted against each other.

Sabinus promised to take no further action until Caesar had resolved the matter of the will of the late king. Josephus states that Sabinus was "eager for gain . . . greedy . . . reckless, insolent."[3]

Once Archelaus had departed for Rome, however, Sabinus immediately sped to Jerusalem and took possession of the palace, acquired Herod's financial accounts, and seized his property. Aware of Sabinus's intentions, Varus marched three legions up to Jerusalem, leaving one legion behind to keep the peace, and then returned with his other troops to Antioch.

CHAOS IN JERUSALEM AND THE REGIONS

Jews from Galilee, Idumea, and Jericho launched attacks on Sabinus and Varus's lone legion in Jerusalem. This was evidence of the Jews' preference for local rather than Roman rule in Israel. Their message was for the intruders to depart and return to Syria.

Meanwhile chaos reigned in the various regions of Herod's kingdom, filling the vacuum of power following the death of Herod and the subsequent incompetence of Archelaus. In Idumea various military groups took up arms against one another. In Galilee Judas, son of Ezekias, also known as Judas the Galilean (or Gaulanite), seized control of Galilee because he "aspired to sovereignty" and "was possessed of a thirst for power and an ambitious desire for royal rank."[4] Simon, a royal slave in Perea, assumed the diadem of kingship and burned down the late king's palaces in Jericho and Betharamphtha. Athronges,

3. Josephus, *Jewish Antiquities* 17.253, 254, 257. Josephus may be portraying Sabinus as a "bad" Roman to balance bad Jews, both of whom combined ultimately to be responsible for the invasion in 66.

4. Josephus, *Jewish War* 2.55; *Jewish Antiquities* 17.10.5.

too, aspired to the throne as a king and appointed himself and his four brothers rulers of Judea.[5] Simon and Athronges died at the hands of Varus's legions.

Josephus comments: "Such was the great madness that settled upon the nation because they had no king of their own to restrain the populace by his pre-eminence, and because the foreigners who came among them to suppress the rebellion were themselves a cause of provocation through their arrogance and greed."[6]

Judas, however, survived the Roman assault in Galilee and reappeared in AD 6 as a coleader of the so-called Fourth Philosophy, the movement opposed to the Roman census in AD 6 that preceded the imposition of the hated poll tax.

Josephus does not explain if these aspirants for royal power did so based on Davidic or Maccabean descent. The critical point, however, was that Caesar appointed "client" kings to the regions conquered by his legions. To self-appoint oneself as a king invited the wrath of Caesar, the indictment of treason, and the terrible punishment, crucifixion.

The thesis of S. G. F. Brandon, that these rebel-leaders were inspired by "zealotism," is close to the mark. He observed that "zealotism" was "a noble expression of Jewish religious faith and one that was sanctioned and inspired by the example of many revered figures of Israel's heroic past."[7] Josephus, however, does not employ the language of "zeal" at this time but reserves it for the faction of that name at the time of the Roman invasion, AD 66–70.

Four decades later when Caiaphas asked Jesus whether he was Christ, Jesus's answer confirmed that he was. The high priest twisted the accusation to Pilate that Jesus was a self-proclaimed "king of the Jews" (Mark 14:61–62; 15:2), which was the *political* crime of treason. Jesus, however, had identified himself to the disciples as the omnipotent "Son of man" who must suffer and die for the redemption of his people (Mark 8:31; 10:45). As the Christ of Jewish prophetic hope, Jesus actually upheld Caesar's role as tax collector and administrator in Judea, a view contrary to the "zealous" mind-set but which was echoed in the writings of Paul and Peter to the churches (Mark 12:13–17; Rom. 13:1–7; 1 Tim. 2:1–2; 1 Pet. 2:13–17). Jesus was "king," but in the sense of

---

5. According to W. R. Farmer, *Maccabees, Zealots, and Josephus* (New York: Columbia University Press, 1956), all Jewish resistance was of Maccabean lineage. This is an interesting theory for which there is little evidence.

6. Josephus, *Jewish Antiquities* 17.277.

7. S. G. F. Brandon, *Jesus and the Zealots* (Manchester: Manchester University Press, 1967), 63–64.

fulfilled prophecy, not at all in the political sense. Jesus had no army, a sure sign that he did not claim to be a king.

HEARINGS IN ROME BEFORE CAESAR AUGUSTUS (JULY–NOVEMBER 4 BC)

Meanwhile in Rome, strong voices were raised against the appointment of Archelaus as king in succession to Herod, ruling all his territories. Archelaus had the support of friends including Nicolaus of Damascus (Herod's court historian),[8] his aunt Salome, and other relatives of the late king. Nicolaus argued tellingly that the recent rioters against Archelaus were actually rioting against Caesar, the arbiter of the kingdom.

Herod Antipas, Archelaus's younger brother, also set out for Rome, claiming that the sixth will appointed him king, in succession to his father. Antipas, who was then only seventeen years old, had the support of Herod's sister Salome and his mother, Malthake. But what weighed most heavily in his favor was the eloquence of Irenaeus, Herod's rhetorician. Also, Sabinus sent messages to Caesar accusing Archelaus but recommending Antipas.

However, the group supporting Antipas realistically recognized his relative youthfulness as a problem for him assuming the absolute kingship immediately. Their preference was for "autonomy" under Antipas, subject to the sovereign supervision of the province of Syria, whose capital was Antioch.

Against the advocacy for Antipas, a group of fifty Jews from Judea supported by eight thousand Jews in Rome also pleaded with Augustus to make Israel an "autonomous" kingdom subject to Antioch, but with Archelaus as king. Once again, the "autonomy" provision was understandable; Archelaus was nineteen years old at the time.

Archelaus fell before Augustus pleading for a favorable decision.

However, voices were raised against this proposal. Herod had been a "cruel tyrant" who had lavished money taken from the Jews for various causes and projects in the Greek world. Worst of all was Archelaus's slaughter of the three thousand during Passover. They urged that Herod's kingdom should now be made part of the province of Syria.

Weeks later (October), faced with these opposing views, Augustus decided on the following resolution:

---

8. Josephus was dependent for his narrative on the writings of Nicolaus of Damascus (now lost).

- Half of Herod's kingdom (Idumea, Judaea, Samaria with Strato's Tower, Sebaste, Joppa, and Jerusalem) was assigned to Archelaus, with the title "ethnarch."
- This was a blow to Archelaus, since the seventh will named him *king* of that region.
- The remaining territory was divided between Herod Antipas (Perea and Galilee) and Philip (Batanea, Trachonitis, and Auranitis), each with the title "tetrarch."

IMPLICATIONS OF AUGUSTUS'S DECISION

Augustus's choice of Archelaus would issue in disastrous results. His failure to punish those who killed the golden eagle martyrs and his release of military force at the Passover with the loss of three thousand Passover pilgrims were not forgotten.

Before the parties in Rome could return to Israel, Varus marched from Syria with two legions and ruthlessly put down the rebellion in Jerusalem, but also in the regions of Judea, Galilee, and Perea.

Josephus is sparing about the details of Archelaus's rule in Judea, Idumea, and Samaria. He does, however, report that the ethnarch "treated not only Jews but also Samaritans with great brutality."[9] The passing reference to Joseph and Mary not settling in Judea is an important window into Archelaus's bad reputation. "But when [Joseph] heard that Archelaus was reigning over Judea in place of his father Herod, he was afraid to go there, and being warned in a dream he withdrew to the district of Galilee. And he went and lived in a city called Nazareth" (Matt. 2:22–23).

In AD 6 representatives of various groups from Judea sent deputies to Caesar to "denounce" their ethnarch. As a result, Augustus banished Archelaus as an exile to Vienna, in Gaul. His property was confiscated to the imperial treasury.

These events must have become part of general knowledge, since Jesus introduces elements into one of his parables. "[Jesus] said therefore, 'A nobleman went into a far country to receive for himself a kingdom and then return. . . . But his citizens hated him and sent a delegation after him, saying, "We do not want this man to reign over us." . . . "But as for these enemies of

9. Josephus, *Jewish War* 2.111.

mine, who did not want me to reign over them, bring them here and slaughter them before me"'" (Luke 19:12, 14, 27).

Herod would not have been happy with Augustus's decision. His seven different wills indicated his passionate desire that his kingdom would remain undivided, subject to Caesar. He was passionately concerned that his kingdom did not fall into the hands of the Maccabean dynasty, from whom his father had seized it.

The Maccabees had united Idumea, Samaria, and Galilee to Judea as a single political entity. Herod, as "client" first of Mark Antony, and subsequently of Augustus, had consolidated the constituent regions as a united Israel. Herod served his Roman masters well by providing stability to the otherwise volatile Levant and as a bulwark against Parthian access to Egypt. True, Herod's grandson Herod Agrippa I ruled a united realm beginning in 41 but ending prematurely in 44. This was the last throw of the dice. The Roman legions marched back into Judea in 66; Galilee now was joined to Judea as a Roman province. The drift into war with Rome was now inevitable.

The arrival of Coponius in AD 6 as the first prefect was followed by two consequences.[10] It consolidated Judea as a region separated from Galilee and Gaulanitis, and it instituted a census as the instrument of direct tax, payable to Caesar. Both of these proved to be disastrous to the future for the homeland of the Jews.

10. In 27 BC Augustus divided the provinces of the empire into imperial and senatorial provinces. Judea was a minor imperial province. Its garrison was composed of less than one Roman legion. Judea was governed by a military prefect, typically belonging to the equestrian order.

11

JUDEA

(AD 6)

The arrival of Roman troops and governors meant that Judea was now a Roman-occupied province (and Galilee after 44). Augustus deemed Judea politically unstable, as reflected by his appointment of *military* governors, referred to as "prefects."[1] The first such prefect was Coponius, but as a measure of the greatness of this event, he was accompanied by the famous general Quirinius. As noted, the Parthian-led war of 40–37 BC indicated the strategic location of Judea.

JUDEA AS A ROMAN PROVINCE

Augustus's momentous decision brought with it several dramatic changes, for example, the relocation of the capital from Jerusalem to Caesarea Maritima, the presence of Roman soldiers, and the introduction of Roman coinage. But more significant were two other changes.

First, Augustus decided on directly taxing the people of Judea. The males of the new province must now pay personal tax directly to Caesar.[2] To inau-

---

1. However, in 41–44 Claudius appointed Herod Agrippa (of Maccabean-Herodian descent) as king of Judea. After his untimely demise in 44, Claudius renamed the governors "procurators," placing greater emphasis on the tax-gathering role. Growing political resistance by the Jews compelled the Romans (initially under Vespasian) to invade the land, 66–74, to subdue the insurrectionists.

2. Fabian E. Udoh, *To Caesar What Is Caesar's: Tribute, Taxes, and Imperial Administration in Early Roman Palestine* (Providence, RI: Brown Judaic Studies, 2000), 207–43.

gurate this new tax, it was necessary to conduct a registration or census of the population.[3]

It is not clear whether the taxes were paid in kind or by coin. It is likewise uncertain whether the tribute was collected by Jewish aristocracy or farmed out to Jewish tax collectors. It is possible that the tax applied to agricultural yield as well as to personal property, based on its value (which explains the necessity for the registration).

The census was opposed by Judas the Galilean (a.k.a. Gaulanite)[4] and Saddok, a Pharisee, who said it was an instrument of the slavery of the Lord's people to the hated gentiles. Their rebellion was defeated by the legions led by the incoming prefect, Coponius.[5]

Josephus refers to this uprising as the expression of a "Fourth Philosophy," the employment of violence to defend the honor of the Lord.[6] Josephus's two great works, *Jewish War* and *Jewish Antiquities*, assume that the invasion of Vespasian in 66 was ultimately attributable to the tax-inspired uprising of Judas and Saddok in 6.

The other dramatic change was the new role and power of the high priest and his council (the Sanhedrin). In effect, the high priest became a "client" ruler of Jerusalem and, most likely, of the whole province, replacing the role played first by Herod the king and then by Archelaus the ethnarch. The high priest and the leading members of his council were Sadducees, whom Josephus typified as "heartless." Furthermore, and profoundly important, the high priests were extremely wealthy through rent from temple merchants and money changers.

The prefect was responsible for appointing the high priest, and the high priest had immense wealth to bribe his way to this appointment. The prefect and the high priest were to a significant degree dependent on one another. In part, this explains the capacity of Caiaphas to overrule Pilate in securing the

---

3. The census in Luke 2:1–5 occurred earlier, during the last days of Herod. It is not referred in other sources.

4. Judas the Gaulanite from Gamla in Galilee, who cofounded the "Fourth Philosophy" in 6 (Josephus, *Jewish Antiquities* 18.3), was one and the same person as Judas the Galilean who claimed the rule of Galilee in 4 BC (Josephus, *Jewish Antiquities* 17.10).

5. The exchange in the temple precincts between Jesus and the Pharisees and Herodians in 33 about paying taxes to Caesar reveals an ongoing and bitter controversy (Mark 12:13–17).

6. The Pharisees were the "first philosophy," the Sadducees the "second," and the Essenes the "third." It is curious that Josephus doesn't employ the vocabulary of "zeal" to the rebellion of Judas and Saddok.

prefect's verdict against Jesus. Whereas the charge against Jesus could have been "blasphemy" (Mark 14:64), issuing in stoning under the auspices of the high priest, it was more expedient to remove the young prophet on political grounds at the hands of the Romans.

As we will indicate, it was Jesus's conflict with these sources of money to the high priest that issued in his arrest, trials, and ultimately crucifixion. Jesus's action in the temple and his known prophecy of its destruction were the source of the hatred and vendetta of Annas, his son-in-law Caiaphas, and several of his sons against Jesus and the first Christians.[7]

HIGH PRIESTS UNDER THE ROMANS (AD 6-41)

High priests were important in Judea at any time. They were especially important to the Romans once the former ethnarchy was made a Roman province. The prefects appointed them, and they governed the holy place and the Holy City. In effect, however, the high priest and the Sanhedrin indirectly ruled Judea.[8]

The high priest and the members of the Sanhedrin, seventy-one in all, were a sacral oligarchy. This council fulfilled the role as client ruler for Caesar, exercised through and under the prefect. Under Roman rule, the high priest reached a pinnacle of importance.

Patronage was the top-down means of controlling the empire. Patrons granted tangible favors to "clients" (money, preferment, property ownership, rents). The "client" was expected to respond to the patron with "friendship" (*amicitia*), practical political loyalty.[9]

Seneca, commenting on the power of Nero Caesar, observed: "By my lips Fortune proclaims what gift she would endow on each human being; from my utterance peoples and cities gather reasons for rejoicing; without my favor and grace no part of the whole world can prosper . . . what cities shall rise, and which shall fall—this is mine to decree."[10] The social and economic conse-

---

7. See pp. 168–69 below.

8. Samaria had its own council, whose power was revealed in the removal of Pontius Pilate (Josephus, *Jewish Antiquities* 18.85–89). The Idumeans may have had their own council, based at Marissa.

9. "From then on Pilate sought to release [Jesus], but the Jews cried out, 'If you release this man, you are not Caesar's *friend*. Everyone who makes himself a king opposes Caesar'" (John 19:12).

10. Seneca, *On Mercy* 1.2–3 (quoted in Warren Carter, *Pontius Pilate: Portraits of a Roman Governor* [Collegeville, MN: Liturgical Press, 2003], 36).

quence was that vast wealth and power was in the hands of a few, and poverty and debt-slavery the lot of the many.

THE FAVORED HOUSE OF ANNAS

According to Josephus, the high priest Joazar, after successfully supervising the registration, "had . . . been overpowered by a popular faction."[11] There is no further explanation. Since Quirinius immediately installed Annas as high priest, I assume the "popular faction" was composed of Annas,[12] his son-in-law, and his sons. It was not a popularity as seen through the eyes of the people but in the Romans' recognition of a priestly dynasty in whom they could confidently entrust the administration of the temple and the Holy City.

High Priests in Palestine, 6–41

Prefects	Dates	High Priests	Dates
Coponius	6–9	Joazar	6
		Annas*	6–15
Ambibulus	9–11		
Rufus	12–14		
Gratus	15–26	Ishmael	15
		Eleazar* (son of Annas)	16
		Simon	17
		Caiaphas* (son-in-law of Annas)	18–37
Pontius Pilate	26–36		

*Family of Annas

A time span of thirty-one years elapsed between the deposition of Joazar (in 6) and the death of Caiaphas (in 37). For no fewer than twenty-nine of those years the high priesthood was held by Annas, his son Eleazar, and his son-in-law Caiaphas.

How can we explain a high priestly continuity that spanned from Augustus (d. 14) to Tiberius (d. 37)? It is assumed that a patron-client relationship existed between successive governors and Annas-Eleazar-Caiaphas; the governors received payment in return for entitlements granted to the high priest.

---

11. Josephus, *Jewish Antiquities* 18.26.
12. Josephus refers to him as Ananus and Ananias.

The high priest created a network of loyal clients within the Sanhedrin, among fellow Sadducees, and among wealthy landowners.

Herod, followed by Archelaus and successive Roman governors, retained custody of the high priests' vestments as a means of controlling the population. The vestments were released to the high priest before the three feasts and then returned to the Antonia Fortress, where they were kept under guard.[13] It is possible that the high priests were forced to pay the prefect for the release of the vestments.

John the Baptist began prophesying in the fifteenth year of Tiberius (28 or 29), during "the high priesthood of Annas and Caiaphas" (Luke 3:1–20). Although Annas ceased being the serving high priest in 15, Luke's reference implies that he remained the de facto high priest, the real power within the pontificate. This is confirmed by John, who refers to Annas as "the high priest" who interrogated Jesus before sending him on to Caiaphas (John 18:13, 22, 24).[14] It appears that Annas remained powerful throughout the years 6–40. It is likely that his wealth and political networks secured the support of successive prefects throughout those years.

Evidently Jesus had become "a person of interest" even before dramatically entering the Holy City. The high priest would have known of Jesus's debates in Galilee with the rabbis from Jerusalem (Mark 3:22; 7:1). The present popularity of Jesus was a timely warning of the possibility of social disturbance and, with it, the vulnerability of the high priest and his house.

Very soon, however, in an astonishing reversal, we witness the chief priests exercising unexpected power over the prefect during the trial of Jesus.

NEPOTISM AND CORRUPTION

The passing reference in Acts 4 to "the priests and the captain of the temple" (v. 1) and to "Annas the high priest and Caiaphas and John and Alexander" is a window into the membership of the Sanhedrin. There was a "captain of the temple" who was most likely responsible to maintain order. The named

---

13. Josephus, *Jewish Antiquities* 18.92–94. Herod, Archelaus, and successive Roman prefects mostly retained custody of the vestments as a means of controlling the population. See further R. A. Horsley, *Jesus and the Politics of Roman Palestine* (Eugene, OR: Wipf & Stock, 2021), 21–40.

14. See also this telling reference: "with Annas the high priest and Caiaphas" (Acts 4:6).

persons "John and Alexander" were probably relatives of Annas or Caiaphas and members of the Sanhedrin.

Surviving from the first century and found in the Talmud is the Lament of Abba Saul, which gives some idea of the politics, nepotism, and corruption of the high priests of that era.

> Woe is me because of the house of Boethus;
> Woe is me because of their staves!
> Woe is me because of the house of Hanin [Annas];
> Woe is me because of their whisperings!
> Woe is me because of the house of Kathros (Kantheras);
> Woe is me because of their pens!
> Woe is me because of the house of Ishmael the son of Phabi;
> Woe is me because of their fists!
> For they are the high priests, and their sons are temple overseers
>   [captains?]
> Their sons-in-law are trustees,
> And their servants beat the people with sticks.[15]

References to the high priests' "sons" and "sons-in-law" point to nepotism. Each "house" exercised violence or political means to gain or retain power, as in the words "their servants beat the people with sticks." The house of Annas does not escape the condemnation of this lament. Presumably their "whisperings" refer to political intrigue, which contributed to their lengthy tenure in Judea. It is before this high priest and Sanhedrin that the young prophet from distant Nazareth must stand.

CONCLUSION

The transition from Herodian to Roman rule in 6 brought with it huge social consequences. Judea was now under the direct rule of the hated gentiles. The Roman occupying forces were now based in Caesarea but, as we will note, could be readily and violently deployed in the Holy City.

The imposition of tax directly paid to Caesar was a constant reminder to the people that they were a vassal state, owned by the gentiles.

15. b. Pesahim 57a Bar.

An unexpected and surprising consequence of annexation was the increased political importance of the high priest and his council. In effect, they became "a client" answerable to Caesar through his incumbent prefect. The great wealth of the high priest gave him considerable leverage over ever-money-hungry governors. The high priest would have been aware of Pilate's vulnerability once Sejanus his patron and protector had been removed and discredited (in 31). This helps explain why the high priest in effect bullied Pilate to condemn and execute Jesus.

12

THE GOVERNOR OF JUDEA
AND THE OUTBREAK OF PROPHECY

Pontius Pilate arrived in Judea in 26 and took up residence in Caesarea Maritima, now capital of the province. Since the year 6, when Augustus annexed Judea, Caesarea had been the garrison base for the prefect's legionary officers and his mainly auxiliary (i.e., non-Roman) soldiers. As military prefect, Pilate's duties included defending the borders of the province, maintaining law and order internally (especially in Jerusalem, which was renowned for religious volatility), and acting as magistrate for capital cases (only the governor exercised the *ius gladii*, "right of the sword").[1]

Pilate's years as prefect of Judea (26–36) were dominated by activities of two popular prophets, John the Baptist (28–31) and Jesus of Nazareth (30–33).

JOHN THE BAPTIST

John was a very significant figure in Jewish history, referred to at length in the New Testament (the Gospels and the Acts of the Apostles) and by Josephus.[2]

Josephus writes positively about John, as do the authors of the Gospels and Acts. An immense number of Jews from Judea and Jerusalem flocked to John in Perea across the Jordan, listening to John's sermons and submitting to baptism at his hands.

---

1. Josephus, *Jewish War* 2.117.
2. Josephus, *Jewish Antiquities* 18.116–119.

Although strictly speaking John did not belong to Pilate's territorial responsibility (Judea and Jerusalem), the prefect would have taken note of significant leaders and movements in adjoining jurisdictions. Accordingly, although based in distant Caesarea Maritima, Pontius Pilate would have been aware of and concerned about John the Baptist and his significant following.

JESUS OF NAZARETH

Even before John was arrested another prophet arose, Jesus from Nazareth in Galilee. Greater crowds gathered to hear the words of this prophet. Pilate would have known about this charismatic figure and his remarkable influence, even though he avoided visiting Caesarea Maritima.

> Jesus withdrew with his disciples to the sea [Lake Galilee], and a great crowd followed, from *Galilee* and *Judea* and *Jerusalem* and *Idumea* and from *beyond the Jordan* and from around *Tyre and Sidon*. (Mark 3:7)

> And [Jesus] went throughout *all Galilee*, teaching in their synagogues and proclaiming the gospel of the kingdom and healing every disease and every affliction among the people. So his fame spread throughout *all Syria*,[3] and they brought him all the sick, those afflicted with various diseases and pains, those oppressed by demons, [those having seizures], and paralytics, and he healed them. And great crowds followed him from *Galilee* and the *Decapolis*, and from *Jerusalem* and *Judea*, and from *beyond the Jordan*. (Matt. 4:23–25)

These texts state that Jesus was followed by "great crowds," from within the internal jurisdictions (Jerusalem, Judea, Idumea, Galilee, Perea) and from beyond those borders (the Decapolis, Tyre and Sidon, all Syria). These regions didn't have physical borders, so that Jesus and those who heard him were free to attend the religious festivals in the Holy City. "And when [Jesus] entered Jerusalem, the whole city was stirred up, saying, 'Who is this?' And the crowds said, 'This is the prophet Jesus, from Nazareth of Galilee'" (Matt. 21:10–11).

3. Probably meaning the eastern Mediterranean seaboard, the Levant.

THE MISSION AND THE MULTITUDE

The Gospel of Mark establishes a close relationship between the Galilean mission of the twelve "apostles" to the towns and villages of Galilee and the wilderness assembly of the five thousand men. The gathering of the multitude was a direct result of their mission throughout Galilee.

Jesus had "called" and "appointed twelve . . . so that they might be with him and he might send them out to preach and have authority to cast out demons" (Mark 3:13–15). Mark reports that "they went out and proclaimed that people should repent. And they cast out many demons and anointed with oil many who were sick and healed them" (Mark 6:12).

Mark doesn't spell out Jesus's objective in sending his disciples to the towns and villages of Galilee. For that we are dependent on Matthew citing the "M" tradition. Jesus says, "Go nowhere among the Gentiles and enter no town of the Samaritans, but go rather to the lost sheep of the house of Israel. And proclaim as you go, saying, 'The kingdom of heaven is at hand.' Heal the sick, raise the dead, cleanse lepers, cast out demons" (Matt. 10:6–8).

Matthew's account states clearly what Mark implies: the message and ministry of the Twelve were exercised ahead of and pointed to an eschatological event, the advent of the kingdom of heaven.

Here, though, there appears to have been a misunderstanding of Jesus's intention. He was referring to his death and resurrection in Jerusalem as the kingdom advent and the instrument of redemption and spiritual deliverance. The disciples and those who heard them, however, understood that the apocalyptic event was to occur immediately, in the wilderness.[4]

This explains, first, the frantic running of men to the place Jesus and the disciples were to meet (Mark 6:33), and second, their seating in groups of hundreds and fifties (Mark 6:40), arguably in military formation. These seating arrangements assisted the disciples to count the number of men who had assembled— five thousand. There were also women and children present (Matt. 14:21).

For the Synoptic Gospels, the *feeding* of the multitude was secondary. Mark reports that because the people were like sheep without a shepherd, Jesus "began to teach them many things" (Mark 6:34). According to Matthew, "He saw a great

---

4. Hugh Montefiore, "Revolt in the Desert," *New Testament Studies* 8 (1961–1962): 135–41.

crowd, and he had compassion on them and healed their sick" (Matt. 14:14). Luke locates the event in Bethsaida, where Jesus "welcomed them and spoke to them of the kingdom of God and cured those who had need of healing" (Luke 9:11).

John, however, is silent regarding Jesus's teaching; all the emphasis is on his perception of the hunger of the crowd and the extensive detail about him feeding this vast crowd with the boy's loaves and fishes. John narrates this event as one of Jesus's signature miracle "signs" and the crowd's recognition of him as "the [Moses] Prophet who [was] to come into the world!" (John 6:14; see also Deut. 18:15; John 1:21; 7:40; Matt. 21:11).

The expectation of the multitude resulted from the disciples' misunderstanding of Jesus's intention in sending his disciples on their mission to the towns and villages of Galilee. For Jesus the advent of the kingdom of God was to occur in Jerusalem, and beyond, whereas for the disciples it was to happen immediately, in the wilderness. The Galileans readily believed the disciples' revelations and ran to the meeting place on the eastern side of the sea.

Consistent with this misunderstanding—attributable to the disciples—the crowds attempted to impose the kingship on Jesus. "When the people saw the sign that he had done, they said, 'This is indeed the Prophet who is to come into the world!' Perceiving then that they were about to come and take him *by force* to make him king, Jesus withdrew again to the mountain by himself" (John 6:14–15). Jesus's reaction, according to Mark, was dramatic: "Immediately he *made* his disciples get into the boat and go before him to the other side, to Bethsaida, while he dismissed the crowd" (Mark 6:45).

When we consider John 6:15 and Mark 6:45 together, we conclude that Jesus was unhappy with the role of the disciples that led to the attempt to impose kingship on him. He withdrew alone, having immediately forced the disciples to sail to Bethsaida. From that time Jesus withdrew from the territory of Herod Antipas and only reentered it later, secretly (Mark 9:30). The people of Galilee had been influenced by the twelve traveling missionaries who had misunderstood Jesus.

The whole episode reveals the difference between the redemptive "kingdom" teaching of Jesus and the external perception of him. The crowds saw Jesus as an apocalyptic prophet because that is how the disciples portrayed him. But that was not how Jesus viewed himself and his mission.

ROMANS AND REBELS

The Romans had reason to be wary of local rebel leaders, for example, Vercingetorix (d. 46 BC), who raised an army that almost overthrew Julius

Caesar in Gaul, or Arminius, who devastatingly defeated Varus in the Battle of Teutoburg Forest, Germany, in 9.

Furthermore, the Holy Land was notoriously volatile. After the death of Herod in 4 BC, Judas in Galilee, Simon in Perea, and Athronges in Judea each attempted to establish himself as a king. As recently as 6, Judas the Galilean (a.k.a. Gaulanite) had led a revolt against the Romans in Judea.[5] Pilate was not to know that Jesus was a man of peace. He had every reason to be aware of and concerned about the potential geopolitical threat posed by the prophet from Nazareth.

Following their interrogation of Jesus, the temple authorities brought him to the prefect. "Then the whole company of them arose and brought [Jesus] before Pilate. And they began to accuse him, saying, 'We found this man misleading our nation and forbidding us to give tribute to Caesar, and saying that he himself is Christ, a king.' And Pilate asked him, 'Are you the King of the Jews?'" (Luke 23:1–3). The accusation of high treason to Pilate by the temple hierarchy, that "[Jesus] opposes payment of taxes to Caesar and claims to be Christ a king," resonates remarkably with the crimes of the notorious Galilean who had in the recent past revolted against Roman rule in Judea. In 6, when Judea was annexed as a Roman province and direct personal tax to Rome was first levied, a man named Judas led an uprising. Judas was a rabbi, a Galilean, and a populist, a convenient and damaging stereotype to apply to Jesus, who was also a Galilean, and a rabbi, and a populist.

PONTIUS PILATE, PREFECT OF JUDEA: REPORTS FROM GALILEE

Although Galilee-Perea was a separate jurisdiction, the governor of Judea doubtless had spies and informers to keep him apprised of any security issues in neighboring regions. There were no secure borders; Galileans frequently traveled to Jerusalem in Judea for the great feasts. As Galilee was a hotbed for radicals, we are right to assume that Pilate was conscious of potential upheavals inspired by Jews from the north coming to the Holy City.

It is more likely than not that after the Passover in 32[6] the military governor heard of radical apocalyptists traveling from town to town throughout Galilee

---

5. Josephus, *Jewish War* 2.118; *Jewish Antiquities* 18.4. Judas had led an uprising circa 4 BC in Galilee after the death of Herod (*Jewish War* 2.56). In one reference Josephus asserts that Judas had ambition for "royal rank" (*Jewish Antiquities* 17.272).

6. Mark and John combine to locate the incident to the time of Passover (John 6:4, 10; Mark 6:39). This would have been the Passover in 32, a full year prior to the "Passover of Death."

followed by a mass gathering on the eastern side of the lake. He would have concluded that the twelve travelers had recruited an army of Galileans who assembled to meet and hear from Jesus, the prophet from Nazareth.

Then, in the Passover in 33, Pilate would have known of the Galilean's mounted entry to Jerusalem to the acclamation of the pilgrims and the people of Jerusalem. The prefect would also have known about the prophet's violent actions in the temple and the disputes between the chief priests and the Galilean pretender.

It makes sense, then, that Pilate's first question on meeting Jesus was, "Are you the King of the Jews?" (Mark 15:2; Matt. 27:11; Luke 23:3; John 18:33). A year earlier Pilate might have concluded that the man from Nazareth was a self-proclaimed prophet-king. Now, however, Pilate changed his mind. This man didn't have a rebel's demeanor and he was not attended by an army. Jesus told him, "My kingdom is not of this world. If my kingdom were of this world, my servants would have been fighting, that I might not be delivered over to the Jews" (John 18:36).

The wily governor knew that Jesus was no "king of the Jews," otherwise he would have arrested his "soldiers," the twelve disciples.

PILATE IN ROMAN PALESTINE

Almost on Pilate's arrival, John the Baptist began preaching and baptizing in the Jordan. Significantly, those who flocked to the waters were from the whole province of Judea and its capital, Jerusalem. This powerful prophet's message inevitably heightened volatility in historically unstable regions.

Then, again almost immediately, Pilate was confronted with an even more popular prophet, Jesus of Nazareth, whose followers had gathered five thousand men to hear him.

13

JESUS, PROPHET AND RABBI

Jesus's disciples addressed him as "Rabbi" ("Teacher"), whereas to Galileans at large he was regarded as a great prophet (Mark 8:28). Jesus the prophet powerfully and publicly proclaimed the imminent coming of the kingdom of God and debated with the scribes about the understanding and application of the law. In private with his disciples, however, Rabbi Jesus explained the meaning of his public utterances.

JESUS AND HIS DISCIPLES

The disciples were a diverse group.[1] The brothers Simon and Andrew had been disciples of John the Baptist (John 1:40), as most likely also were their fishing partners James and John Zebedee. Such was John's impact that he was thought to have been the Christ, the returning Elijah, or the Moses-Prophet (John 1:19–21). Two of Jesus's disciples were polar opposites: the *Cananaean*/"zealot," Simon, and the tax collector, Levi (a.k.a. Matthew). Judas, who betrayed Jesus to the chief priests, may have been motivated by pro-Roman sympathy as well as greed. The Gospels name the remaining five but provide no further detail.

---

1. As listed in Matt. 10:1–4, Mark 3:16–19, and Luke 6:14–16.

THE ESOTERIC TEACHING OF JESUS

Jesus explained in private what he had said in public but which the disciples had not understood. For example, Mark records Jesus's teaching about the imminent advent of the kingdom of God by a cluster of parables: the soils, the lamp, the measure, the harvest, and the mustard seed. Mark then adds, "With many such parables he spoke the word to them, as they were able to hear it. He did not speak to them without a parable, but *privately* to his own disciples he explained everything" (Mark 4:33–34).

Another example of Jesus's private explanation is recorded following his dispute with Pharisees over purity rules, which Jesus's disciples are accused of not upholding "according to the tradition of the elders." Mark then reports that "when he had *entered the house* and left the people, his disciples asked him about the parable," whereupon he explained its meaning (Mark 7:1, 5, 17).

The Gospel of Matthew also notes Jesus's private revelations to his inner circle: "At that time Jesus declared, 'I thank you, Father, Lord of heaven and earth, that you have *hidden* these things from the wise and understanding and *revealed* them to little children; yes, Father, for such was your gracious will. All things have been handed over to me by my Father, and no one knows the Son except the Father, and no one knows the Father except the Son and anyone to whom the Son chooses to reveal him'" (Matt. 11:25–27). This public face of Jesus to crowds, religious leaders, and needy individuals and his private face to his twelve chosen "apprentices" may be articulated as denoting Jesus's exoteric profile and his esoteric teaching.[2]

A consequence of Jesus's public teaching and private explanation was that Jesus was easily viewed one way by the crowds and another way by the Twelve. It is likely that the populace and the religious leaders and officials viewed Jesus quite differently, that is, politically, as a leader to follow and a potential threat to public order.

CAESAREA PHILIPPI

The climax of Jesus's private disclosure to the disciples occurred in Caesarea Philippi, in Iturea and Trachonitis, the tetrarchy of Herod Philip. They had been with him for more than two years, witnessing his miracles and hearing

2. B. F. Meyer, *The Aims of Jesus* (London: SCM, 1979), 202–19.

his teachings to the crowds in public and to them in private.[3] For Jesus this was a critical moment. He knew that he was the Father's "beloved Son" (Mark 1:1, 11; 9:7; 12:6; 13:32; cf. 14:36) whose pathway was to Jerusalem, where he would face rejection and death, from which he would be resurrected.

These outside and inside aspects of Jesus are especially displayed in the conversation between Jesus and the Twelve at Caesarea Philippi, the turning point of Mark's narrative. First, Jesus asked, "Who do people say that I am?" The disciples replied: they think you are another John the Baptist, Elijah, or one of the prophets. In other words, the general populace had recognized Jesus as a prophet of significant distinction, the equal of John the Baptist, Elijah, or another of the great prophets of God. It is noted that John the Baptist and Elijah publicly denounced leaders who were acting contrary to the law of God.

Jesus then pointedly asked them who *they* thought he was. Peter, speaking for the group, declared, "You are the Christ" (Mark 8:29).[4] Based on the multitudes who assembled to hear him, the profound nature of his teaching, and his numerous miracles, it is likely that they had reached that conclusion beforehand. For a thousand years the prophets had repeatedly promised the coming of a second David, the Lord's anointed king, deliverer of God's people. The holy land of the Lord was occupied by the gentiles and was enduring shameful brutality through Caesar's present representative, the prefect Pontius Pilate. The very name *Caesarea* Philippi reminded them of Caesar's oppressive military presence throughout that whole region.

The disciples' response to Jesus's two questions revealed public opinion ("he is a prophet"), and their response revealed their private understanding ("you are the Christ").

To their response (through Peter), however, Jesus made the most surprising and shocking revelation. They expected a messianic victory from him, but he spoke of suffering, rejection, and death at the hands of the gentiles whom he was expected to defeat. They did not understand this, nor what "resurrec-

---

3. Jesus's reputation as a healer had even reached John the Baptist in prison at remote Machaerus (Matt. 11:2).

4. Jesus's own words about his ministry, "the blind receive their sight and the lame walk, lepers are cleansed and the deaf hear, and the dead are raised up, and the poor have good news preached to them" (Matt. 11:5), echo Isaiah's prophecy of the deeds of the Coming One: "Then the eyes of the blind shall be opened, / and the ears of the deaf unstopped; / then shall the lame man leap like a deer, / and the tongue of the mute sing for joy" (Isa. 35:5–6).

tion" meant. Furthermore, he told his disciples that they must be prepared to follow him to death.

Jesus pointedly walked ahead of them from Caesarea Philippi to Jerusalem, repeating his predictions of what would befall him there and his challenge to them to follow him come what may. Jesus's demand to the disciples was for an obedience that was as absolute to him as his was to the Father.

Nevertheless, Jesus did not embrace the title "the Christ" at Caesarea Philippi, but rather the enigmatic "Son of Man." He had seldom referred to himself by that title beforehand, but from Caesarea Philippi it was his almost constant self-identification, including at the Sanhedrin trial (Mark 14:62). While some have argued that it was merely the equivalent of the first-person pronoun "I," it is more likely to be his reference to the sovereign and celestial figure in Daniel 7, to whom was given a "kingdom, that all peoples, nations, and languages should serve him" (Dan. 7:14).

THE MESSAGE OF JESUS IN THE GOSPEL OF MARK

Almost from its beginning the Gospel of Mark focuses on Jesus's future; for example, he speaks of the bridegroom being "taken away." Mark refers to the plot between the Pharisees and the Herodians to "destroy him" (Mark 2:20; 3:6). At Caesarea Philippi, and afterward, Jesus's almost total focus was on his journey to Jerusalem, where he will face death but be resurrected on the third day.

So, what did Jesus say about the effects of the future events?

Spiritual Liberation

The first half of the Gospel of Mark is characterized by Jesus casting out unclean spirits (1:23; 3:15, 22; 5:2; 7:25; 9:17). This became known in the scribal academies in Jerusalem, who sent learned men to challenge him. This they did by accusing him of casting out demons by the power of Beelzebul,[5] that is, the devil. It is evident that these scholars did not dispute the fact of the exorcisms, only the source of Jesus's power to exorcise, by the prince of demons.

Jesus responded with a parable about a "strong man" who held captives in his house but who was overcome by a stronger man (Jesus himself) who liberated the captives (3:27). Given the centrality in this gospel of the death of

---

5. Beelzebul was a Philistine deity.

Jesus, we are right to conclude that it was to be the divine instrument of this spiritual, universal deliverance.

The second half of this gospel is devoted to Jesus's journey to Jerusalem, his arrival, his arrest, his trial, and his crucifixion. Although Mark's intention is understated, it seems that what happened to Jesus when he died and was resurrected was the potential overpowering of Satan to open the prison for the deliverance of his slaves.

In short, Jesus's answer to the scribes from Jerusalem is to be understood as finding its deeper meaning in the crucifixion of Jesus, the truly "strong man" who liberated those who were previously the spiritual slaves of Satan.

Redemption

On their way to Jerusalem the Zebedee brothers sought priority and privilege in the upcoming kingdom of God. In response, Jesus memorably replied that "the Son of Man came not to be served but to serve, and to give his life as a ransom (*lytron*) for (*anti*) many" (10:45). A *lytron* was a sum of money or similar as a payment for the freedom of a slave. Here Jesus is referring to slaves of evil powers and an individual's bondage to them. The notion of freedom connects this saying with Jesus's words about liberating the strong man's prisoners.

Mark structures his narrative to leave us in no doubt that the death of Jesus will be that instrument of redemption.

A Message of Hope

While the themes of spiritual liberation and redemption are prominent in Mark, the narrative of the arrest, trials, and crucifixion raises a question. Why does Mark (and the other gospel writers) need to provide such extensive detail? Why not simply say in a few words that the authorities arrested and crucified Jesus? That would be sufficient for the readers and hearers to understand that his death had secured their freedom and redemption.

There must be another reason for the detailed nature of Mark's account, and for that matter, those of the other three Gospels.

Mark understood well about inequality and injustice in the Roman world. Wealth and power were the preserve of the few. The great majority were the poor; slaves represented 10 percent of the population. These had no access to wealth or justice. The head of the family (*paterfamilias*, "father of the family") had the (theoretical) authority to punish, even kill, members of his household.

Owners of slaves had the legal capacity to punish, torture, even crucify slaves whom they deemed disobedient. Slaves frequently were tattooed or compelled to wear riveted collars, bearing the names and addresses of their owners (to bring runaway slaves home).

Mark's Gospel tells the story of a good and innocent man who was tortured and unjustly crucified but who was vindicated by God through resurrection. Mark's mentor, Peter, appealed to slaves of cruel masters to follow the non-vengeful attitude of Christ, who, when he suffered unjustly, entrusted himself to the God who judges justly (1 Pet. 2:21–23).

Mark's narrative was a message to the poor and the slaves. It was to set before them the example of the innocently suffering Jesus, who placed himself in the hands of the just God. Understood in the context of cruelty and injustice to the poor and defenseless, Mark's narrative is to be understood as an example of nonvengeance, faith, and a message of hope.

JESUS'S MESSAGE TO THE NATIONS

Jesus did not see his ministry confined to the Holy Land and the historic covenantal people. Rather, based on his prospective redemptive acts in Jerusalem—his vicarious death and triumphant resurrection—the blessings of his Father would be brought to all the peoples of the world.

The confession by a Roman centurion that the crucified Jesus was "truly the Son of God," as recorded by Mark, signified that many in the Roman world would soon honor Jesus instead of the Caesar (Mark 15:39). One of Caesar's titles was "son of God." Mark understood that the gospel was God's "good news" for the nations, for the world, about the true "Son of God," the crucified Jesus.

The gospel must first be proclaimed to *all nations*. (Mark 13:10)

Wherever the gospel is proclaimed in *the whole world* . . . (Mark 14:9)

Jesus's private instruction and explanation to the disciples equipped them for their mission in Galilee, and beyond that, for their mission to the nations. Post-Easter, under the presidency of Peter, the disciples located biblical texts that had prophesied Jesus and his ministry. Furthermore, they formulated and formatted the "traditions" of the Last Supper and Jesus's resurrection appearances, which in turn most likely they "delivered" to the newly "called" Paul and doubtless to others (Gal. 1:18; 2:2; 2:20). Both "traditions" explain the death of

Jesus vicariously (Christ died *hyper*, "for" others) in the letters of Paul, Peter, John, and the Letter to the Hebrews.[6]

Jesus's coming to Jerusalem is paradoxical. On the one hand, the temple authorities and the Roman governor willfully condemned an innocent man to execution, whereas on the other, that death followed by his resurrection was "of God," redemptive for all peoples. Although apparently contradictory, each statement is true, and both taken together are true.

THE PUBLIC PERCEPTION OF JESUS

The prophet Jesus was widely known, not only in his home tetrarchy, Galilee, but throughout the other jurisdictions, Judea and Iturea-Trachonitis as well as the seaboard Hellenistic republics and the Decapolis. The governor, Pilate, and the temple authorities would have been aware of Jesus's extensive movements, as they would have regarding those of John the Baptist. His meeting with five thousand men would have been common knowledge throughout the length and breadth of the land. It would have been widely understood that the healer and exorcist from Nazareth was proclaiming an apocalyptic message, the imminent arrival of the kingdom of God. Furthermore, rumors of his long journey from the north to the Holy City for Passover would have come to the attention of the governor of the province and the senior priests in the Sanhedrin.

A critical question is: How can we explain the readiness and ability of the disciples to accurately proclaim the message of Jesus immediately after his death? The book of Acts credibly attributes this astonishing ability to the inspiration of the Spirit of God. There is, however, a parallel explanation. It is that for three years the disciples had been schooled by their rabbi in his public (*exoteric*) discourse, as recorded in the gospels, but no less in his private (*esoteric*) explanations and elaborations. Initially they had been slow to learn and understand Jesus's teaching, but by the Feast of Pentecost circa 33, enabled by the Holy Spirit, and led by Peter, they were ready publicly to declare that their resurrected Master was the God-promised, resurrected Anointed One. Jesus's *exoteric* teaching and *esoteric* explanations to the Twelve should not be underestimated but are key to understanding the gospel message and the canon of the New Testament.

---

6. Gal. 2:20 (for example of many); Heb. 2:9; 5:1; 6:20; 7:25, 27; 1 Pet. 2:21; 1 John 3:16; cf. Rev. 1:5.

14

THE GALILEAN BLASPHEMER

Blasphemy was disrespectful speech about God or disrespectful action directed toward God. Darrell Bock[1] cites several examples, including pronouncing or misusing the divine name, mocking God, mocking the Torah, idolatry, profaning the Sabbath, and speaking against Israel. Broadly speaking, blasphemy rejects the Creator-creature paradigm.

The Gospels record several examples of the charge of blasphemy against Jesus.

JESUS'S HEALING OF THE PARALYTIC

In Mark 2:1–12 Jesus declared to the paralytic, "Your sins are *forgiven*," whose passive voice could have been taken to mean "God forgives your sins." The scribes, however, took Jesus's words as blasphemy since "Who can forgive sins but God alone?" Jesus doesn't seek refuge in a passive understanding of his words but affirms, "The Son of Man has authority on earth to forgive sins."

This was not an isolated incident. Mark, our major source for Jesus's actions in Galilee, records Jesus violating the fasting rules, eating with unclean people, breaking the Sabbath, supposedly engaging in sorcery, and flouting the purity laws (Mark 2:18; 2:15–17; 2:24; 3:22; 7:1–2).

---

1. Darrell Bock, *Blasphemy and Exaltation in Judaism: The Charge against Jesus in Mk 14:53–65* (Grand Rapids: Baker Books, 2000), 30–112.

We can be confident that the priestly and scribal hierarchies in Jerusalem came to hear of this influential Galilean blasphemer. The charismatic Jesus was attended by vast crowds in a theologically heterodox jurisdiction that was at risk of slipping away altogether from the control of the Jerusalem-based high priest and the preeminent scribes.

JESUS'S CLAIM, "I AND THE FATHER ARE ONE"

John, our major authority for Jesus's deeds and words in Jerusalem, is no less informative about Jesus's reputation as a blasphemer in the Holy City.

In Jerusalem, at the Feast of Hanukkah, when challenged about his supposed claim to be the Christ, Jesus replied, "The works that I do in my Father's name bear witness about me." He then declared, "I and the Father are one" (John 10:30). The Jews who were present were scandalized not so much by Jesus's "works" but by his claim to be "one" with the "Father." This they took to be blasphemy against the name of the Lord, and in response those present took up stones to execute him. It is noted that Leviticus 24:10–23 mandates stoning for the crime of blasphemy. Jesus escaped and fled from Jerusalem to Bethany across the Jordan, which was in the jurisdiction of Herod Antipas.

The high priest later convened an emergency meeting of the Sanhedrin to consider the steps that must be taken against Jesus, who, however, was not present at the time. The immediate reason for this informal gathering was Jesus's raising of Lazarus, and the furor it inspired in the Holy City. However, the knowledge of Jesus's blasphemous claim to be "one with the Father," for which he would have been stoned, must have weighed heavily on the minds of the council members, especially with the Passover fast approaching.

This amounted to what we would regard as a "warrant" for Jesus's apprehension once he appeared in Jerusalem.

JESUS'S CLEARING OF THE TEMPLE: MARK 11:15–18

One has only to consider the fanatical zeal of the priests defending the temple from the Romans in 70 to sense the religious importance of this holy place. This, however, did not preserve the sanctity of the temple precincts from corrupt exploitation. As we will note,[2] Caiaphas had recently set up a market in the Court

---

2. See pp. 100–102 below.

of the Gentiles where sacrifices were sold and iconic Roman coins were changed for aniconic Tyrian coins.[3] Mark records Jesus's dramatic action driving "out those who sold and those who bought" and overturning "the tables of the moneychangers and the seats of those who sold pigeons" (Mark 11:15–18).

In the following heated exchange with representatives of the high priest, Jesus declared that his "authority" for these actions was his identity as the "beloved Son" of God.

We will discuss this critical incident later.[4]

It concludes with the chief priests, the scribes, and the elders attempting to arrest Jesus but failing to do so. The language of blasphemy is not employed in this passage, but we are left in no doubt that had these temple leaders been successful in capturing Jesus, the charge of blasphemy would have followed.

THE SANHEDRIN TRIAL: MARK 14:61–65

To anticipate later discussion of the trial of Jesus before the Caiaphas-led Sanhedrin, we note that to Caiaphas's question, "Are you the Christ, the Son of the Blessed?" Jesus replied, "I am." He then added, "You will see the Son of Man seated at the right hand of Power and coming with the clouds of heaven." The gathered assembly unanimously declared Jesus's words blasphemy and condemned him to death.

The readers' expectation would have been that death by stoning would follow, as it did a few years later to Stephen.

As we will note later, the high priest Caiaphas did not proceed with the stoning of Jesus for blasphemy, as he might have done, but handed him to Pilate with the political charge that Jesus claimed to be "king of the Jews." Caiaphas would go to any lengths to avoid stoning Jesus and making him a martyr to the Jewish temple hierarchy. Let the Jews blame the Romans for the death of the popular Galilean.

---

3. William Lane, *The Gospel according to Mark* (Grand Rapids: Eerdmans, 1974), 403. According to Lane (404), these sales and exchanges of currency had been conducted on the Mount of Olives, which is close to the temple.

4. See pp. 102–6 below.

15

ANNAS AND CAIAPHAS

Quirinius appointed Annas high priest in 6, to be replaced by the prefect Gratus in 15. After a flurry of depositions of high priests, in 18 Gratus appointed Annas's son-in-law Caiaphas, who remained in that office until his death in 36. Annas, however, remained the real power in the high priesthood and the governance of Jerusalem and the temple until his death in 40.

THE ANNAS DYNASTY

Annas (known by Josephus as Ananias and Ananus) with his five sons belonged to the party of the Sadducees, whom Josephus described as "more heartless than any of the other Jews," in contrast to the Pharisees, who were "more lenient."[1]

Apart from the appointment of Caiaphas, no fewer than five of Annas's sons became high priests: Eleazar (16–17), Jonathan (36–37), Theophilus (37–41) Matthias (42–43?), and Annas II (62). It is evident from the Gospels and the book of Acts that Annas retained the title "high priest" (Luke 3:1–2; John 18:13–24; Acts 4:6). Wherever we observe them, Annas, his son-in-law, and his sons are hostile to Jesus, his followers, and his brother James.[2]

1. Josephus, *Jewish Antiquities* 20.199; also 13.294.
2. Acts 4:5–8; Josephus, *Jewish Antiquities* 20.200. See chap. 24, "The Annas Vendetta."

ANNAS, HIGH PRIEST

Josephus described Annas as "a sort of perpetual high priest . . . perhaps the occasion that former high priests kept their titles ever afterwards."[3] Annas was a kind of "godfather" or éminence grise.

Annas accumulated huge wealth through his control of the sale of animals for sacrifice, rents from money changers, and other income-producing activities in and around the temple. It is likely that the huge wealth Annas accumulated from the temple merchants and money changers provided the resources for effectively "purchasing" from the Roman governor the appointment of his son-in-law and his five sons to the office of high priest.

Under Annas and Caiaphas the sale of sacrifices and the exchange of coins had been relocated from the Mount of Olives to the Court of the Gentiles. This became the occasion of two evils: the extortionate cost of animal sacrifices[4] and money changing, and the creation of a noisy venue that had been set aside for the gentiles' worship.

HIGH PRIEST CAIAPHAS

Even from this distance in time, we reasonably assume that it was the powerful influence of Annas that secured the appointment of Caiaphas (in 18).[5] Given the monetary practices of the Roman world, it is also reasonable to believe that the prefect benefited financially from his appointment.

Caiaphas exercised rule as high priest for eighteen years, being dismissed in 36 by Vitellius, governor of Syria.[6] We do not know why Caiaphas lost the

3. Josephus, *Jewish Antiquities* 20.204. It is noted that high priests were appointed for life (Num. 35:25; cf. m. Horayot 3.5; m. Megillah 1.9; m. Makkot 2.6; t. Yoma 1.4).

4. m. Kerithot 1.7 reports the intervention of Rabban Simeon b. Gamaliel, who forced the reduction of price for a pair of doves as needed by a poor woman who had suffered multiple miscarriages.

5. Helen K. Bond, *Caiaphas, Friend of Rome and Judge of Jesus* (Louisville: Westminster John Knox, 2004), 141–43, interprets the four evangelists as pursuing their apologetic concerns to a degree that diminishes their usefulness as historical sources.

6. It may be significant that Mark does not name Caiaphas as high priest, suggesting an early date for the writing of that gospel (before or soon after that high priest was replaced). Matthew and Luke, who depend on Mark, supply the name Caiaphas, suggesting a later date of authorship of those gospels. The Gospel of John names Caiaphas.

high priesthood. He was, however, succeeded by Jonathan, the second son of Annas, which suggests that the patriarchal father-in-law was responsible for this loss of office. Various hints in the Gospels suggest that Caiaphas was always in the shadow of his father-in-law, who, as we noted, retained the title "high priest."

Caiaphas's final decade in office coincided almost exactly with Pilate's tenure as prefect of Judea.[7] Since the high priest held office at the pleasure of the prefect, it is likely that some of the wealth of the Annas family found its way to Pilate's pocket.

ANNAS'S MANSION

It is widely believed that prominent within the complex of six structures discovered in the Jewish Quarter of the Old City Jerusalem[8] was the very large Palace of Annas (footprint 6,500 square feet, with an upper story). The palace has four *mikva'ot* (ritual baths), supporting the hypothesis of a building for deeply religious usage. According to Josephus, "the victors [Romans] set fire to the house of Ananias (Annas) the high priest" when they overcame the city in 70.[9]

It is likely that Caiaphas was located within the Palace of Annas, which was also where some members of the Sanhedrin most likely assembled on the night Jesus was arrested. It is plausibly suggested that Caiaphas was gathering members of the council during Annas's interrogation of Jesus.

THE COURT OF THE GENTILES

Prior to 30, the Mount of Olives was considered in effect part of the holy temple precincts. There were four markets for the sale of sacrificial animals,[10] all subject to the oversight of the Sanhedrin. As recently as three years earlier, however, these markets had been transferred to the Court of the Gentiles,

---

7. In 1990 a superior-quality ossuary (receptacle for bones of those previously interred) was discovered that bore the name Caiaphas. It contained the remains of a man aged sixty, a woman, two children, and two infants. It provides archaeological support for the writings of Josephus and the Gospels.

8. Now the Wohl Museum.

9. Josephus, *Jewish War* 2.426.

10. y. Ta'anit 4.8.

which was under the direct control of Caiaphas,[11] indicating his vested interest in the steady flow of money to the high priest. Josephus specifically refers to the immense wealth of Annas,[12] high priest and father-in-law of Caiaphas. We are not left wondering about the source of Annas's wealth.

Since the high priest enjoyed exclusive access to and use of the entire sacred complex, it comes as no surprise that price gouging and other corrupt practices occurred in and around the temple. When Jesus cleared the merchants and money changers from the Court of the Gentiles, he was recorded as saying, "Is it not written, 'My house shall be called a house of prayer for all the nations'? But you have made it a den of robbers."[13] Jesus's words sealed his fate.

The office of high priest brought Annas and his sons' great wealth. According to Josephus, "The high priest Ananias [Annas] . . . increased in glory every day, and this to a great degree, and had obtained the favour and esteem of the citizens in a signal manner; for he was a great hoarder up of money."[14] This ascription of popularity, however, is not found in the Lament of Abba Saul surviving in the Talmud, quoted in full earlier:

> Woe is me because of the house of Hanin [Annas];
> Woe is me because of their whisperings! (t. Pesahim 57a)

Jesus's clearance of the vendors and money changers from the Court of the Gentiles affected the flow of money from the temple to Annas and Caiaphas, as well as exposing Jesus to the charge of blasphemous behavior in the temple and in his dialogue with temple authorities. The two high priests, as well as the cohort of chief priests, had strong motives to be rid of Jesus the Galilean.

JESUS IN JERUSALEM

Jesus was no stranger to Jerusalem and its temple. His many visits to the Holy City and its holy place (e.g., Matt. 21:23; 26:55; John 7:14) would have informed

11. William L. Lane, *The Gospel according to* Mark (Grand Rapids: Eerdmans, 1974), 403, citing V. Epstein, "The Historicity of the Gospel accounts of the Cleansing of the Temple," *Zeitschrift für die neutestamentliche Wissenschaft* 55 (1964): 42–58.

12. Josephus, *Jewish Antiquities* 20.204.

13. Mark 11:17, quoting Jer. 7:11 on the corruption of the temple in his day.

14. Josephus, *Jewish Antiquities* 20.204.

him of its culture and practice. Why, then, did Jesus only drive out the merchants and money changers on this one occasion (apart from John's account at the beginning of Jesus's public ministry—John 2:13–16)?

There are two connected answers. One is that it was now close to the Passover when the sale of animal sacrifices would have been at its peak. Josephus observed that at Passover in 66 an astonishing 255,000 lambs were needed.[15] The rent from sellers of sacrifices and money changers that flowed into the temple bank flowed on into the pockets of high priests Annas and Caiaphas, a flow that increased during the great festivals.

The other of Jesus's related acts—the cursing of the fig tree—created the opportunity for Jesus to teach the parable of the beloved Son and to allude to the psalm of the rejected "stone" (Mark 12:10; Ps. 118:22). These teachings effectively secured the trial of Jesus, which was loaded against him, issuing in a guilty verdict and crucifixion.

The Earlier Meeting

The Gospel of John records a meeting of the Sanhedrin following Jesus's raising of Lazarus. This was prior to Jesus's "triumphal entry" to Jerusalem.[16] At that informal meeting Caiaphas said, "Nor do you understand that it is better for you that one man should die for the people, not that the whole nation should perish" (John 11:50). This remark tacitly recognized the powerful reputation of that "one man," Jesus, who, if mishandled, could bring the destruction of the nation.

The members of the Sanhedrin were concerned that were they to allow Jesus to continue performing "signs," then everyone would believe him, and that the Romans would come and destroy the holy place and the nation (John 11:48). John commented that he did not say this on his own authority, but unwittingly prophesied that Jesus was about to die for the nation (John 11:51). John recognized a deeper meaning in Caiaphas's cynical comment that it is better for one innocent man to die to preserve the nation. Without Caiaphas realizing it, God spoke through him, that the death of Jesus would bring true salvation to the nation. After this meeting, the Sanhedrin decided to put plans into motion to kill Jesus (John 11:53).

15. Josephus, *Jewish War* 6.424.
16. See John 11:45–53.

This earlier meeting of the Sanhedrin finds an echo in a much later talmu-
dic source. "On the eve of Passover Jesus was hanged and a herald went out
40 days before (and cried): He is to be stoned because he practiced magic
and beguiled and led Israel astray. Anyone who knows any justification on
his behalf should come and testify for him! But there was no defence found
for him and so he was hanged on the eve of Passover."[17] This tradition located
the death of Jesus to the "eve of Passover" in agreement with the Gospels
but reveals distinctively that for forty days beforehand a herald declared that
Jesus had already been previously condemned to be stoned for blasphemy.
This tradition is at variance with the broad chronology of the Gospels but may
find agreement with the meeting of the Sanhedrin following Jesus's raising
of Lazarus, as recorded by John. Either way this tractate confirms the public
nature of Jesus's presence in Jerusalem at that fateful Passover.

John's account locates the seizure of Jesus at night and, moreover, enu-
merates a very large arresting force of Roman soldiers and temple authorities. According to John, it was a *speira* (sizable cohort) of soldiers under the
command of a *chiliarchos* (captain of a thousand) together with "officers from
the chief priests and Pharisees" (temple guards). The secretive mode of arrest
and a very large military-style capture of Jesus point to the threat that he was
seen to present both to the temple authorities and to the Roman prefect.

This charismatic prophet who had attracted huge followings in the north
had come now to the Holy City, and at Passover. The high priests Annas and
Caiaphas and the Roman authorities agreed that this dangerous leader must
be imprisoned, and his followers dispersed.

The End of the Temple

It is likely that Jesus's private prophecy of the destruction of the temple
(Mark 13:1-2) was also understood more publicly. Centuries earlier Jeremiah
was to suffer for his verbal assaults against the temple (Jer. 7:1-4). Jesus's
words about a mountain cast into the sea were easily understood as referring
to the end of the temple (Mark 11:23). Rumors that the young prophet from
Galilee was speaking of the end of the temple (Mark 13:1-36) would have come
to the attention of the custodians of the temple.

---

17. b. Sanhedrin 43a.

"By What Authority?"

Following Jesus's dramatic mounted arrival in Jerusalem, he went immediately to the temple and "looked around at everything." He did not remain, however, "as it was already late." Mark implies that he would have done then what he did the next day, expel the vendors and money changers.

Returning the next day, he pronounced a curse on a fruitless fig tree and then physically expelled the merchants and money changers from the Court of the Gentiles. The events are connected: the fruitless fig tree was a symbol of the corrupted temple leadership.

Upon hearing this, the chief priests and the senior Pharisees "were seeking a way to destroy him, for they feared him, because all the crowd was astonished at his teaching" (Mark 11:18). The next day, walking in the temple, the chief priests, scribes, and elders—representing the three groups of the Sanhedrin—confronted him, asking: "By what authority are you doing these things, or who gave you this authority to do them?" (Mark 11:28). This question was pious pretense, as if to say, "God gave us the authority to preside in his house, but who are you to desecrate it? Are you a recognizably ordained rabbi?"

Their veiled assertion was that "Caesar has bestowed on us—the house of Annas—the authority to preside over the temple." The term "authority" translates the Greek *exousia*, which translates the Latin *imperium*, the supreme authority Caesar conferred on his provincial governors. In the person of the prefect, you met the one who authorized him, the ruling Caesar. The Sanhedrin, through their representatives, were saying to Jesus, "Our authority is from Caesar (and, therefore, God), but who are you to be doing these things against us?"

Jesus replied with the parable of a vineyard whose owner, having gone to another country, leased it to tenants (Mark 12:1–12). When the owner sent servants to receive the rent (in kind), the tenants beat them and sent them away empty-handed. The owner continued to send servants, whom the tenants now killed. Finally, the owner sent his own "beloved Son" (*huios agapētos*), expecting that the tenants would respect him. However, the tenants killed him on the assumption that the vineyard would then be theirs.

Jesus's "parable" (cast in the form of an allegory) opened his mind to his interrogators and to the readers of Mark's words. God is the owner of the vineyard, his historic people; the tenants are successive local religious leaders, including the present high priests; the servants were the prophets sent by God to his people; God's "beloved Son" is Jesus, the heir of the vineyard whom the tenants will kill. In consequence, God will give the vineyard to others. The Roman centurion's recognition of Jesus as "the Son of God" is Mark's hint that God's future is with "others," that is, the gentiles (Mark 15:39).

This is Jesus's own account of the story of God's dealings with his people and leaders who have killed prophets and who are about to kill him. Remarkably, Jesus identified himself as God's "beloved Son." Mark's readers will recall that the Father addressed Jesus as his "beloved Son" at the baptism and the transfiguration (Mark 1:11; 9:7; also 13:32—the Son).

Jesus's parable was both his assertion of divine authority and his strident condemnation of the corruption of the guardians of the temple, the high priests Annas and Caiaphas. The consequences proved to be astonishing. The high priests then initiated Jesus's arrest and placed him before the Sanhedrin, upon which they "delivered" Jesus to Pilate, on the contrived accusation that he claimed to be "king of the Jews." Such was the high priests' hatred that they effectively bullied Pilate against his will to condemn Jesus to crucifixion.

More was to follow their removal of Jesus: the stoning of Stephen, the execution of James Zebedee, and the stoning of James, brother of the Lord. It was nothing short of an Annas-inspired vendetta against Jesus and the early Christians.[18]

Jesus's "parable" claiming the "authority" of the "beloved Son" was his death sentence. It was now a matter of time and opportunity before Jesus's words about his demise would be fulfilled.

THE HIGH PRIESTS' SCHEMES

An important question is: Why didn't the high priests seek to remove Jesus by stoning on the charge of blasphemy but insisted that Pilate crucify Jesus as "king of the Jews"? There was an earlier attempt to stone Jesus for blasphemy, which had failed (John 10:31, 39–40). Later the high priests condemned Stephen for blasphemy and executed him by stoning. It appears that they had done so with the approval of Pilate, the governor. So why did they not have Jesus removed by stoning?

The likely reason is that Jesus was a popular figure, and they knew the blame would rest on their shoulders. Herod Antipas had become unpopular for his killing of John the Baptist (Mark 11:33). Far better, they appeared to have

---

18. See chapter 24, "The Annas Vendetta."

reasoned, for Jesus to be crucified for the *political* crime of claiming to be king of the Jews. Pilate and the hated Roman occupiers would bear the criticism for removing Jesus. Besides, they would have thought that crucifying Jesus would spell the end of his movement. If his disciples faced crucifixion, they would quickly reject Jesus and return to their fishing, farming, and toll collecting.

THE ARREST OF JESUS AND THE POWER OF ANNAS AND PILATE

Since the main arresting body was Roman soldiers and temple officers, it is evident that Annas and Pilate had agreed about the threat posed by Jesus. The captors took Jesus first to Annas for interrogation by him alone, which is evidence for his continuing de facto power and authority. Only then was Jesus sent to Caiaphas for a more detailed trial, after which he was handed over to the Roman authorities.[19]

The complex procedures reveal the intricacies of the power of Annas, on the one hand, and the power of Pontius Pilate, on the other. Not least, however, they disclose the threat they felt from Jesus's presence in the Holy City.

19. According to Andreas J. Köstenberger, *A Handbook on the Jewish Roots of the Christian Faith*, ed. Craig Evans and David Mishkin (Peabody, MA: Hendrickson, 2019), "the Gospels provide historically accurate accounts of Jesus' trials," 164.

16

PONTIUS PILATE

Pontius Pilate was prefect of Judea from 26 to 36. He belonged to the Roman equestrian order, which signified membership of a family of less status than the senatorial families, and an officer of limited administrative and military experience. His immediate superior was the governor of the province of Syria to the north.

THE OFFICE OF PREFECT

Prefects typically served for 2–3 years, making Pilate's tenure unusually long. His decade-long appointment coincided with the final ten years of Caiaphas's incumbency as high priest in the temple in Jerusalem. It is possible that, notwithstanding his disagreement with Caiaphas during the trial of Jesus, their alliance issued in significant wealth finding its way to the Roman governor.

Whereas the capital of Judea in the Herodian era had been Jerusalem, the Romans relocated their headquarters and garrison to Caesarea Maritima. The prefect received from Caesar the *ius gladii* ("right of the sword"), the authority to exercise capital punishment. It seems, however, that the prefect could delegate that power to the high priest where blasphemy had occurred, as in the case of the allegations against Stephen (Acts 6:13).

The prefect was the commander of the military force, which in Judea was not for the most part composed of Roman legionaries but of locally trained auxiliaries drawn from Syria and other non-Jewish sources. The prefect was also a magistrate presiding over civil and capital cases throughout Judea. It was expected that Roman military officers should, in times of peace, engage in the building of roads and other infrastructure like aqueducts. Pilate fulfilled this expectation by restoring and extending an aqueduct in Jerusalem. The prefect of Judea was responsible for the collection of taxes and their distribution, including to Caesar.

In broad strategic terms, the prefect was responsible for law-and-order issues in Judea, but also in adjoining territories Galilee and Iturea and Trachonitis. Invasion by the Parthians was an ever-present threat. The rise of a young charismatic prophet from Nazareth would have come to the attention of the prefect in Caesarea.

TIBERIUS AND PREFECTS OF JUDEA

Pilate was governor of a notably volatile province, yet a province of significant geopolitical importance. Although Tiberius's years (14–37) were marked by quietness in the East,[1] the potential for politico-religious violence was ever present. For this reason, Judea remained a military province with a prefect appointed by the Caesar, and not a civilian province with a governor appointed by the Senate, and for a one-year term.

Under Augustus the governors of Judea were appointed for three years (Coponius, 6–9; Ambibulus, 9–11; Rufus, 12–14), whereas Tiberius dispatched them for a decade (Gratus, 15–26; Pilate, 26–36). While Tiberius joked that his long-term appointments issued in less "blood sucking" corruption by governors,[2] concern for Judea's strategic military stability may have been a more fundamental reason.

PONTIUS PILATE, HIS NAME

This prefect's names do not cast light on his persona. The praenomen *Pontius* suggests membership of an old Samnite family, the *Pontii*. The cognomen *Pilatus* could mean "hairy" or more likely "armed with spears (*pila*)," suggesting a successful military history. For an otherwise obscure figure, there are numer-

1. Tacitus, *The Histories* 5.9, observed: *sub Tiberio quies*, "Under Tiberius all was quiet."
2. Tiberius's "Parable of the Flies" (Josephus, *Jewish Antiquities* 18.174–176, Loeb translation, L. H. Feldman).

ous historical references to Pilate: Josephus, Philo, Tacitus, the four Gospels, the Acts of the Apostles, and Paul's first letter to Timothy. There are further references to Pilate inscribed on coins minted in 29, 30, and 31.

Another and critical source for Pilate is his inscription in Caesarea Maritima, which appears to be a dedication to Sailors of Tiberium with the name of the dedicatee, Pontius Pilatus, and very importantly, his title, *Praefectus* of Judea. It has been suggested that the inscription was to honor sailors who approached the lighthouse from the dangers of the sea.

PONTIUS PILATE, LUCIUS AELIUS SEJANUS, AND TIBERIUS CAESAR

The Roman trial of Jesus cannot be considered independently of geopolitical affairs in Rome. Pontius Pilate's years as prefect of Judea began in 26. It is a moot point whether he was appointed by Tiberius Caesar or by the now all-powerful praetorian prefect, Lucius Aelius Sejanus.

A critical date is 26, the year Tiberius took up permanent residence on the island of Capri, leaving Sejanus all-powerful in Rome and the empire. For the next five years, Pilate, along with other provincial governors, would have had to answer to Sejanus.

Many of Pilate's actions as prefect of Judea appear to have been calculatedly anti-Semitic. So, was Sejanus an anti-Semite, and was Pilate acting under his instructions in implementing provocative policies in Judea?

According to Philo, Sejanus was unquestionably anti-Semitic:[3]

Flaccus Avillius [governor of Egypt, 33–38] succeeded Sejanus in his hatred and hostile designs against the Jewish nation.[4]

. . . Sejanus who was desirous to destroy our nation . . . [5]

Philo's comments are consistent with the proposal that Pilate's anti-Semitic policies were in fulfillment of the program of the all-powerful Sejanus in the years 26–31.

3. Tacitus, *Annals of Imperial Rome* 3.72; 4.2, 72; Suetonius, *Tiberius* 65; Dio Cassius, *Roman History* 8.2, 4, 7. E. M. Smallwood, "Some Notes on the Jews under Tiberius," *Latomus* 15 (1956): 325.

4. Philo, *Flaccus* 1.1.

5. Philo, *Embassy to Gaius* 160.

PREFECT OF JUDEA, 26–31

Josephus is singularly expansive in chronicling Pontius Pilate's hostile acts as prefect of Judea.[6] It is difficult to avoid the conclusion that Sejanus was the inspiration for these incidents.[7]

Soon after his arrival, Pilate marched his troops from Caesarea to Jerusalem.[8] For the first time the military standards bore idolatrous icons, specifically busts of the Caesar (Tiberius). Their arrival occurred under the cover of darkness. Once daylight arrived, the population walked to Caesarea and for some days implored Pilate to remove the images from the standards. Eventually, Pilate ordered the removal of the images. Josephus is in no doubt about Pilate's motive: "[he] took a bold step in subversion of Jewish practices."[9] Similarly unprecedented, apparently, was the issuing of coins bearing the offensive *lituus* and *simpulum* as used in Roman cultic practice. These actions cannot be explained away on the grounds of cultural innocence. They were calculated and deliberate.

By now Pilate must have been aware of Jewish sensibilities. Nevertheless, the governor proceeded with the construction of an aqueduct bringing water to Jerusalem. To pay for this otherwise worthy project he looted the sacred treasury (*Corbonas*).[10] This calculated action provided his troops, who were disguised as Jews, the opportunity to fall on the protesters, many of whom were killed and wounded.

From Luke's Gospel we read of the assault of Pilate's soldiers on pilgrims from Galilee who were in Jerusalem for Passover. They slaughtered the Galileans in the act of sacrificing the Passover lambs (Luke 13:1–2).

There are references to Pilate's calculated brutality toward his Jewish subjects between his arrival in Judea in 26 and his trial of Jesus in 33. The trial narratives cast light on the consequences of Pilate's provocative policies toward the Jews. The two insurrectionists (*stasiastai*) crucified with Jesus, along with the robber Barabbas (*lēstēs*, a rebel), their leader, had participated in an otherwise unknown uprising (*stasis*) against Roman rule (Mark 15:7). It is highly likely that this rebellion had been provoked by Pilate's actions.

6. See Josephus, *Jewish Antiquities* 18.55–63.

7. P. L. Maier, "Sejanus, Pilate and the Date of the Crucifixion," *Church History* 37 (1968): 8–9.

8. Josephus, *Jewish War* 2.169–174; *Jewish Antiquities* 18.55–59.

9. Josephus, *Jewish Antiquities* 18.55.

10. Josephus, *Jewish Antiquities* 18.60–62.

PILATE'S AWARENESS OF JESUS

Jesus became a public figure after his baptism, which is dated to 28 or 29. Pilate, the recently arrived prefect, could not have been unaware that great crowds gathered to hear Jesus of Nazareth in Galilee.[11]

Jesus's calculated arrival in the Holy City ahead of the Passover would have been brought to the notice of the governor. Furthermore, there were whispers that in Jesus's announcement of the dawning of the kingdom of God (Mark 1:14–15), he was implicitly claiming to be "king of the Jews." Pilate was aware that the crucifixion must occur before the Sabbath.[12]

As noted, the Romans had suffered humiliating defeat from self-styled local kings in Gaul and Germany, as well as in Judea itself a few years earlier.[13]

AFTER THE FALL OF SEJANUS, 31–33

At the height of Sejanus's powers, Tiberius at last became aware of the dangerous ambitions of the praetorian prefect. Still in Capri, Tiberius convened a meeting of the Senate, whose members condemned Sejanus to death. He was strangled and his body torn apart. Mob violence was directed against any whose names were linked with Sejanus. The Senate declared him *damnatio memoriae*, his name expunged from public records, statues, even coins bearing his name. Tiberius secured the killing of Sejanus's children. Treason trials followed, directed to any who had the slightest connection with the former praetorian prefect. Arrests, trials, and executions dominated Roman life for many months.

As the likely appointee of Sejanus in Judea, the prefect Pontius Pilate had reason to believe that Tiberius's wrath could reach across the waters to him. The members of the temple hierarchy, doubtless aware of this, were able to direct the prefect's actions to their own ends.

11. See earlier, Mark 3:7–8.

12. So Andreas J. Köstenberger, *A Handbook on the Jewish Roots of the Christian Faith*, ed. Craig Evans and David Mishkin (Peabody, MA: Hendrickson, 2019), 165, citing b. Sanhedrin 35b. Furthermore, Roman officials worked only until late morning (Köstenberger, *Handbook*, 165, citing Sherwin-White).

13. Josephus, *Jewish Antiquities* 18.4–10.

Tiberius's Letter

Furthermore, Tiberius took urgent steps to defuse anti-Semitism in the provinces, especially in Judea, the ancestral home of the Jews. To that end, Tiberius Caesar sent a missive to his governors, chronicled by Philo: "[Tiberius] sent commands to all the governors of the provinces in every country to comfort those of our nation in their respective cities, as the punishment intended to be inflicted, was not to be inflicted upon all, but only on the guilty; and they were but few. And he ordered them to change none of the existing customs, but to look upon them as pledges, since the men were peaceful in their dispositions and natural characters, and their laws trained them and disposed them to quiet and stability."[14]

Pilate would not have missed Tiberius's reference to the "few" who were "guilty." He would have understood that as governor of the Jewish homeland, the Caesar's encyclical was first and foremost directed to him.

The Golden Shields

Pilate's most curious action was his creation of gilded shields dedicated to Tiberius, which the governor placed in the Praetorium. "They had no image work traced on them nor anything else forbidden by the law."[15] Although the shields were aniconic, they bore the name of Tiberius and were almost certainly offensive to Jewish scruples.[16] Four Herodian princes, led by Herod Antipas, complained to Tiberius, who ordered the removal of the shields.

Amid political turmoil after the fall of Sejanus, this may have been Pilate's ill-conceived action to strengthen his position in Judea. He sought to ingratiate himself to Tiberius while being inoffensive to the Jews. The reaction by the people and the princes reflects the deep and justifiable suspicion of the people toward Pilate.[17]

The incident of the gilded shields occurred in the post-Sejanus situation.[18] Pilate was now accountable to a new master, Tiberius, who, aware of the polit-

14. Philo, *Embassy to Gaius* 161.
15. Philo, *Embassy to Gaius* 299–305.
16. P. S. Davies, "The Meaning of Philo's Text about the Gilded Shields," *Journal of Theological Studies* 37 (1986): 109–14.
17. Philo, *Embassy to Gaius* 299–305.
18. E. M. Smallwood, "Philo and Josephus as Historians of the Same Events," in

ical realities involving the Jews, forbade further harassment of them. This will explain Pilate's speedy removal of the shields, which he would not have done during Sejanus's incumbency. In the new situation when Tiberius was again undisputed ruler, the Jewish temple hierarchy had the upper hand regarding Pilate, especially in the light of his past behavior toward the Jewish people. It was this "new" situation that explains the "new" Pilate as we encounter him in the Gospels in his relationship to the Jewish leadership at the trial of Jesus.

PHILO ON PONTIUS PILATE

Philo is renowned for his extremely negative appraisal of Pontius Pilate, prefect of Judea. "He was a man of very inflexible disposition, and very merciless as well as very obstinate . . . his corruption, and his acts of insolence, and his rapine, and his habit of insulting people, and his cruelty, and his continual murders of people untried and uncondemned, and his never ending, and gratuitous, and most grievous inhumanity."[19] This was Philo's judgment based on Pilate's ill-fated creation of the aniconic golden shields and his (initial) refusal to remove them from the palace of Herod Antipas in Jerusalem.

There are, however, several reasons for moderating Philo's extreme verdict on Pilate. To begin, Philo was angry with Pilate for creating the golden shields and for refusing to remove them. Furthermore, Philo's description varies from the Gospels' presentation of the governor at the trial of Jesus, where he is a vacillating figure. Again, Josephus may be attributing the incidents of the standards and the removal of money from the sacred treasury to Pilate's ignorance of Jewish scruples. Finally, Philo's portrayal of Pilate is somewhat stereotypical. According to one authority, "Philo presents officials like Pilate, Sejanus, Capito and the emperor Gaius Caligula as typically hating Jews, exhibiting fear and devising false accusations."[20]

These considerations suggest that we should moderate to some degree Philo's appraisal of Pontius Pilate.

Josephus, Judaism, and Christianity, ed. L. H. Feldman and G. Hata (Leiden: Brill, 1987), 126–28.

19. Philo, *Embassy to Gaius* 302.

20. Warren Carter, *Pontius Pilate* (Collegeville, MN: Michael Glazier, 2003), 16.

THEORIES ABOUT PONTIUS PILATE

Naturally the divergences between Philo/Josephus and the Gospels regarding Pilate have attracted the attention of scholars, and several theories have been proposed to account for them. We review two such views and propose a third as the most likely approximation of the person of the governor under whom Jesus "suffered."

There is, first, the view that the tough governor as portrayed by Philo and Josephus is correct and the accommodating Pilate of the Gospels is a falsification. According to this reconstruction, which S. G. F. Brandon propounded in 1967,[21] Jesus was in fact an anti-Roman insurrectionist (or an advocate of insurrection). Since the early church needed the good will of the Roman authorities, its founder's true sympathies must be masked. Hence the Gospels present Jesus as innocent, a victim of Jewish machinations, with an indecisive governor portrayed as coerced to execute Jesus against his better moral judgment.

It is likely that the Romans were indeed aware of and concerned about the new messianic sect from Judea. In his account of the fire in Rome in 64, Tacitus described the popular apprehension of the spread of this "superstition" (*superstitio*, sect) to Rome and of its strength there.[22]

The gospel writers' sensitivity to this opinion may be reflected at several points. In his account of the feeding of the five thousand, Mark significantly omits the assertion found in John that the Galilean crowd attempted to make Jesus "king," followed by Mark's account that suggests that something like that had occurred (cf. John 6:15 with Mark 6:45–46).

Luke's version of Jesus's trial by Pilate and his interrogation by Herod the tetrarch is careful to establish that Jesus did not engage in any treasonable kingship activities, whether in Galilee or Judea (Luke 23:1–16).

Sensitivity to damaging opinion does not, of course, make that opinion true. The accusation of high treason to Pilate by the temple hierarchy, that "[Jesus] opposes payment of taxes to Caesar and claims to be Messiah, a king" (Luke 23:2 NIV), resonates remarkably with the crimes of a notorious Galilean who had in the not-too-distant past—the year 6—revolted against Roman rule

21. S. G. F. Brandon, *Jesus and the Zealots* (Manchester: Manchester University Press, 1967).

22. Tacitus, *Annals* 15.44.

in Judea. The uprising of Judas the Galilean at the time Judea was annexed as a Roman province, when direct personal tax to Rome was first levied, was doubtless well remembered by Roman officials in Rome.

The Roman military governors took seriously charges of this kind. One of their major responsibilities was to maintain peace and order within the provinces. The Roman military administration was severe not only regarding leaders of movements but also regarding associates and followers of those leaders who revolted against them. It is assumed that Pilate carefully investigated these charges against Jesus and not only executed him for treason, as he did, but would also have acted severely against his followers, which he did not.

Had Jesus been the insurrectionist of Brandon's reconstruction, the Romans would have stamped out the Jesus movement then and there, as they had in the case of Judas's following.[23]

In short, the possible presence of some apologetic elements in the Gospels portraying Jesus as a nonrevolutionary does not prove that he was a revolutionary, nor does it invalidate the essential integrity of the Gospels in their presentation of Pilate as a rather compromised figure at that time.

A second theory, advanced by Brian McGing in 1991, proposed that the major sources are in fact in fundamental agreement, despite apparent divergences.[24] According to this line of argument, Pilate was a governor loyal to his emperor Tiberius and that his actions toward Jews and Samaritans, when compared to the actions of other governors, were relatively unremarkable. In fact, his ten-year incumbency was one of relative calm.

Pilate's behavior toward Jesus could be adequately accounted for by his ignorance of Jewish culture and politics along with a certain personal indecisiveness. There may have been just enough smoke, as it were, in the case of Jesus to justify extinguishing the fire. In any case, what importance attached to one Jew? And did not the accused's stubborn silence in the face of interrogation amount to contempt of court (*contumacia*), something abhorrent to Romans?

While this reconstruction upholds the broad historicity of the Gospels in the face of the Brandon alternative, it scarcely does justice to Philo's and Josephus's accounts of Pontius Pilate. Indeed, so far as we know, it was the provocative actions of Pilate after his arrival in Judea in 26 that broke the calm that had

---

23. B. McGing, "Pontius Pilate and the Sources," *Catholic Biblical Quarterly* 53, no. 3 (1991): 416–38.

24. McGing, "Pontius Pilate," 416–38.

prevailed since Judas's rebellion twenty years earlier. In his brief chronological survey of Jewish history from the arrival of Pompey in 63 BC to the outbreak of the war with Rome in 66, Tacitus was to comment, *sub Tiberio quies*, "under Tiberius all was quiet."[25] This was to change during the next five years while the Praetorian prefect Lucius Aelius Sejanus was de facto ruler in Rome.

As noted, Pilate's introduction to Jerusalem of military standards bearing idolatrous icons was without precedent; previous governors had used unornamented standards. Issuing coins bearing the offensive captions and the use of the *lituus* and *simpulum* was similarly unusual. These actions cannot be explained away on the grounds of cultural ignorance. They were calculated and deliberate. Actions such as the seizure of money from the sacred treasury for the construction of an aqueduct in Jerusalem[26] and the slaughter of the Galileans in the act of sacrificing the Passover lambs (Luke 23:1–2) are quite consistent with the provocatively introduced iconic standards and coins noted above.

The two insurrectionists crucified with Jesus, along with Barabbas, had participated in an otherwise unknown uprising against Roman rule (Mark 15:7). Most likely this disturbance was also provoked by Pilate's actions.

Pilate's appointment in Judea effectively ended when he was dispatched to Rome to account for the slaughter of Samaritans on Mount Gerizim.[27] Josephus does nothing to qualify or downplay his report that the Samaritans complained that their people had gathered at Mount Gerizim, "not as rebels against the Romans," but as "refugees from the persecution of Pilate."[28]

Josephus's is but a milder and briefer version of Philo's portrayal of Pilate as "naturally inflexible, a blend of self-will and relentlessness."[29] Even allowing for some rhetorical excess by Philo, the violence of the episodes recorded by Josephus and Luke's brief but chilling reference to the slaughter of the Galileans may well justify Philo's verdict on Pontius Pilate.

But how can this Pilate be reconciled with the governor who comes before us in the Gospels?

A third reconstruction, which is associated with E. M. Smallwood and P. L. Maier, contends that both Philo and Josephus have portrayed Pilate correctly

25. Tacitus, *Histories* 5.9. See further P. W. Barnett, "Under Tiberius All Was Quiet," *New Testament Studies* 21 (1975): 564–71.

26. Josephus, *Jewish Antiquities* 18.60–62.

27. Josephus, *Jewish Antiquities* 18.85–89.

28. Josephus, *Jewish Antiquities* 18.88.

29. Philo, *Embassy to Gaius* 301, 302.

but that at the trial of Jesus, due to changed political circumstances in Rome, Pilate had been forced to act out of character.[30] Thus, each of the major sources can be viewed as historically consistent.

According to this opinion, Pilate's appointment to Judea coincided with the years of Sejanus's appointment as Praetorian prefect. It will be remembered that Tiberius continued to remain on the island of Capri during those years, leaving Sejanus as actual ruler in Rome and the empire.

Philo the Jew of Alexandria states that Sejanus "wished to make away with (our) nation," knowing that the Jewish people were loyal to Tiberius.[31] It is likely that Sejanus was ambitious to grasp imperial power in Rome. It appears to be no coincidence that Pilate "decided to overturn the laws of the Jews" at the very time the anti-Semite Sejanus was at the height of his powers in Rome.

Under interrogation by the chief priests, Jesus accepted the charge that he was the Son of Man, which led to the accusation of blasphemy against him (Mark 14:64). But when they brought him to Pilate, they converted the religious charge of blasphemy to one more recognizable and culpable for the Roman mind, the political charge of treason.

Thus, in each of the four Gospels Pilate asks the political question of the accused, "Are you the King of the Jews?" (Mark 15:2; cf. 14:61; see John 18:33). Jesus's agreement with this charge would have been, in effect, a denial of Tiberius's kingship in Judea. Upon inquiry, however, Pilate decided that he must release Jesus. The charge of treason was not substantiated. But in the "new" situation after the fall of Sejanus, the chief priests were able to intimidate the governor: "If you release this man, you are not Caesar's friend. Everyone who makes himself a king opposes Caesar," then, adding ominously, "We have no king but Caesar" (John 19:12, 15).

The man who had ridden roughshod over the Jewish people was now at the mercy of their leaders. And he knew it. One false move and his appointment would be canceled and his career finished. Pilate acquiesced, handing Jesus over to the execution squad for crucifixion, on the charge of treason, that he was "the king of the Jews."

---

30. The leading advocate of this reconstruction is P. L. Maier, "Sejanus, Pilate and the Date of the Crucifixion," *Church History* 37 (1968): 3–13; "The Episode of the Golden Roman Shields in Jerusalem," *Harvard Theology Review* 42 (1969): 109–21.

31. Philo, *Embassy to Gaius* 160. See Smallwood, "Some Notes on the Jews under Tiberius," 325.

THE HISTORICAL PONTIUS PILATE

Pontius Pilate poses a major problem for the historian. The three main sources present him rather differently. Philo's comments about Pilate are extremely hostile, Josephus's somewhat less so. How, then, are we able to reconcile the ruthless figure of Philo and Josephus with the governor of the Gospels who is unable to discharge a prisoner whom he wished to set free?

The most likely answer is that Pilate was an anti-Semite and a bully who came to Judea determined to break the spirit of the Jewish people. So how are we to account for the rather weak figure who, although finding Jesus innocent of the charge "king of the Jews," succumbed to the demands of the temple authorities that he must be crucified?

The temple authorities would know of the passing of Sejanus, Pilate's patron and protector, and Tiberius's seizure of power and of his determination to stamp out anti-Semitism in the provinces. Pilate's calculated assault on his Jewish subjects must have been well known.

For their part, the chief priests and the Pharisees would have been aware of Jesus's attitudes subverting the Sabbath, fasting, and the purity rules in Galilee and his blasphemy in Jerusalem claiming to be "one with the Father." His popularity following the raising of Lazarus alarmed the members of the Sanhedrin to the point that they saw their tenure of the temple and their rule of the Holy City to be at risk (John 11:47–48). Their hostility would have reached its peak with Jesus's expulsion of traders and money changers from the Court of the Gentiles. They were determined to be rid of the Galilean whatever the cost, including the possible opposition of the Roman governor.

As noted, the high priests could have petitioned Pilate for permission to stone Jesus for blasphemy. Far better, they reasoned, for him to be crucified by the Romans. Let Pilate take the blame!

THE SAMARITAN INCIDENT AND THE RECALL OF PILATE

Pilate's end as prefect of Judea came because of his mismanagement of an incident in Samaria.[32] A local prophet claimed to know the location of the lost sacred vessels on Mount Gerizim, the Samaritans' holy mountain. Armed Samaritans gathered at a village, Tirathana, from which they planned to ascend

32. Josephus, *Jewish Antiquities* 18.85–90.

the mountain. Pilate arrived with cavalry, killed some Samaritans, and took many prisoners, whom they also killed. Among those killed were "principal leaders and those who were most influential among the Samaritans." Pilate may have believed that discovery of the sacred vessels would inspire wholesale uprising against Rome.

As noted, Josephus does nothing to qualify or downplay his report that the Samaritans complained that their people had gathered at Mount Gerizim, "not as rebels against the Romans," but as "refugees from the persecution of Pilate."[33]

Pilate's heavy-handed response to the Samaritan event cost him dearly. The Council of the Samaritans complained to Vitellius, governor of Syria, about Pilate's excessive military response. Vitellius forthwith sent Pilate to Rome for trial and appointed Marcellus as prefect of Judea. Tiberius died before Pilate reached Rome. After serving throughout 26–36 as prefect of Judea, Pontius Pilate disappears from the annals of history.

Timeline: Pontius Pilate Prefect of Judea, AD 26–36

26	Pontius Pilate arrives in Judea, appointed by Tiberius or Sejanus
	Brings Roman standards with embossed figures of the emperor into Jerusalem[34]
	Jewish delegation to Caesarea to plead for their removal
	Pilate seizes money from *Corbonas* for construction of aqueduct[35]
	In Jerusalem his soldiers (in mufti) kill many
31	Death of Sejanus
	Treason trials in Rome
	Sejanus declared *damnatio memoriae*
	Incident of the golden shields[36]
	Tiberius writes to the governors[37]
?32	Pilate's soldiers slaughter Galileans in Jerusalem at Passover (Luke 13:1)
	Source of enmity between Pilate and Herod Antipas?
	Uprising in Jerusalem involving Barabbas (Mark 15:7; Acts 3:14)

---

33. Josephus, *Jewish Antiquities* 18.88.
34. Josephus, *Jewish Antiquities* 18.55–59; *Jewish War* 2.169–174.
35. Josephus, *Jewish Antiquities* 18.60–62; *Jewish War* 2.175–177.
36. Philo, *Embassy to Gaius* 299–305.
37. Philo, *Embassy to Gaius* 161.

17

HEROD ANTIPAS

Herod Antipas is important for the study of Christian origins. Jesus's life span (ca. 6 BC–AD 33) was enclosed within Antipas's rule of Galilee (4 BC–AD 39). Furthermore, Herod Antipas interrogated Jesus as part of Pilate's trial of Jesus (Luke 23:6–16).

Antipas was the grandson of Antipater the Idumean, son to Herod the "Great" and the Samaritan Malthake, and younger brother to Archelaus. Herod Antipas, therefore, was not in any biological sense a Jew.

THE DIVISION OF HEROD'S KINGDOM

One of Herod's most deeply held objectives was to find a son to inherit his undivided kingdom, testament to which was his creation of no fewer than seven successive wills.

In his later years Herod executed possible successors: in 7 BC Aristobulus and Alexander, sons of his Maccabean wife, Mariamne I; in 5 BC Antipater, his eldest son, to Doris.

In his fifth will Herod named Antipas as king, his sole heir, but later decided to divide his kingdom three ways. Archelaus was to be king of Judea, Idumea, and Samaria; Antipas was to be tetrarch of Galilee and Perea; Philip was to be tetrarch of Iturea-Trachonitis.

The three named heirs traveled to Rome to argue their cases before Caesar Augustus, who ratified Herod's final will, with the single change that Archelaus would not be "king" but *ethnarch* ("ruler of a nation") of Judea.

This meant that half of Herod's kingdom was to be ruled by Archelaus, with the remaining half divided between Antipas and Philip. Archelaus was sent into exile in 6, and Philip died in 34. Antipas, however, remained tetrarch of Galilee until his exile in 39. The Gospels generally refer to Antipas as "tetrarch," except that Mark also refers to him as "king."[1] Jesus referred disparagingly to Antipas as "that fox" (Luke 13:32), although scholars disagree about the meaning.

ANTIPAS'S EARLY YEARS

Antipas was born circa 20 BC. As a child he was sent to Rome for education, where he would have learned Latin and Greek to add to his prior understanding of Aramaic and Hebrew. As well, he met current and future leaders of the Roman world.

On his return from Rome in 4 BC, he found Galilee in turmoil following the death of Herod earlier that year. Each part of Herod's kingdom was under threat from opportunistic warlords. Athronges and his brothers had attempted to seize Judea; Simon had captured Perea; and Judas, son of Ezekias, had attempted to make Galilee his own fiefdom.

Ezekias had earlier captured Sepphoris, administrative capital of Galilee, looted money and weapons, arming his followers for revolt against Herodian rule. Before Antipas returned, Varus, legate of Syria (based in Antioch), at the head of his legions, burned down the city and sold the inhabitants into slavery. On arrival Antipas renamed the city Autocratis and rebuilt it as the "ornament of the Galilee" and constructed a new wall around Betharamphtha in Perea, which he renamed Julias, the name of the wife of Augustus.[2]

Antipas's territories—Galilee and Perea—did not have a common border. Perea was militarily vulnerable because it shared a frontier with the potentially hostile Nabateans, whose capital was Petra. At some point after his return, Herod Antipas married the Nabatean princess Phasaelis, daughter of King Aretas IV. It was a political marriage.

Following the military campaigns, it was necessary to rebuild his principal cities, Sepphoris in Galilee and Julias in Perea. In 17 Antipas began to create a new capital, Tiberias, on the western side of the lake.

---

1. Mark 6:14, 22, 25, 26, 27. This may reflect Antipas's aspirational use of the title "king." However, the parallel passage (Matt. 14:1) refers to "Herod the tetrarch."
2. Josephus, *Jewish Antiquities* 18.27.

TOPOGRAPHY

Josephus was familiar with Galilee, having led the Jewish forces against the Roman legions in 66. He described Galilee as divided into upper and lower parts and bounded by Samaria and Scythopolis (Beth Shean) to the south; by Hippos, Gadara, and Gaulanitis to the east; by Tyre to the north; and adjacent to Ptolemais to the west.

He further observed that the two Galilees—upper and lower—had always resisted hostile invasion due to the numbers and courage of the men of the region.[3]

He describes the land of Galilee as "everywhere . . . rich in soil and pasturage . . . producing . . . a variety of trees . . . [so that] every inch of the soil has been cultivated . . . there is not a parcel of waste land."[4] Further, "the towns . . . are thickly distributed . . . and the villages all so densely populated that the smallest of them contains above fifteen thousand inhabitants."[5]

Josephus is likewise lyrical about the body of freshwater known variously as Lake Gennesaret, Lake Ginosar, and Lake Tiberias. He gives its dimensions, incorrectly, as "a length of thirty furlongs and inland to a depth of twenty." This harp-shaped lake is twenty-one kilometers long and thirteen kilometers wide. The lake has numerous small harbors indicating extensive travel by boat for people and transport of produce. More than twenty species of fish supported numerous fishermen, who sold their catch to local people or for pickling.

THE HERODIANS

The two primary references to the Herodians are in the Gospel of Mark (Mark 3:6; 12:13; cf. Matt. 22:16). The suffix -*ianoi* indicates "a faction," in this case one supportive of Herod Antipas. Of various suggestions, the most likely is that its members were influential Galileans who supported Herod the tetrarch's ambition to be "king" not only of Galilee but of the undivided realm of his late father, Herod the "Great." That had been the intent of Herod's fifth will, which, however, was superseded by his final will.

Mark's account of the attendees at Antipas's birthday celebration may provide a clue about the membership of the Herodians. "Herod on his birthday

---

3. Josephus, *Jewish War* 3.39.
4. Josephus, *Jewish War* 3.42.
5. Josephus's statistics appear to be overstated.

gave a banquet for his nobles (*megistanoi*) and military (*chiliarchoi*) commanders and the leading men (*prōtoi*) of Galilee" (Mark 6:21).

These wealthy, powerful, and influential men most likely were the leaders
of the pro-Herod faction, who supported him and advocated his cause. We
can readily understand this faction's opposition to the prefect of Judea, whose
appointment, bolstered by his auxiliary legions, was the chief obstacle to Antipas's hopes of kingship over a reunited realm.

SETTLEMENTS IN GALILEE

On arrival in his tetrarchy in 4 BC, Antipas found its capital, Sepphoris, in
ruins, which he rebuilt. Although Sepphoris remained his biggest city, he
relocated his capital and his place of residence to his newly built Tiberias,
which was more centrally located. Tiberias, named after the present emperor, was mostly populated with gentiles. Its internal culture was decidedly
Hellenistic.

Doubtless inspired by his father's achievements as a builder, the young
tetrarch engaged in the renovation and construction of significant cities; first
he restored Sepphoris and then created the new capital, Tiberias. Under Antipas, the previously rural Galilee became to a significant degree urbanized. It
is likely that many previously agriculturally based Galileans were attracted to
these cities, leaving the farming estates with fewer laborers.

Antipas's two major settlements, Sepphoris and Tiberias, were not re-
ligiously "Jewish." Mosaics in Sepphoris portray pagan banquets. Its synagogue is decorated with the signs of the zodiac. Although these may date
to a later era, there is no reason to question an earlier non-Jewish religious
culture. Antipas's new city, Tiberias, was also un-Jewish in character; it was
built on a graveyard and its court and lifestyle were Hellenistic in character.
There is no record of Jesus visiting Sepphoris or Tiberias. Little is known of
Betharamphtha Julias.

Luke informs us that Antipas's "household manager" in Tiberias was Chuza,
whose wife, Joanna, was among a group of wealthy women who financially
supported Jesus and the disciples (Luke 8:3). Joanna was among the women
who traveled to Jerusalem with Jesus, and who found his burial tomb empty
(Luke 24:10). Luke also refers to Manaen, a member of Herod the tetrarch's
court (in Tiberias), who became a leader in the church in Antioch (Acts 13:1).

The Gospels are silent about Jesus's visits to the largest settlements in Galilee, Sepphoris and Tiberias, both of which appear to have been the centers

of the Herodians' influence. We readily imagine these to have been the cities where the Herodians lived, leaving their farming estates in the hands of stewards. For Jesus to visit these cities would be to risk capture and execution, following the fate of the great prophet John the Baptist.

Rather, Jesus and the twelve disciple-missionaries would have directed their attention to the 204 villages of Galilee.[6] These probably ranged in population from several dozens to several hundreds. Archaeological inquiry has located a cluster of synagogues around the northwestern and northeastern quadrants of the lake,[7] prominent among them, according to Jesus, were Capernaum, Chorazin, and Bethsaida (Matt. 11:20–21). Based on current thinking, it appears that Jesus taught in either Aramaic or Greek, depending on the language spoken in the village.[8]

WEALTH AND POVERTY

According to Josephus, both Galilee proper and Perea were in different ways agriculturally rich. Josephus remarks that Galilee's "soil is universally rich and fruitful" and that the region is "full of the plantations of trees of all sorts."[9] Regarding Perea he observes that while "the greater part of it is desert, and rough, and much less disposed for the production of the milder kinds of fruits," yet "it produces all kinds of fruits, and its plains are planted with trees of all sorts, while yet the olive tree, the vine, and the palm trees, are chiefly cultivated there."[10]

Furthermore, the great freshwater lake had abundant quantities of fish and supported vibrant fishing and pickling industries.

Numerous travelers passed through Antipas's territories, whether Galilee or Perea. Toll collectors were stationed on major thoroughfares, like the Via

6. Josephus, *Life* 285. The villages, large and small (*kōmai*), appear to have had a village president (*kōmarch*), an administrative arrangement that went back to Ptolemaic times.

7. J. J. Rousseau and Rami Arav, *Jesus and His World* (Minneapolis: Fortress, 1995), 271.

8. Stanley E. Porter, "Jesus and the Use of Greek: A Response to Maurice Casey," *Bulletin of Biblical Research* 10, no. 1 (2000): 71–87; G. Scott Gleaves, *Did Jesus Speak Greek?* (Eugene, OR: Wipf & Stock, 2015).

9. Josephus, *Jewish War* 3.2.

10. Josephus, *Jewish War* 3.2.

Maris, that passed by Capernaum. Part of Antipas's considerable wealth flowed to him through an array of taxes and tolls.

Most of Antipas's subjects were poor. There was, however, a small middle class whose members owned their property (for example, the father of the prodigal, and the boat-owning father of the Zebedee brothers) and a small upper echelon as represented by the Herodians.

It is not known how Antipas raised the funds for his building projects. Most likely he owned large estates from which he derived considerable income. Moreover, as noted, he ruthlessly levied taxes from his subjects. It is reasonably assumed that most of the Galileans and Pereans were poor and in debt.

JESUS'S DEBATES WITH THE SCRIBES FROM JERUSALEM

The Gospel of Mark reports three confrontations in Galilee between Jerusalem-based scribes and Jesus:

Mark	Location	Issue
2:6	Capernaum	Jesus's implied authority to forgive sins
3:22	Capernaum	Jesus's dependence on Beelzebul for casting out demons
7:1	Gennesaret	Jesus's disciples breaking purity rules

These incidents reveal the concerns of the leading scribes (senior Pharisees, Bible scholars) regarding the influence of this new leader in Galilee. On three counts he was a blasphemer: only God could forgive sins; only God's power could be invoked to drive out demons; the whole structure of Jewish religion depended on purity. These were extremely serious charges.

Rabban Johanan ben Zakkai, from Arav in Galilee, was a later contemporary of Jesus. Later, from Jerusalem, he began collecting the judgments of the rabbis that evolved as the Mishnah, published circa 200.

The point to note is ben Zakkai's low view of law-based religion in Galilee. He is famous for observing, "O Galilee, O Galilee, why do you hate the Torah?" It is true that he became prominent after the mid-first century, that is, some decades after Jesus, and that he was railing against the influence of the Sadducees.

Nevertheless, his low view of Galilee's practice of the Torah may have echoed the concerns of the senior scribes in Jerusalem several decades earlier.

We reasonably assume that the Jerusalem establishment feared the influence of Jesus contributing to the loss of Galilee to their historic faith.

Jesus's arrival in Jerusalem for Passover 33 would have attracted the attention of the senior scribes in the Holy City. Scribes were well represented in the membership of the Sanhedrin, before whom Jesus was tried. We assume that Jesus's current "crime" regarding his desecration of the temple was seen as a continuation of his blasphemous actions in Galilee.

A SECURE RULER

Thanks to the loyal support of his Herodian faction ("the nobles," "the commanders," and "the leading men"), Antipas's tetrarchy enjoyed political stability throughout the years of his tenure from 4 BC to AD 39. Furthermore, the Roman occupation of Judea in 6 provided military protection when in 6 Judas the Galilean led the revolt against payment of taxes to the Roman Caesar.

Antipas's years of good fortune ended in 36. He had made a diplomatic error that lost him the vital protection of Vitellius, military legate in Antioch. This military hiatus provided Aretas IV, king of the Nabateans, the long-awaited opportunity to wreak revenge on Antipas, who had divorced the king's daughter some years earlier. In that year the Nabateans destroyed Antipas's army. Josephus reports that the Jews interpreted Antipas's defeat as God's punishment for the murder of John the Baptist.[11]

ANTIPAS, HERODIAS, JOHN THE BAPTIST, AND JESUS

As noted, it was probably for political convenience that Herod Antipas married Phasaelis, daughter of Aretas; the marriage was a bond to secure a friendly border between Perea and Nabatea. Although Antipas and Phasaelis had been married for "a long time," the tetrarch had decided to marry Herodias, despite her existing marriage to his half brother, Philip.[12] Herodias demanded that

---

11. Josephus stated that "Herod had put him to death, though he was a good man and had exhorted the Jews to lead righteous lives" (*Jewish Antiquities* 18.116–119); cf. Mark 11:32.

12. Josephus, *Jewish Antiquities* 18.109–110; Mark 6:17. Philip's precise identity is debated. See Harold Hoehner, *Herod Antipas* (Grand Rapids: Zondervan, 1980), 131–36.

Antipas "oust the daughter of Aretas."[13] Phasaelis, however, discovered the plan and fled to Petra.

Antipas's marriage to Herodias attracted the condemnation of the popular prophet John the Baptist, whom he imprisoned and later executed (Mark 6:21–29).[14] John had baptized Jesus in the Jordan; their respective ministries overlapped for a period (John 3:22–24).

Herod the tetrarch, domiciled in Tiberias, must have heard of Jesus and the crowds who gathered to hear him. The mission of the Twelve to the villages of Galilee had come to his attention with such force that he thought John the Baptist had been resurrected (Mark 6:14). At its aftermath, when Jesus fed the multitude, an attempt was made to impose the kingship on him, which he refused (John 6:15; Mark 6:45). From that time, according to Mark, Jesus withdrew from Antipas's jurisdiction to the regions of Tyre, Sidon, the Decapolis, and Gaulanitis (Mark 7:31; 8:27; 9:2, 30). There is abundant evidence that Jesus often withdrew from Antipas's tetrarchy.[15]

Jesus compared Herod Antipas with John the Baptist. While John belonged to the distinguished body of prophets, the tetrarch was a mere "reed shaken by the wind," a man who dressed in "soft clothes" living in a "king's house" (Matt. 11:7–15).

On his final journey to Jerusalem, some Pharisees warned Jesus "to get away from here, for Herod [Antipas] wants to kill you" (Luke 13:31). The tetrarch had imprisoned and killed one trouble-making prophet, would he not hesitate to kill another whose following was greater? It was on that occasion that Jesus referred to Herod Antipas as "that fox."

Curiously, as we shall see, when Antipas had the opportunity to condemn Jesus, he did not do so. Rather, he handed him back to Pontius Pilate. Luke, who reports this, does not give a reason. One likely explanation is that having killed one popular prophet, he was not prepared to risk being blamed for killing another.[16] Far better, he may have surmised, to leave the fate of the Nazarene to the Romans.

---

13. Josephus, *Jewish Antiquities* 18.110.

14. Josephus, *Jewish Antiquities* 18.118–119.

15. Hoehner, *Herod Antipas*, 317–30.

16. Philo, *Embassy to Gaius* 300, mentions the presence of the four sons of Herod being in Jerusalem, one of whom would have been Herod Antipas, tetrarch of Galilee.

THE EXILE OF HEROD ANTIPAS IN 39

Tiberius died in 37 and was succeeded by Gaius Caligula. The new emperor, an old friend of Herod Agrippa I, appointed him "king" of Philip's former tetrarchy, Iturea-Trachonitis. His arrival at his jurisdiction infuriated Antipas, but even more so Herodias. Although Antipas was "content with his tranquillity and wary of the Roman bustle,"[17] Herodias goaded him to go to Caligula and demand appointment as "king" over the region he had faithfully served for so many years as "tetrarch." Caligula was unimpressed and stripped Antipas of his tetrarchy, exiled the tetrarch and Herodias to Spain, and united the former tetrarch's territories to Agrippa, now under his rule as "king."

17. Josephus, *Jewish Antiquities* 18.245.

Part 3

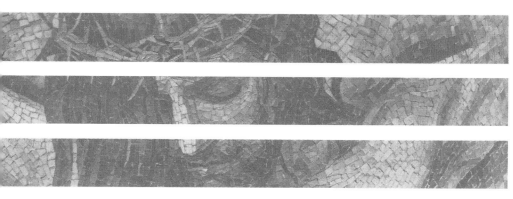

THE TRIALS
OF JESUS

18

THE JEWISH TRIALS

The Gospel of John provides the most comprehensive overview of the trials of Jesus on the evening preceding the crucifixion. A combined cohort of Roman soldiers and Jewish temple officials arrested Jesus in a garden across the Kidron Valley and brought him bound to the senior high priest, Annas (John 18:12–13, 19–23).

PRELIMINARY INTERROGATION BY HIGH PRIEST ANNAS

It is the measure of Annas's absolute importance that the arrested Jesus was brought first to him. John records that "the high priest" (i.e., Annas) then questioned Jesus "about his disciples and his teaching."

We are right to suppose that Annas wanted to know if Jesus posed a political threat that would issue in civil disturbance in the Holy City during the imminent Passover. Annas understood that the Romans would not abide lawless and riotous behavior. While Annas's vast wealth probably helped secure Pilate's lengthy tenure as prefect, the high priest knew this bribery would count for nothing if the arrival of Jesus in Jerusalem provoked civil disobedience.

It is not likely that Annas's fears were allayed by his interrogation of Jesus, whose denials would have come across as disrespectful, for which he was struck by one of the officers.

Annas then sent Jesus to the incumbent high priest Caiaphas (John 18:24; Mark 14:53), who had assembled the Jewish council to examine the Galilean rabbi (Mark 14:53, 55). It is likely that Caiaphas was located within the spacious

Palace of Annas, which was also the place where some members of the San-hedrin were assembling. It is plausibly suggested that Caiaphas was gathering members of the council during Annas's interrogation of Jesus.

Unlike Mark, followed by Matthew and (briefly) by Luke, John gives no details of Caiaphas's inquiry, but merely states that he sent Jesus to the governor's headquarters (the Praetorium, former palace of Herod) (Mark 15:1). John makes it clear that his interest is the Roman trials by Pilate, which he records at length.

CAIAPHAS'S TRIAL

According to Mark, followed by Matthew and Luke, the trial under Caiaphas involved "the whole Council" (Mark 14:55). From John we learn that it followed soon after Annas's interrogation, which was probably located within the senior high priest's palace.

The Mishnah tractate Sanhedrin gives a different understanding of capital trials. It asserts that forty years before the destruction of the temple (i.e., in 30), the Sanhedrin did not have jurisdiction over capital cases, confirming John 18:31: "The Jews said to [Pilate], 'It is not lawful for us to put anyone to death.'"

However, the publication of the Mishnah is dated to circa 200 (much later than the trial of Jesus) and is formalistic in character. It is noted that the stoning of Stephen occurred after the inquiry of and in the presence of the high priest and witnesses to Stephen's offensive words. This was not a lynching. It is reasonable to suggest that the capital punishment of Stephen under the auspices of the high priest occurred with the permission of the prefect, Pontius Pilate.

I concur with the following statement: "Recent studies argue that the Sanhedrin in Jerusalem was, at this time, not a permanent administrative institution but a consultative body convened ad hoc by the incumbent or a former high priest for the purpose of deliberating political questions as well as investigating religious offences."[1]

Caiaphas, son-in-law of Annas, enjoyed long tenure of the office of high priest, most likely at the pleasure of his father-in-law, Annas. His decade-long incumbency coincided exactly with Pontius Pilate's decade as prefect (ca. 26–36). It is reasonable to infer that Caiaphas and Pilate enjoyed practical working relationships and held a common concern regarding charismatic regional

---

1. David W. Chapman and Eckhard J. Schnabel, *The Trial and Crucifixion of Jesus* (Tübingen: Mohr Siebeck, 2015), 16.

leaders like Jesus of Nazareth. It is likely that both men reaped great wealth during their respective administrations.

Lucius Vitellus, governor of Syria, removed Caiaphas in 36. In the next year, Pilate was recalled to Rome over his excessive response to a threatened uprising in Samaria.

It is possible that Caiaphas and Pilate shared a common concern for Jesus's announcement of the dawn of a "kingdom" and hints they heard that this leader was a "messiah." Jesus's mounted entry to Jerusalem, his acclaimed arrival in the city, and his violent actions in the temple would have increased their fears. After all, the uprisings of Judas (in Galilee), Simon (in Perea), and Athronges (in Judea) had occurred in living memory, in 4 BC, following the death of Herod. The uprising of Judas the Galilean and Saddok the Pharisee in 6 was even more recent.

For the Jewish trial of Jesus, we are chiefly dependent on Mark's account. Apart from several departures (which I will note), Matthew merely echoes Mark, often repeating his words. Luke also depends on Mark but omits any reference to Jesus's alleged threat to destroy the temple.

According to John, the elder high priest Annas interrogated Jesus and then handed him over to incumbent high priest Caiaphas, for which no detail is recorded, except that Caiaphas delivered Jesus to officers who led Jesus to the headquarters (Praetorium) of the governor (John 18:28).

THE SANHEDRIN TRIAL ACCORDING TO MARK

It is striking that the high priest and the council were determined to convict Jesus of blasphemy, but blasphemy based on eyewitness testimony. This was to satisfy Deuteronomy 19:15. "A single witness shall not suffice against a person for any crime or for any wrong in connection with any offense that he has committed. Only on the evidence of two witnesses or of three witnesses shall a charge be established."[2]

The Witnesses

Reference to "witnesses" in Mark's narrative helpfully signals court procedures at that time. In this case, however, the Sanhedrin leaders perverted the worthy principle of integrity.

---

2. Various texts in the New Testament reflect this requirement: Matt. 18:16; John 7:51; 8:17; 2 Cor. 13:1; 1 Tim. 5:19; Heb. 10:28.

Had the high priest and council ignored this stricture in the trial of a popular, charismatic figure and proceeded to stone him to death, there would have been serious social and political consequences, especially at Passover season, as he and they well knew.

The "chief priests" (the top echelon of priests closest the high priest) and the "whole council" sought false witnesses who could testify against Jesus and thus secure a verdict against him. Mark doesn't inform his readers about their respective testimonies, except that they could not agree about the details of Jesus's alleged blasphemous words or acts. Presumably these related to the clearing of the temple.

However, some bore witness to Jesus's alleged words three or so years earlier, which were recorded by John, when Jesus cleared vendors and money changers from the temple. In John's account Jesus said, "Destroy this temple, and in three days I will raise it up" (John 2:19). John explained, "But [Jesus] was talking about the temple of his body" (John 2:21). According to Mark, however, several reported that they had heard Jesus say, "*I* will destroy this temple that is made with hands, and in three days *I* will build another, not made with hands" (Mark 14:58).

The latter version was a blasphemous statement of intention whereas, as recorded by John, Jesus had promised to rebuild the temple after three days in the event it had been destroyed. Several bore witness to having heard Jesus back then, but they did not agree as to the details, and so their testimony was of no use.

That line of prosecution having failed, the high priest asked Jesus directly about these testimonies that went back to Jesus's very recent expulsion of the traders and money changers from the temple. According to Mark, "Jesus remained silent and made no answer."

"Are You the Son of the Blessed?"

Other attempts to secure conviction having failed, the high priest asked Jesus directly, "Are you the Christ, the Son of the Blessed?" We recall that "the chief priests and the scribes and the elders" had challenged Jesus's "authority" to clear the merchants and money changers from the temple. (Mark 11:27–12:12). In Jesus's reply, he identified himself as "a beloved son." They immediately sought to arrest him, doubtless with the intention of stoning him for this blasphemy. They were unsuccessful then, but now they have him in custody, ready to confirm his guilt.

To that critical question Jesus replied, "I am,[3] and you will see the Son of Man seated at the right hand of Power, and coming with the clouds of heaven" (Mark 14:62). Jesus replied astonishingly that he was, indeed, the Son of the Blessed but also the celestial Son of Man as prophesied by Daniel (7:13–14) who would be seated at the right hand of Power and who would come (as judge) with the clouds of heaven. The high priest had heard enough. "'You have heard his blasphemy. What is your decision?' And they all condemned him as deserving death" (Mark 14:63–64).

THE SYNOPTISTS' ACCOUNTS OF THE TRIAL

Comparison of the Gospels of Matthew and Luke with the Gospel of Mark suggests that these two texts depended on the Gospel of Mark. Luke significantly abbreviates Mark whereas Matthew follows Mark closely but amplifies that text as he deems necessary. Mark and Matthew are concerned to do justice to the forensic process.

The major divergence is that in Mark the false witnesses testified that Jesus said, "I will destroy this temple . . . and in three days I will build another," whereas in Matthew two testified that Jesus said, "I am able to destroy this temple of God and to rebuild it in three days."

Luke omits altogether references to the destruction of the temple. To their question, "Are you the Son of God?" Jesus replies, "You have said so."

Mark 14:53–65	Matthew 26:57–68	Luke 22:66–70
[53] And they led Jesus to the high priest. And all the chief priests and the elders and the scribes came together.	[57] Then those who had seized Jesus led him to Caiaphas the high priest, where the scribes and the elders had gathered.	[66] When day came, the assembly of the elders of the people gathered together, both chief priests and scribes. And they led him away to their council, and they said,

3. In Matthew's account (26:64), Jesus's response to the question is noncommittal, "You have said so."

Mark 14:53–65	Matthew 26:57–68	Luke 22:66–70
55 Now the chief priests and the whole Council were seeking testimony against Jesus to put him to death, but they found none.	59 Now the chief priests and the whole Council were seeking false testimony against Jesus that they might put him to death, 60 but they found none,	
56 For many bore false witness against him, but their testimony did not agree.	though many false witnesses came forward. At last, two came forward 61 and said,	
57 And some stood up and bore false witness against him, saying,	"This man said, 'I am able to destroy the temple of God, and to rebuild it in three days.'"	
58 "We heard him say, 'I will destroy this temple that is made with hands, and in three days I will build another, not made with hands.'"	62 And the high priest stood up and said, "Have you no answer to make? What is it that these men testify against you?"	
59 Yet even about this their testimony did not agree.	63 But Jesus remained silent.	
60 And the high priest stood up in the midst and asked Jesus, "Have you no answer to make? What is it that these men testify against you?"		
61 But he remained silent and made no answer. Again, the high priest asked him,	And the high priest said to him, "I adjure you by the living God, tell us if you are the Christ, the Son of God."	67 "If you are the Christ, tell us." But he said to them, "If I tell you, you will not believe, 68 and if I ask you, you will not answer.

Mark 14:53-65

"Are you the Christ, the Son of the Blessed?" [62] And Jesus said, "I am, and you will see the Son of Man seated at the right hand of Power and coming with the clouds of heaven." [63] And the high priest tore his garments and said, "What further witnesses do we need? [64] You have heard his blasphemy. What is your decision?" And they all condemned him as deserving death. [65] And some began to spit on him and to cover his face and to strike him, saying to him, "Prophesy!" And the guards received him with blows.

Matthew 26:57-68

[64] Jesus said to him, "You have said so. But I tell you, from now on you will see the Son of Man seated at the right hand of Power and coming on the clouds of heaven." [65] Then the high priest tore his robes and said, "He has uttered blasphemy. What further witnesses do we need? You have now heard his blasphemy. [66] What is your judgment?" They answered, "He deserves death." [67] Then they spit in his face and struck him. And some slapped him, [68] saying, "Prophesy to us, you Christ! Who is it that struck you?"

Luke 22:66-70

[69] But from now on the Son of Man shall be seated at the right hand of the power of God." [70] So they all said, "Are you the Son of God, then?" And he said to them, "You say that I am." [71] Then they said, "What further testimony do we need? We have heard it ourselves from his own lips."

From Mark's account it appears that the authorities adopted a twofold approach against Jesus. The first was to establish that he had declared his intention to destroy the temple. This related to John's account of Jesus clearing the temple several years earlier when he referred to the destruction of the temple (John 2:13-16).

However, the witnesses to Jesus's words could not agree, so the high priest moved on to another issue, Jesus's identity. His question was, "Are you the Christ, the Son of the Blessed?" The high priest had good reason to seek his answer, for "the chief priests and the scribes and the elders," when seeking Jesus's "authority" to clear the vendors and money changers from the temple, had heard him refer to himself as the "beloved Son" of God. If Jesus confirmed this, it would mean that he admitted making a blasphemous statement, for which he faced death.

Jesus did not resile from that claim, for it lay at the heart of his identity. But he immediately added, "and you will see the Son of Man seated at the right hand of Power and coming with the clouds of heaven." If Son of God was his identity, "Son of Man enthroned and returning [as judge]" was his vocation (quoting Dan. 7:13–14). Earlier Jesus had announced the imminent arrival of the kingdom of God (Mark 1:14–15). The celestial triumph of the Son of God as the enthroned Son of Man would mark the beginning of the kingdom of God.

There was no place for the temple or its officers in that kingdom, which was poised to overtake them and reduce them to impotence. The judges had heard enough. This was blasphemy and provoked a violent outburst against the prisoner.

Their decision reached, "as soon as it was morning, the chief priests held a consultation with the elders and scribes and the whole Council. And they bound Jesus and led him away and delivered him over to Pilate" (Mark 15:1).

THE UNWANTED TRIAL

Caiaphas found Jesus guilty of blasphemy but handed him over to the Romans for trial and certain execution. However, the high priest didn't seek Pilate's permission to execute Jesus by stoning, a viable option, but delivered him to Pilate for a trial against Jesus's alleged *political* crime claiming to be a "king of the Jews."

What makes best sense of this mystery is that Caiaphas feared social and political consequences of stoning a charismatic and popular figure, whom many regarded as a prophet. The people at large were hostile at Antipas's execution of John the Baptist (Mark 11:32). Who knows what might happen if they killed Jesus? Better by far, I imagine Caiaphas thinking, for the Romans to get rid of this troublesome man. Most likely Caiaphas could have received Pilate's permission to stone Jesus but prudently chose not to request it.

Caiaphas had good reason to be happy as his officers took Jesus, now severely beaten, to the Roman governor. The troublesome Galilean was now Pilate's problem, not his.

19

THE ROMAN TRIAL OF JESUS
ACCORDING TO MARK, MATTHEW, AND LUKE

The view taken here is that Matthew and Luke follow Mark's account, but with their own distinctive nuances. In each account, those involved were Jesus, the temple authorities, and Pilate, the governor. Matthew and Luke follow Mark in identifying the religious leaders as unrelenting accusers and Pilate as acquiescing in their demands, but under protest.

Are these portrayals credible, especially that of a Roman governor acceding to the demands of local people? Have these writers exculpated Pilate to make life easier for Christians within the Roman Empire?

MARK

The chief priests, elders, and scribes brought Jesus to the prefect, Pontius Pilate (Mark 15:1.)[1] In the Sanhedrin meeting they found that Jesus was guilty of "blasphemy," for which they could have sought Pilate's approval to have Jesus stoned. It seems likely, however, that they did not want to risk the opprobrium of the population of Jerusalem at large; Jesus was a charismatic figure with a large following in Judea as well as in Galilee.

They decided to make Jesus Pilate's problem by changing Jesus's alleged guilt from a matter of religion to one of politics. This explains Pilate's immediate question to Jesus, "Are you the King of the Jews?" (Mark 15:2). If guilty,

---

1. This section explores Mark 15:2–15.

Jesus was doomed to immediate crucifixion for treason. Only Caesar had the authority to appoint local client kings.

Jesus's reply, "You have said so," in effect pushes the matter back to Pilate, as if to say, "Is that what you think?" Otherwise, Jesus did not respond.

That line of questioning came to an end, so that the temple authorities "accused him of many things." Mark doesn't elaborate, but they probably were thinking of his recent desecration of the temple and the outrageous parable of the vineyard, where Jesus asserted that he was the "beloved Son" of God who foretold the end of the high priest's tenure of the holy place. Once again Jesus remained silent, to the astonishment of Pilate, who concluded his interrogation of Jesus.

Pilate would have been torn by conflicting motives. On the one hand, he would have been the recipient of money from the wealthy senior high priest, Annas. His days as governor were coming to an end, and he would not wish to forfeit the perquisites that would allow him to return to Rome with considerable riches. On the other, however, he would have been aware of having a bad reputation. The incidents of the iconic military standards, the plundering of the sacred *Corban*, and the installation of the aniconic shields in the Praetorium were well known. With his protector Sejanus gone, followed by a reign of terror against his supporters, and Tiberius's letter to his governors demanding care of the Jews, this governor was aware of his vulnerability to dismissal. Three years later, Pilate was indeed sent to Rome for trial on account of his harsh treatment of the Samaritans.[2]

Pilate saw the solution to his quandary in invoking the Paschal Privilege, whereby it was possible to release one felon at the Passover. He doubtless saw this as a way of avoiding having to decide about Jesus; he could simply release him without charge.

Many doubt the existence of this custom, since it is not referred to in the writings of Josephus or the Old Testament. It is, however, to be found in the Gospel of John (John 18:39), which is written independently of Mark's Gospel. Furthermore, it is consistent with the original event of the Passover, the liberation of the Hebrews from their slavery in Egypt.[3] Presumably, the Paschal

---

2. Josephus, *Jewish Antiquities* 18.87–89.

3. According to m. Pesahim 8.6a, "they may slaughter for one . . . whom they have promised to bring out of prison."

Privilege antedated the Roman rule in 6 and had been part of trials from earlier generations, perhaps going back to Maccabean times.

The attending crowd was clearly hostile to Jesus, although the reason is not given. The most likely explanation is that they had been influenced by the chief priests, perhaps for financial gain. Whatever their motivation, it was the crowd that urged Pilate to invoke the Passover pardon, but not for Jesus. Perhaps they were disappointed that Jesus had not displayed messianic leadership against the Romans following his triumphant entry to the city.

Whatever the reason, they made a precise proposal to the prefect, that he release Barabbas, who had been imprisoned for his part in a recent anti-Roman insurrection. We have no further information about this incident, but given the unpopularity of the Roman occupation, there is no reason to doubt it.

Pilate made two attempts to release "the king of the Jews," but the crowd cried out for his crucifixion.

Pilate's weakness submitting to cries of the crowd for Jesus's blood is imaginable. He was dependent on finances provided by the wealthy Annas and Caiaphas. He had earned a reputation for cruelty toward the Jews and could not afford another negative report for crucifying a harmless rabbi. Not least, Sejanus, his patron and protector—who was an anti-Semite—was now dead (October 31) and decreed by the Senate to be of "damned memory." Meanwhile, Tiberius had written to his governors to provide due care of his Jewish subjects.[4] The temple leaders knew this and used it against the governor.

MATTHEW

Matthew (in 27:11–26) follows closely Mark's narrative, including his choice of words. There are, however, several amplifications that Matthew makes. He adds "elders" to Mark's "chief priests." Matthew gives to Pilate his title, "governor." Whereas Mark states that the chief priests accused Jesus of "other matters," Matthew restricts the accusation to being "king of the Jews." Mark reports that the accusers brought many charges against Jesus, while Matthew states that they "testified" against him. For Mark Barabbas was a "murderer" in the insurrection, whereas for Matthew he was a "notorious prisoner." In Mark's account Jesus is accused of being "king of the Jews," but for Matthew

4. Philo, *Embassy to Gaius* 161.

he was "Jesus who is called Christ" (stated twice). According to Matthew, the chief priests and elders sought to "destroy" Jesus.

The net effect of Matthew's additions is to intensify the role of the chief priests and elders to secure Pilate's decision against Jesus. It is implied that the temple authorities and the crowd had a hold over Pilate, but Matthew (following Mark) doesn't disclose what it was.

Matthew adds two critical details. One was Pilate's wife's dream based on which she warned the governor, "Have nothing to do with that righteous man." Matthew's text implies that Pilate was responsive to this advice. The consequence of this intercession was that Pilate pleaded with the chief priests and elders to release Jesus, not Barabbas. When they did not accede, Pilate dramatically "washed his hands"; there was nothing more he could do. The chief priests and elders and the gathered crowd must have their way.

Matthew's redaction of Mark presents the two parties culpable for the crucifixion of Jesus: the religious authorities and their crowds actively so, Pilate passively.

LUKE

Luke's version, in 23:1–5, is stated more briefly but is significantly different at this point: those who brought Jesus to Pilate began by describing the nature of his alleged kingship. "We found this man misleading our nation and forbidding us to give tribute to Caesar, and saying that he himself is Christ, a king" (Luke 23:2). According to them, this man, like Judas the Galilean, forbade paying the poll tax to Caesar (although Jesus had specifically directed the payment of the tax when recently asked about his policy on that explosive question [Mark 12:17]). Furthermore, according to Luke, he claimed to be Christ (Messiah), a king.

When Pilate asked Jesus directly, "Are you the King of the Jews?" Luke, following Mark, quotes Jesus, "You have said so." Then, according to Luke, Pilate immediately declared, "I find no guilt in this man."

The temple leaders immediately responded, "He stirs up the people, teaching throughout all Judea, from Galilee even to this place."

Pilate summoned the accusers and reiterated his nonguilty verdict of the charges they made against Jesus. The priestly accusers demanded the release of Barabbas; although Luke made no reference to the issue of the Paschal Privilege, nevertheless it is implied. Pilate protested the innocence of Jesus, desiring to release him, but the accusers demanded his crucifixion. Once more Pilate pleaded Jesus's innocence, but his enemies demanded his crucifixion.

Pilate acquiesced. He released Barabbas, but "delivered Jesus over to their will."

Luke, like Mark and Matthew, saw the initiative and impetus for Jesus's execution with the temple authorities. Although Pilate sought to release Jesus, such was the insistence of the religious leaders that the governor fell in with their demands and released Barabbas.

There are several distinctives in Luke's account noted above: his failure to refer by name to the Paschal Privilege and the addition of the damning accusations against Jesus:

v. 2   Jesus had influenced the nation,
           had forbidden the payment of "tribute" tax to Caesar,
           was claiming to be Christ, a king
v. 5   Jesus stirs up the people,
           teaching throughout all Judea,
           from Galilee to Jerusalem

The spokesmen for the high priest had cleverly fashioned Jesus of Nazareth in the shape of Judas the Galilean,[5] who claimed to have been a king, and who in AD 6, in opposition to the new poll tax, had brought his insurrection from Galilee to Judea.

The message was clear: the Roman prefect must immediately execute this second Galilean, anti-Roman rebel-king.

Remarkably, however, in Luke's account, after examining the charges, Pilate found no grounds for executing Jesus. Significantly, Herod the tetrarch of Galilee, to whom Pilate had sent Jesus, also found no guilt in him (Luke 23:15).

No less than three times Pilate declared Jesus's innocence: first after the initial detailed accusation (23:14); next after refusing to release Barabbas (23:20); a third time after the accusers' call for Jesus's crucifixion (23:22).

But Pilate was not able to withstand the vehemence of their demands. He released Barabbas and handed Jesus over to the soldiers for crucifixion.

Luke, in keeping with Mark and Matthew, portrayed the governor as unable to withstand the demands of the temple leaders and their supporting

5. Josephus, *Jewish War* 2.118, 433; 7.253; *Jewish Antiquities* 18.4–10, 23–25.

crowd. But neither he nor they explain how the all-powerful military prefect caved in before the face of these protests.

The temple authorities had determined that Jesus must die. He had violated the sanctity of the temple (the Court of the Gentiles) by driving out the vendors and the money changers, and he had claimed the authority of the Son of God in doing so. So, Jesus must die, but not at their hands. This will explain why they bullied the prefect into condemning Jesus, despite his misgivings.

THE JEWISH TRIAL AND THE ROMAN TRIAL

Mark's version of the Roman trial is silent about the witnesses to the earlier reference to the destruction and rebuilding of the temple. By contrast, the Roman version emphasizes the issue of Jesus's kingship of the Jews and introduces the Paschal Privilege as a way Pilate can be free of executing Jesus.

Matthew follows Mark in the accusation that Jesus could destroy and rebuild the temple, and in claiming to be the celestial Son of Man and the Son of God. Of the four evangelists, only Matthew refers to Pilate's wife's dream and to the prefect washing his hands of the guilt of Jesus's fate.

Luke portrays the authorities accusing Jesus as a latter-day Judas the Galilean, an anti-Roman rebel-king, and worthy of execution.

Unsurprisingly, the three synoptists' versions of the Jewish trial and of the Roman trial tend to complement rather than contradict one another. This Jesus was a blasphemer in claiming to be Son of Man and Son of God. Furthermore, according to the accusers, he claimed to be "king of the Jews." Luke's account tellingly places Jesus in the mold of Judas, the Galilean rebel king.

EXPLAINING PILATE

Based on the synoptists' accounts, we are left to guess what kind of power these accusers held over Pilate.

Pilate, with his patron Sejanus dead, now lacked a protector in Rome. Tiberius, who had retaken the reins of power after 31, had sent clear messages to his governors about their responsibility to provide due protection to the Jewish people in their care,[6] something Pilate had previously failed to do.

Furthermore, Jesus was able to be portrayed as a self-proclaimed king with a considerable following, whose responsibility it was for Pilate to crucify for trea-

---

6. Philo, *Embassy to Gaius* 161.

son. Given Jesus's outward similarity to the rebel-king Judas the Galilean, the governor would have faced difficulty explaining why he did not crucify him.

Not least, Pilate would have been looking to the wealthy Annas family for financial benefits ahead of his return to Rome in coming months.

Perhaps the clue to understanding Pilate's weakness is the incident of the aniconic golden shields, which he installed later in Herod's palace.[7] This was Pilate's pathetic attempt to please Tiberius, whose name, with Pilate's, was inscribed on the shields, but without religious effigies that would offend Jewish scruples.

Pilate, however, miscalculated about the hoped-for effects of this strategy. Such was the outcry by the Jews that Pilate wrote a self-serving letter to Tiberius, only to be directed to remove the shields.[8]

The golden shields incident reveals Pilate's vulnerability to complaints against him in Judea as directed to Caesar and is consistent with the Synoptic Gospels' portrayal of him as subject to the demands of the local Jewish leadership.

7. Philo, *Embassy to Gaius* 289.
8. Philo, *Embassy to Gaius* 302.

20

THE ROMAN TRIAL ACCORDING TO JOHN

John's account of the trial of Jesus differs from that of the synoptists and is considerably longer. There is no easy way to explain the differences between John's version and those of Mark, Matthew, and Luke.

The narrative is made good sense by the assumption that there was a courtyard or similar in the grounds of the Praetorium, which had previously been Herod's palace. It was a very large complex that extended from the present Jaffa Gate for a considerable distance to the south.[1]

According to John, the priestly accusers brought the bound Jesus early to the Praetorium but did not enter for fear of defilement from contact with gentiles; it was the Passover. Because they would not come into the building, the prefect must come out to them and then retreat inside to pursue his trial of Jesus.

18:28–32	outside	Pilate and the temple authorities
18:33–38a	inside	Pilate and Jesus
18:38b–40	outside	Pilate and the temple authorities
19:1–3	inside	Pilate, soldiers flog and mock Jesus
19:4–8	outside	Pilate, Jesus, and the temple authorities

1. Most scholars reject the belief that the trial of Jesus occurred near the Antonia Fortress, notwithstanding the popular belief that the Via Dolorosa began there. The overwhelming opinion of archaeologists is that Pilate's trial of Jesus occurred within Herod's palace complex, by then known as the Praetorium.

| 19:9–11 | inside | Pilate and Jesus |
| 19:12–16 | outside | Pilate, Jesus, and the temple authorities |

In the *outside* scenes, the dialogue was between Pilate and those who accused Jesus. Pilate, acting in his role as judge, began by formally asking the temple authorities, "What accusation (*katēgoria*) do you bring against this man?"

Instead of allowing due process to run its course, the accusers rudely turned on Pilate, "If this man were not doing evil, we would not have delivered him over to you." As in the Synoptics, the captors' manner of addressing the governor suggests that they had the upper hand.

Pilate's response, "Take him yourselves and judge him by your own law," implies that it was within their power to pass judgment on Jesus. That authority resided in the Caesar who delegated it to his provincial governors who, however, could authorize local leaders to conduct their own trial for blasphemy and execute offenders by stoning.

Now *inside* the Praetorium Pilate began a private interrogation of Jesus directed to the charge that he claimed to be "king of the Jews." In response, the accused asked his interrogator whether this accusation issued from him or from others. Pilate replied that the initiative for Jesus's arrest did not issue from him but from Jesus's "own nation and the chief priests." This is consistent with the synoptists' version of the trial.

Pilate then asked, "What have you done?" In reply Jesus declared, "My kingdom is not of this world," the evidence for which was that Jesus's servants did not physically oppose his arrest. His servants were not military, therefore his was not an ordinary or imaginable "kingdom" that Jesus had proclaimed. The absence of an army supporting Jesus was proof positive that he was no pretender-king; a claimed kingship presupposed an army. In effect, Pilate recognized this; he made no attempt to round up Jesus's followers.

Nevertheless, Pilate took the reference to a "kingdom" to mean that Jesus was in some other sense a king, to which Jesus responds, "You say that I am a king." Jesus, however, immediately rejects the notion he is a king by asserting, "For this purpose I was born and for this purpose I have come into the world—to bear witness to the truth," that is eternal, otherworldly truth. "Everyone who is of the truth listens to my voice."

To this Pilate made his famous reply, "What is truth?" This was probably a cynical remark by a world-weary governor contemptuous of the pathetic figure in front of him who was far from king-like.

Pilate then went *outside* to inform the temple leaders and the supporting crowd, "I find no guilt (*aitia*) in him." He then sought to release Jesus by means of the Paschal Privilege. But they demanded, "not this man, but Barabbas." Barabbas is described as a "robber" (*lēstēs*, better, an insurrectionist).

Pilate returned *inside* understanding that Jesus must die, despite his own misgivings and his attempt to convince the chief priests of Jesus's innocence of their charges. As in the synoptists' accounts, it is evident that the Jewish leaders possessed dominant power over the Roman governor.

It was Roman practice to torture and humiliate a felon prior to the crucifixion. John records that they "flogged" Jesus, which was by cords with metal tips that excoriated the flesh. By way of mockery, they placed a crown of thorns on his head and dressed him in a purple robe and addressed him, "Hail, king of the Jews." The soldiers struck him with their hands.

Pilate believed that Jesus was innocent of the claim to be "king of the Jews," yet he weakly fell in with the accusations of the temple authorities. As governor, Pilate was responsible to administer justice, but to his shame, he became the actual instrument of injustice.

Pilate brought the beaten and humiliated Jesus *outside* to the accusers, inexplicably claiming to find no guilt (*aitia*) in him; Jesus had not confessed under torture. He found Jesus blameless of the accusation while parading him laughingly as a king. The governor's words "Behold the man" were probably in mockery of the Jews, as if to say, "You are saying that *this* man is king of the Jews?" Undeterred and unashamed, the chief priests and the officers cried out, "crucify him, crucify him."

Now again *inside* the Praetorium, Pilate expressed curiosity about Jesus. He is not a king, at least not in the commonly understood sense of a leader having an army. But Pilate was intrigued: Where does this man come from?

Pilate took Jesus's silence to be disrespectful: "You will not speak to me? Do you not know that I have authority (*exousia*, Latin *imperium*) to release you and authority to crucify (*staurōsai*) you?" Jesus responded, "You would have no authority over me at all unless it had been given you from above." Let Pilate understand that despite the appearance that political appointments are made by the emperor, the reality is that all authority is from God and those who bear it are accountable to God. All secondary powers are likewise answerable to God, including as exercised by Caiaphas, who has committed "the greater sin" in handing over the innocent Jesus to Pilate.

For the last time Pilate returned to the courtyard of the Praetorium, where he confronted "the Jews" (i.e., the temple leaders) by repeatedly seeking to release Jesus. John's account makes clear what the synoptists imply: the Jews' hold over Pilate was his exposure to the claim that he had not been Caesar's "friend" (*philos*), that is, his loyal client-governor. Fundamental to a governor's duty was to preserve the Pax Romana in the province where he was sent, to protect Roman interests. Toleration of a local, self-appointed local king would represent a governor's most fundamental failure.

Weeks earlier "the Jews" had attempted to have Jesus stoned for the blasphemy of saying "I and the Father are one," but he escaped (John 10:30). Later, following Jesus's raising of Lazarus, the Sanhedrin determined that Jesus must die (John 11:50). Jesus's fate was sealed when he expelled the sellers of sacrifices and the money changers from the Court of the Gentiles, followed by his allegory that identified him as "the beloved Son" whom the chief priests would kill and for which the vineyard would be taken from them (Mark 12:9).

Now that at last the temple authorities had dispatched Jesus to Pilate, there was no way they would countenance the felon's release. Defeated, Pilate mounted the judgment seat (*bēma*), and doubtless ironically declared to the Jews, "Behold your king." They cried out, "Away with him, away with him, crucify him!" Pilate asked, "Shall I crucify your king?" to which they replied insincerely, "We have no king but Caesar."

John's words, "So he (Pilate) delivered him over to *them* to be crucified," call for comment. To whom did Pilate "deliver" Jesus? Although the context suggests it was to the Jews, that cannot be a correct understanding. To our knowledge Jews did not crucify felons. Most likely, John means us to understand that Pilate "delivered" Jesus to the Roman execution squad.

The Romans had formal words for someone to be crucified, *ibis im crucem*, "you shall mount the cross." Pilate may have uttered those terrible words to Jesus as he was hoisted on the crossbar (*stauros*) upon the pole already in the ground.

John captures the same basic narrative of the synoptists, that for identifiable reasons the temple leaders were immovably committed to executing Jesus, not by their hands but by Pilate's. Furthermore, as in Mark, Matthew, and Luke, the Fourth Evangelist portrays Pilate as a weak figure dominated by the Jews' demand for the crucifixion of Jesus. John uniquely points to Pilate's obligations to Tiberius (as Caesar's "friend," i.e., client). John makes no mention of Pilate's prior dependence on his patron Sejanus (now deceased), or Tiberius's letter to his governors about the Jews, although these are reasonably inferred despite the silence of the four Gospels.

John's account is interwoven with theological insights, for example, that Jesus was "king-like" in his dignity and demeanor and that the prefect was a weak figure, even comically so as he shuttled between the chief priests outside and Jesus inside. At the same time, John employs terms that convey the impression of historical probity, for example, "accusation" (*katēgoria*), "guilt" (*aitia*), "derived authority" (*exousia*), "insurrectionist" (*lēstēs*), "friend of Caesar" (*philos tou Kaisaros*), "judgment seat" (*bēma*), the "stone pavement (*lithostrōtos*), "cross" (*stauros*), "to crucify" (*staurōsai*), and a legal caption (*titlon*) to identify the crucified man's crime. John's details are consistent with Roman trial procedure.

More than the other gospels, the Gospel of John takes a special interest in the arrest and trials of Jesus. His narrative has an accumulation of credible details that deserves careful reflection. John's capacity to write theologically may blunt our understanding of the degree to which he also manages to write historically and in a manner that is legally, topographically, and culturally credible.

John understates what happened next. Jesus, bearing his own cross (crossbar, *stauros*), went to Golgotha ("the place of a skull"), where the soldiers crucified him. Pilate wrote an inscription (*titlon*), "Jesus of Nazareth king of the Jews" (in three languages), and attached it to the cross.

"The chief priests of the Jews" took exception to Pilate's words, demanding the alteration, "This man said, I am king of the Jews." They did not want to be held responsible for bringing about the death of the king of the Jews, but of a pretender who claimed to be king of the Jews. Pilate, in his final effort to resist the Jews' hold over him, replied, "What I have written I have written."

It is not easy to reconcile the various gospel accounts of that fateful night. Where Matthew and Luke depend on Mark, a coherent picture emerges. For the arrest of Jesus, however, we depend on Mark 14:43–50 and John 18:1–12, which are not easy to reconcile. Likewise difficult to account for are the disparate accounts of Mark 15:2–15 and John 18:28–40. The best way forward is to accept each version and learn from its insights.

21

HEROD ANTIPAS, JESUS, AND PILATE

(LUKE 23:6–16)

When Pilate heard the accusation of the chief priests that Jesus had stirred up the people "throughout all Judea, from Galilee even to this place," and that he was a Galilean, he decided to send him to Herod Antipas, tetrarch of Galilee.

It is likely that Pilate had already heard about the prophet-healer from Nazareth, including that a large crowd had gathered, following a campaign of visitation by his disciples throughout Galilee.

Pilate, however, had decided that Jesus was no king of the Jews. Nevertheless, it was prudent to know the opinion of Herod Antipas, who was visiting Jerusalem for the Passover.

Thus, Jesus met Antipas face-to-face for this one and only time. Antipas had heard about Jesus, no doubt by rumor, but also by information from Joanna, wife of Antipas's household manager, Chuza (Luke 8:3). Jesus remained silent, although Antipas interrogated him at length.

Nevertheless, Antipas sent Jesus back to Pilate, reporting that the Nazarene had done nothing worthy of death. This is curious, since earlier it was reported to Jesus that the tetrarch was seeking to kill him (Luke 13:31). Antipas had condemned John the Baptist to death but found no comparable fault in Jesus. Why, then, did he pass up the opportunity to be rid of the Galilean? Most likely, he would be glad to allow the prefect to face a hostile reaction to that onerous task. His execution of the revered John the Baptist brought him severe criticism. His hands would not be colored with the blood of another popular prophet (Mark 11:32).

Beforehand, there had been "enmity" between the prefect of Judea and
the tetrarch of Galilee. Luke gives no explanation, but he does refer to Pilate's murder of Galileans at a Passover in Jerusalem (Luke 13:1). The common agreement about Jesus by Pilate and Antipas became the basis of a new
friendship between the two men. Nevertheless, Antipas complained to Tiberius when Pilate brought gilded shields into the Praetorium.[1] Their friendship
was short-lived.

1. Philo, *Embassy to Gaius* 299–305.

22

THE TESTIMONIUM FLAVIANUM

Josephus wrote *Jewish Antiquities* in the thirteenth year of Domitian, that is, in 99. The so-called *Testimonium Flavianum* is Josephus's brief account of the trial of Jesus. Josephus was not a Christian, but there is a good case that his narrative of the trial of Jesus and his comments about it are his attempt to see it through Christian eyes.

It is right that this historically important document should be bracketed with the four canonical documents for the details from those gospels that it innocently confirms.

Josephus locates Jesus in the time of Pontius Pilate, under whose hand he was tried, condemned, and crucified. Although Jesus was a popular figure, unlike so many in Josephus's catalogue of key individuals like Judas the Galilean, this Jesus was not an insurrectionist or a "sign prophet" like Theudas or the Egyptian.

JESUS THE RABBI

Josephus locates Jesus in the time of Pontius Pilate, governor of Judea, circa 26–36, under whose hand he was condemned and crucified.

> About this time there lived Jesus, a wise man, if indeed one ought to call him a man. For he was one who wrought surprising feats and was a teacher of such people as accept the truth gladly. He won over many Jews and

many of the Greeks. He was the Christ. When Pilate, upon hearing him accused by men of the highest standing among us, had condemned him to be crucified, those who had in the first place come to love him did not give up their affection for him. On the third day he appeared to them restored to life, for the prophets of God had prophesied these and countless other marvellous things about him. And the tribe of Christians, so called after him, has still to this day not disappeared.[1]

Scholarly opinion overwhelmingly rejects much of this text as either spurious or heavily interpolated. Josephus was a dedicated Jew, and (to our knowledge) no Christian. Statements such as "if indeed one ought to call him a man ... he was the Messiah ... on the third day he appeared to them restored to life ... the prophets of God had prophesied these and countless other marvellous things about him" are Christian in character, and Josephus was a loyal Pharisee.

As well, the Christian apologist Origen, writing in the third century (d. 254), asserted that Josephus did not believe Jesus was the Messiah.[2] This would mean that the Christian statements would have been interpolated into Josephus's text between the middle of the third century and the first quarter of the fourth century. Eusebius, writing in the early years of the next century, quotes Josephus's text exactly on no less than three occasions.[3]

Of the many alternative explanations for the *Testimonium Flavianum*, one is most widely believed. It is that removal of the "Christian" statements above leaves a short reference to Jesus as wonder-worker and teacher whom Pontius Pilate crucified, but whose followers were still present when Josephus wrote his *Antiquities* during the 90s.

THE INTEGRITY OF THE *TESTIMONIUM FLAVIANUM*

Despite the weight of negative opinion about its integrity, there are several reasons to accept the whole *Testimonium* as genuine.

Among these is the practical issue of emending texts in antiquity. Unlike in the age of computers, when cut and paste occurs with ease, in the years be-

1. Josephus, *Jewish Antiquities* 18.63–64.
2. Origen, *Contra Celsum* 1.47; *Commentary on Matthew* 10.17: Josephus "did not accept Jesus as Christ."
3. Eusebius, *Demonstratio* 3.5.102–103; *History of the Church* 1.11.7–8; *Theophany* 5.44.562.

tween Josephus writing in the 90s and Eusebius writing from 324, emending a text meant rewriting the whole scroll. It is noted that all the extant Greek manuscripts of *Jewish Antiquities*—Ambrosianus in the eleventh century, Vaticanus in the fourteenth century, and Marcianus in the fifteenth century—have identical, full versions of the *Testimonium*.

Furthermore, the manner of the writing of the whole passage is coherent and hangs together as a complete statement, with its own internal logic intact.

Provocative Statement	Jesus, a wise man, if indeed one ought to call him a man
Substantiation	For [*gar*] (a) he was one who wrought surprising feats, and
	(b) he was a teacher of such people as accept the truth gladly.
Amplification	He won over many Jews and many of the Greeks [*Hellēnikoi*].
Conclusion	He was the Messiah [*Christos*].
His triumph	When Pilate condemned him to be crucified, those who loved him did not give up their affection for him.
His vindication	On the third day he appeared to them restored to life.
Verification	And the tribe of Christians [*Christianoi*], so called after him, has still to this day not disappeared.

Furthermore, the passage is a semi-*inclusio*:

"he was *the Christ*."

"And the tribe *of Christians*, so called after him,[4]
has still to this day not disappeared."

The *Testimonium* is a complete statement. The assertion that an interpolator has taken a minimalist statement and added in "Christian" items fails to recognize that the *Testimonium* as cited by Josephus is a complete, grammatically logical whole.

---

4. Tacitus, *Annals of Imperial Rome* 15.44, comments that *Christus* was the founder of the name *Christian*.

This, however, is not to say that Josephus the Pharisee personally believed what he wrote about Jesus. This would explain Origen's comment that Josephus did not believe Jesus was the Messiah, that is, he was not a dedicated disciple of Jesus. Rather, Josephus was merely accurately reporting what "the tribe of Christians" believed about Jesus. Given his disdain of insurgents and prophets, it is understandable that he writes positively about the nonviolent Jesus (as he also had regarding John the Baptist).

WRITTEN FROM ROME IN THE 90S

Josephus wrote the *Jewish Antiquities* from Rome in the 90s, where Christian beliefs were widely known, especially in the years since Nero's pogrom against the Christians in 64. Josephus's closing remark: "the tribe *of Christians* . . . has still to this day not disappeared" is positive. Of the many prophets and rebels listed by Josephus from 6, not one of them (to our knowledge) survived beyond the fiery catastrophe, August-September 70. Only the "tribe" of Christians survived, and it appears, flourished.

Paul's letter to the Romans is dated to the middle-late 50s, the first letter of Peter to the early 60s, and the Gospel of Mark from the mid-50s to the mid-60s. The latter texts—First Peter and the Gospel of Mark—were written from Rome.[5] By the time Josephus wrote *Jewish Antiquities* in the 90s, Rome had become a world center of Christianity.

Close examination of Josephus's text suggests that he had been exposed to and was aware of the details about Christ and of Christian origins in Judea and of Christianity's significant presence in Rome. Josephus's *Jewish War*, written in the 70s, makes no reference to Jesus, whereas his *Jewish Antiquities*, written in the 90s, has extended comments about Jesus and John the Baptist. These later references suggest that for Josephus both John and Jesus were respected figures.

CONSISTENCY WITH THE GOSPELS

His initial statement that Jesus was a "wise man" is consistent with the Gospels' many references to him as a "rabbi." The text immediately qualifies this by "*if indeed* one ought to call him a man," a judgment found in Christian texts (e.g., Je-

---

5. Rome as the provenance for 1 Peter is indicated by 5:13: "She who is in Babylon . . . sends you greetings," and for the Gospel of Mark by its numerous Latinisms.

sus as "the man of heaven" [1 Cor. 15:48]). This Josephus immediately explains: "*For,*" on the one hand "he wrought surprising feats" (i.e., the many miracles recorded in the Gospels) and, on the other (also prominent in the Gospels), "he was a teacher . . . of the truth." As a result of Jesus's twofold acts (miracles and teaching), he "won over many Jews and many of the Greeks" (so, John 12:20). Such was Jesus's fame in these two matters that many held him to be the Messiah. At Caesarea Philippi Peter, speaking for the Twelve, declared Jesus to be "the Christ," whereupon Jesus led his followers up to Jerusalem. Later, *Jewish Antiquities* 20.200 reports that Jesus was "the *so-called* Messiah," implying a widely held view that, however, Josephus most likely did not share.

Consistent with the Gospels' accounts is Josephus's comment that "men of the highest standing among us" (i.e., the temple authorities) accused him as Messiah and consequently Pilate (the Roman prefect) "condemned" him (as Messiah, or, in the Gospels, as "king of the Jews").

Nevertheless, "those who had come to love him did not give up their affection for him," a statement reflecting the poignant reaction of his disciples to his crucifixion, an affection his followers in Rome continued to feel.

The radical assertion "on the third day he appeared to them restored to life . . . for the prophets of God had prophesied these and countless other marvellous things about him" accords exactly with Paul's "received" apostolic "tradition": "he was raised on the third day in accordance with the Scriptures" (1 Cor. 15:4).

THE STRIPPED-DOWN VERSION

Based on the view that the "Christian" items in the text are inauthentic, several attempts have been made to remove these and restate Josephus's unamended text. The following is but one of several reconstructions.

> About this time there lived Jesus, a wise man. He won over many Jews and many of the Greeks. He was the [so-called] Christ. When Pilate, upon hearing him accused by men of the highest standing among us, had condemned him to be crucified, those who had in the first place come to love him did not give up their affection for him. And the tribe of Christians, so called after him, has still to this day not disappeared.

The resulting "Jesus" is a benign teacher and miracle worker who was loved by his followers, not someone who would have been a threat to either the high priest or Caesar's incumbent prefect, who would warrant being arrested, tried, and crucified. He does not give the impression of being a bellicose leader and rebel against Rome. References to him as "the Christ" or "the so-called Christ" are open to interpretation as halfhearted or even sarcastic.

CONCLUSION

Josephus regards the era from 6 to 70 as a discrete unit of time that began with Judas's insurrection against the Roman tax in Judea in 6 and ended with Titus's destruction of the holy place in 70. Between those polar dates Josephus chronicled various insurgents and prophets who, with two exceptions, gave expression to the fatal "Fourth Philosophy" that led to and presaged the destruction of the Holy City and its holy place. Those exceptions were John the Baptist and "Jesus, the wise man . . . [said to be] the Christ," whose "tribe" was not extinguished in the great fire of Rome in 64 but which continued to flourish at the time Josephus wrote *Antiquities*, in the 90s in Rome.

It is worth noting two other relevant passages in Josephus's *Jewish Antiquities*: regarding John the Baptist (18.116–119) and James, brother of Jesus (20.200). While some question the integrity of these passages, most authorities regard them as genuine. A majority would add, however, that Josephus does not connect John the Baptist with Jesus the wise man.

Before the critical era there was almost universal regard for the *Testimonium Flavianum*. Not only was it regarded as authentic, for many it was revered almost as scripture.

Opinion on the authenticity of the *Testimonium*, however, is varied. Louis H. Feldman, translator of the Loeb edition of *Jewish Antiquities*, surveyed the relevant literature from 1937 to 1980.[6] Feldman noted that 4 scholars regarded the *Testimonium Flavianum* as entirely genuine, 6 as mostly genuine; 20 accepted it with some interpolations, 9 with several interpolations; and 13 regarded it as being totally an interpolation.

According to J. P. Meier,[7] the received text is not Josephan, but we can get back to the original by removing the three Christian statements: "if indeed one ought to call him a man"; "who wrought surprising feats"; "on the third day he appeared to them alive."

---

6. Louis H. Feldman, *Josephus and Modern Scholarship* (Berlin: de Gruyter, 1984).
7. J. P. Meier, *A Marginal Jew*, vol. 1, *Rethinking the Historical Jesus* (New York: Doubleday, 1991).

Part 4

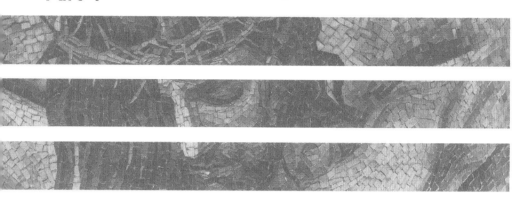

AFTER JESUS: THE BIRTH OF THE CHURCH

23

THE LAMB WITHOUT BLEMISH
IN THE GOSPEL OF MARK

Throughout the Gospel of Mark, the author reveals himself as a master of bare, uninterpreted narrative, and of highly significant single references.

A BARE, UNINTERRUPTED NARRATIVE OF JESUS'S TRIALS

A powerful example is Mark's lengthy narratives of the Sanhedrin and Roman trials (twenty-six verses; Mark 14:53–65; 15:2–15), whereas there is just one reference to the actual death of Jesus (Mark 15:37). What is Mark wanting his audience to conclude? Most likely this writer pointed to four reciprocal and connected realities: Jesus's desertion and denial by his followers, his dignified innocence under trial, the blameworthy behavior of his judges, and his quiet courage in death.

From his opening lines Mark has introduced Jesus as "the Son of God," an identity twice confirmed as "beloved Son" by the voice of the Father from heaven, three times by Jesus himself, and once by a Roman centurion (1:1; 1:11; 9:7; 12:6; 13:32; 14:61; 15:39). His self-identification as the Son of God before temple authorities and the Sanhedrin provoked the charge of blasphemy that sealed his death (14:61–62).

Despite Jesus's exalted identity, from the beginning he knew that premature death awaited him. He understood well that the unlikely union of Galilean Pharisees and the Herodians[1] over his breaching of the Sabbath would spell

1. The Herodians appear to have been wealthy and powerful supporters of the

his death (3:6). From the incident at Caesarea Philippi to his arrival in Jerusalem, he referred repeatedly to his rejection, death, and resurrection. From its beginning, Mark's whole narrative points arrow-like to the death of Jesus.

Mark intends us to understand that God will reveal his blessings through the death of his Son in Jerusalem. He alludes to these throughout his narrative.

Immediately following his baptism and temptations, Jesus announced the imminent advent of the kingdom of God (1:14–15). In Jerusalem, under trial by the Sanhedrin, he declared that he was the Son of God but also the returning, celestial Son of Man (14:62). That would be the epoch of the kingdom of God he proclaimed in Galilee.

Challenged by his disciples' failure to fast, he declared himself to be "the bridegroom" who will bring a time of sadness when he is "taken away" from them, his "bride-to-be" (2:20). Mark doesn't explain Jesus's precise intention, except to infer that postresurrection Jesus would become bridegroom of his people, the true Israel.

Jesus's exorcisms in Galilee were yet another practice that attracted the criticism of the scribes from Jerusalem (3:22–23). His answer explained the present exorcisms while at the same time being prophetic. "But no one can enter a strong man's house and plunder his goods, unless he first binds the strong man. Then indeed he may plunder his house" (3:27). The "strong man" is Satan, who holds humanity captive in his "house." Jesus is the (infinitely) stronger man who will "bind" the "strong man" and so "plunder his house," that is, liberate his prisoners.

This is an astonishing statement pointing beyond Jesus in Galilee to Jesus in Jerusalem. By his sacrificial death and his victorious resurrection, Jesus will bind Satan and release his prisoners *cosmically*.

Another example of Mark's subtlety is his report of the conversation between Jesus and the man possessed with the "unclean spirits." "What is your name?" asked Jesus, to which he replied, "My name is *Legion*, for we are many" (Mark 5:9). In 63 BC Pompey the "Great" invaded and Romanized Palestine, which possibly explains how someone living in the remote region to the east of the lake would know a Latin word. Beyond that, however, Mark seems to be making a point, again in a nuanced way: the entire Roman people are like the man Legion, under the thrall of unclean spirits, awaiting the coming of Jesus to expel them. This message would not be lost on Mark's Roman readers.

---

tetrarch of Galilee, Herod Antipas. It is possible that they sought to have him appointed sole ruler of a united Israel.

Equally astonishing was Jesus's response to the request of the sons of Zebedee seeking places of authority beside Jesus in his glory (10:37). It is evident that they did not understand the pathway of suffering that lay before them when Jesus spoke of "a cup" and "a baptism." Furthermore, and most importantly, they saw their hoped-for recognition and authority in terms of the Roman world where rulers "lord it over" the people and grind that "authority" down upon them. Jesus's response is breathtaking. "But it shall not be so among you. But whoever would be great among you must be your servant, and whoever would be first among you must be slave of all. For even the Son of Man came not to be served but to serve, and to give his life as *a ransom* for many" (10:43–45).

Now close to Jerusalem, Jesus made that remarkable statement. He came as a servant, the Son of Man who came not to be served but to serve: to give his life as a ransom for many, that is, for their liberation. Here he echoes the promised achievement of the truly "strong" man liberating Satan's prisoners.

The word of great interest is "ransom" (*lytron*), which, apart from Matthew's echoing it (Matt. 20:28), occurs only here in the New Testament. Jesus's critical word focuses attention on his death, the giving of his life for a defined merciful act of service "for many," that is, for the redemption of humanity. This single reference, more than any other, opens the door to the understanding of the whole gospel.

Critical here is the little word "for," which translates Greek *anti*, meaning "instead of," "in place of." The vicarious intent is unmistakable. Mark means us to understand that Jesus's death, when it comes, will be "redemptive," "liberating" in an ultimate sense.

What, then, does Mark intend us to think about the trials of Jesus at the hands, first, of the Sanhedrin, then of Pilate? In each, Jesus was blameless, the object of unjust and corrupted judges and the recipient of physical cruelty. The divine mystery is: By which means did God employ wicked cruelty toward the righteous Jesus to set free the prisoners of the "strong man"?

Is there an allusion here by Mark relative to the words of Peter in his first letter? This is not altogether unlikely since Mark wrote his gospel under the authority of Peter, his mentor. We note that Peter in his letter used the rare verb *lytroō* (redeem),[2] a near relative of the noun *lytron*. "You were *ransomed* from the futile ways inherited from your forefathers, not with perishable things such as silver or gold, but with the precious blood of Christ, like that of a lamb without blemish or spot" (1 Pet. 1:18–19).

---

2. The verb *lytroomai* only appears in Luke 24:21, Titus 2:14, and 1 Pet. 1:18.

It is possible (but admittedly not certain) that Mark's narrative of the blameless Jesus under corrupt trials allusively corresponds with Peter's reference to him as "a lamb without blemish or spot."

Mark is a skillful and spiritually insightful writer. Furthermore, he expects his audience to notice and understand the clues within his narrative that point to Jesus in Jerusalem; his sense of desertion and denial; his innocence under corrupt trials; his courageous, uncomplaining death; and his resurrection.

A NEW SACRIFICE AND A NEW LOVE-BASED ETHIC

A sense of mystery underlies the gospel of Jesus. Under the old covenant, sins were expunged *cultically*, through the offering of animal sacrifices in the holy place at the hands of holy men. With Jesus's redemption of the world, however, his sacrifice did not have a religious setting. There was no temple, no priests, no slain animals. That setting was secular and political, and Jesus was executed unjustly and with cruelty.

It occurred in the hours of Jesus's crucifixion climaxed by his death midafternoon Friday. Those were hours of darkness signifying a cosmic redemption. They were preceded by evils of the previous night when Jesus faced a series of corruptly conducted trials.

At every point the events of that night and of the day following were unjust and brutal, a wicked misuse of power. Completely absent was any sense of a duty of care for the man on trial. Meanwhile, Jesus was abandoned by followers and friends, apart from the women and the Beloved Disciple.

From Caesarea Philippi to Gethsemane, Jesus foreshadowed what was to happen, but most clearly of all in his acts and words at the Last Supper earlier "that night": "And he took bread, and when he had given thanks, he broke it and gave it to them, saying, 'This is my body, which is given for (*hyper*)[3] you. Do this in remembrance of me.' And likewise the cup after they had eaten, saying, 'This cup that is poured out for you is the new covenant in my blood'" (Luke 22:19–20).[4] Jesus's actions and words anticipated the trials and beatings that were to unfold later that night, climaxing the next day in his death by crucifixion.

This, then, was the setting for the event that issued in the redemption of the world. Its setting was not religious but political.

---

3. Jesus's use of *hyper* is vicarious.
4. See Exod. 24:3–8; Jer. 31:31–34.

Significant, too, was Jesus's expected response, which was not "religious," legalistic, or cultic but trust-based toward Jesus and love-based toward others. This is the consistent message from Jesus in the Gospels and from his disciples in the letters.

Most important of all, these are the words of the one who was, and knew he was, the "beloved Son" of his *Abba*, Father. He endured that horrific night and the next day for others, for their redemption through simple trust in *Abba* expressed in the loving care of others.

CONCLUSION

Mark quotes Jesus promising liberty to those imprisoned by the "strong man" and that his death would be a ransom for many. The climax of his gospel occurs when Jesus reached Jerusalem at Passover. Mark records the events of that final night, when Jesus was betrayed, arrested, deserted, and denied.

Jesus's words at the Last Supper, when he foreshadowed his vicarious death, explained the earlier promised liberation and redemption.

One of the characteristics of this gospel is the writer's expectation that the readers have attended carefully to his words. Mark assumes that they will connect the earlier references to liberty and redemption to the desertion, denials, arrest, trials, beatings, crucifixion, and his death.

Strikingly, Jesus did not achieve universal redemption and spiritual liberation by cultic acts in a holy place, by the sacrifice of animals, at the hands of holy men. Rather, the sacrifice of Jesus was his mistrial, accompanied by brutal beatings, followed by crucifixion, issuing in his death.

Consistently, his call to follow him was devoid of reference to cultic, temple-related acts. Rather, as the apostle Paul observed, by the exercise of faith, hope, and love.

24

THE ANNAS VENDETTA

The evidence from the four Gospels combines to attribute the blame for Jesus's execution to the high priests, Annas and his son-in-law Caiaphas. The high priests were determined to remove Jesus, but by the hand of Pilate, which is the reason they bullied the governor to crucify the young prophet. His blood would be on the hands of the Roman occupiers. Furthermore, crucifixion of the leader would spell the end of his movement.

Based on the reports of the mission of the Twelve in Galilee and the possible military-style assembly of the five thousand men, Pilate may have believed Jesus to be a peasant-king whose ambition was to conquer first Galilee and then Judea.

Pilate's interrogation of the Galilean, however, quickly corrected any ideas that the man standing before him was a pretender-king. His demeanor was anything but bellicose, and there was no army, just a ragged assortment of fishermen, artisans, and a tax collector.

The governor's efforts to release Jesus were blocked by members of the crowd, but ultimately by the senior high priest, Annas. His motives are not difficult to discern. This clever prophet was undermining the orthodox basis of the Jewish religion, the temple and the priesthood. A formidable scholar, though self-taught, this man humiliated the rabbis who debated with him. Furthermore, he was attended by significant and growing crowds. Worst of all was his pretentious entry to the Holy City and his provocative assault on the merchants and money changers in the Court of the Gentiles.

In Annas's hands were two formidable weapons. One was the high priest's awareness that Pilate was politically vulnerable since the removal of his protector, Sejanus, who had been executed less than two years earlier. For Pilate there could be no openness to the charge that he had released a "king of the Jews." Annas, through his operatives, exploited this mercilessly. Second, although not mentioned, was Annas's great wealth that gave him the capacity to bribe and control the incumbent governor of Judea.

Such was Annas's power that the outcome of Jesus's trial was never in doubt. Pilate delivered Jesus into the hands of the execution squad, and he was crucified under the *titulus*, "king of the Jews."

In brief, the narratives when combined lay the blame for Jesus's mistrial and execution at the feet of Annas. There is no basis for thinking the early Christians falsely inculpated the Jew Annas and exonerated the Roman Pilate to exploit the then current racial stereotypes. The Fourth Gospel points its finger at Annas, and through him, at Caiaphas.

AFTER THE EXECUTION OF JESUS

The experience of Roman governance was that the execution of a cult leader spelled the end of his movement. The story line running through the texts of the New Testament, however, points instead to the church's continuation and expansion. The crucifixion and the resurrection were the twin triggers for the rapid rise and spread of Christianity, empowered by the dramatic infusion of the Spirit of God.

The Arrest of Peter and John

According to the book of Acts, the followers of the crucified one were immediately proclaiming "the resurrection of the dead" (Acts 4:2). They were arrested by "the priests and the captain of the temple" (Acts 4:1) and the next day arraigned before the "rulers and elders and scribes gathered together in Jerusalem, with Annas the high priest and Caiaphas and John and Alexander, and all who were of the high-priestly family" (4:5–6), that is, a plenary meeting of the Sanhedrin. We note the pointed and prominent reference to Annas, which serves to reinforce our understanding of the antipathy of that man to Jesus and the movement he inspired.

The followers of the now-deceased Jesus were gathering crowds asserting that he was the resurrected Christ. The authorities dismissed Peter and John as "uneducated and common," that is, as not belonging to the educated, rabbinic class.[1] They did, however, recognize that they had "been with Jesus," deeply influenced by him, his life, and his teaching.

Stephen in the Diaspora Synagogues in Jerusalem

The book of Acts refers to Stephen preaching in the synagogues of the Freedmen, the Cyrenians, the Alexandrians, the Cilicians, and the Asians (6:8–9).[2] It is understandable that Stephen visited the synagogues of diaspora Jews since, as a "Hellenist," he too was a Jew whose origin was not in the Holy Land.

Thanks to archaeological labors we have the so-called Theodotus inscription discovered in 1913 in the southern part of the City of David, Jerusalem, dated to the first century. The dedication reads:

> Theodotos son of Vettenus, priest and head of the synagogue (*archisynágōgos*), son of a head of the synagogue, and grandson of a head of the synagogue, built the synagogue for the reading of the law and for the teaching of the commandments, as well as the guest room, the chambers, and the water fittings as an inn for those in need from abroad, the synagogue which his fathers founded with the elders and Simonides.[3]

This valuable inscription, written in Greek, identified a synagogue and inn for Jewish pilgrims "from abroad." Among its many points of interest, the inscription attests a synagogue for special needs, providing tangential evidence of synagogues for specific national groups, as indicated by Acts 6:8–9.

Stephen's systematic and motivated visits to these synagogues provoked fierce resistance. The book of Acts doesn't report Stephen's words, but the reports of those who disputed with him: "We have heard him speak blasphemous words against Moses and God" (6:11). Subsequently these disputants arraigned Stephen before the Sanhedrin: "This man never ceases to speak words against this holy place and the law, for we have heard him say that this

---

1. Indicated in Acts 4:13 by the epithets *agrammatoi* (uneducated in the law) and *idiōtai* (technically unqualified).

2. It is more likely that Luke is referring to five discrete synagogues than that the one synagogue had such a diversity of membership. "Freedmen" may have been Jews enslaved by Romans, taken to Rome, then manumitted and returned to Judea.

3. John S. Kloppenborg, "Dating Theodotus (CIJ II 1404)," *Journal of Jewish Studies* 51 (2000): 243–80.

Jesus of Nazareth will destroy this place and will change the customs that Moses delivered to us" (6:13–14).

Luke describes these accusations as those of "false witnesses." Nevertheless, the accusations must have been sustainable, even if exaggerated and unqualified. It is true that Jesus prophesied the destruction of the temple (through not at his hands), and he did repeatedly dispute with the Pharisees over interpretation of the law of Moses.

The Acts narrative doesn't identify those who "brought [Stephen] before the Council." For two reasons Luke means us to understand that among them was Saul (later, Paul). First, the narrative suddenly introduces him: "the witnesses [to Stephen's stoning for blasphemy] laid down their garments at the feet of a young man named Saul" (7:58). Secondly, later in Acts the author has Paul say, "I am a Jew, from Tarsus in *Cilicia* . . ." (21:39), a reference that connects with one of the synagogues whose members disputed with Stephen and were likely among those who brought Stephen before the Sanhedrin, charged with blasphemy, the penalty for which was stoning.

Consistent with this reconstruction are Paul's own words: "For you have heard of my former life in Judaism, how I persecuted the church of God violently and tried to destroy it. And I was advancing in Judaism beyond many of my own age among my people, so extremely zealous was I for the traditions of my fathers" (Gal. 1:13–14).

We readily imagine the "extremely zealous" young member (arguably leader) of the Synagogue of the Cilicians worsted in debate with Stephen and being one of those who charged Stephen with blasphemy before the Sanhedrin, whose presidents were Annas and Caiaphas.

ANNAS, PONTIUS PILATE, AND THE EXECUTION OF STEPHEN

While the *ius gladii* limited the exercise of capital punishment to the Roman prefect, it is all but certain that Annas and Caiaphas tried and executed Stephen with the approval of Pontius Pilate. The trial of Jesus revealed the high priests' power over Pilate. They would have their way again to remove Stephen, a serious troublemaker.

The Role of Saul in the Stoning of Stephen

References in the book of Acts to "the witnesses" (Acts 7:58) are to those members of the five named synagogues who had disputed unsuccessfully with Stephen and who had brought their accusations of blasphemy to Annas and Caiaphas.

While it may appear that Saul's was the minor role of an onlooker who looked after the clothes of the executioners, it is more likely that he was their leader. The prescribed mode of stoning was set out in the Mishnah:

> Four cubits from place of stoning the accused is stripped.
> The drop twice the height of a man
> One of the witnesses pushes the offender
> He is turned face up
> If the fall didn't kill, a stone is dropped on his heart.[4]

As leader of the executing group, Saul would have cast the first stone on Stephen.

Saul as the Executor of Annas's Vendetta

Following the narrative of the book of Acts, the high priests Annas and Caiaphas now conferred authority upon Saul for the destruction of the Jesus movement in Jerusalem. Evidently, they were impressed by his "zeal" and ruthless efficiency displayed in debates with Stephen, his effective accusation of Stephen's blasphemy to the Sanhedrin, and his leadership in the execution of the offender.

The book of Acts gives no fewer than four accounts of Saul's assaults on the members of the church in Jerusalem that followed the stoning of Stephen.[5]

Saul led groups of officials from door to door to arrest the believers. These he took for trial in the synagogues, where some would have been subjected to the forty lashes less one;[6] others were taken for stoning for blasphemy. The assault was so severely effective that the members of the church "were all scattered throughout the regions of Judea and Samaria" (Acts 8:1).

Only the apostles remained in the Holy City, perhaps to care pastorally for those few who were unable to flee, but also to be a foundation for the church in Jerusalem once the persecutions eventually ceased. When Saul, now a be-

---

4. m. Sanhedrin 6.1–4. Although written in the second century, this tractate's reference is likely to the era of the New Testament.

5. The book of Acts makes multiple references to Saul's violent assaults on the members of the church in Jerusalem: 8:3; 9:1; 22:4–5; 26:9–10.

6. Paul was himself subject to this punishment five times (2 Cor. 11:24). For reference to the forty stripes less one as punishment in the synagogues, see m. Makkoth 3.11–15.

liever, returned to Jerusalem, he lodged with Cephas, saw James the brother of the Lord, and met other apostles (Gal. 1:18–20).

Such was Saul's murderous hatred of the fugitive followers of Jesus that he was determined to extradite them in chains from Damascus back to Jerusalem for trial and punishment. To that end he secured letters of authority from the high priest (Caiaphas?) to the synagogues in Damascus (Acts 9:1; 22:5; 26:11–12).

This is further evidence of the high priests' appreciation of Saul's deadly dedication and efficiency. While the focus of the narrative rests on Saul, we must not lose sight of the determined hatred of Annas and Caiaphas toward first Jesus, then his followers, including Stephen. Having secured the death of the Galilean, they would not rest until the remains of his leaders and followers were expunged from the Holy Land and the Holy City.

We can do no more than speculate about the high priests' reasons. Most likely they viewed Jesus's assault on the vendors and money changers in the Court of the Gentiles as an intolerable precedent to be imitated by other misguided radicals. This same Jesus was known to prophesy the destruction of the temple. Furthermore, reports from Galilee, but also from Jerusalem, pointed to Jesus as a formidable prophet who had been heeded and followed by large crowds in Galilee, the surrounding principalities, and even in Jerusalem itself. It is by no means unlikely that the high priests Annas and Caiaphas feared the loss of their power base to this young man. They had displayed the upper hand against the governor in the trial of Jesus, but they clearly understood that the Romans could destroy the Supreme Council itself if the followers of the Galilean caused trouble.

Saul's Volte-Face and Fall from Grace

Saul's volte-face from persecutor of the church and its faith (Gal. 1:13, 23) to become its most eminent advocate is often and correctly noted. From Jerusalem, in an arc round to Illyricum (Rom. 15:19), in just twenty-three years, Paul the apostle proclaimed the message of the Son of God in no fewer than seven Roman provinces and composed and sent nine powerful pastoral epistles to the churches he founded.[7] More than anyone else among the followers of Jesus of Nazareth, this man changed the course of history.

7. Paul did not establish the Christian movement in Rome, but many whose names are given in Rom. 16 were part of his mission in the East.

What is not so often noted, as it deserves to be, is that Saul's conversion would have radically changed his relationship with the high priests Annas and Caiaphas and the Sanhedrin. Previously, as their trusted and efficient weapon against the followers of Jesus, Saul would have been viewed as a rising star in the upper echelons of the religious establishment in Jerusalem. His intellectual brilliance and indomitable energy would have marked his future as a senior rabbi in the school of the Pharisees and member of the Sanhedrin.

Saul's would have been viewed as an astonishing fall from grace. Thirty years later he wrote from prison in Rome to the church in Philippi, "For his [Jesus's] sake I have suffered the loss of all things" (Phil. 3:8). The gifted and precocious young Saul must leave the Holy City and return to the obscurity of his place of origin, Tarsus in Syria and Cilicia. During the next decade he would sustain himself by tentmaking, an unclean trade; tents were made of leather, cured by horses' urine. His proclamation of "Christ crucified" in the synagogues of that province issued in no fewer than five severe beatings (2 Cor. 11:24).[8] For the next dozen or so years in the provinces of Macedonia, Achaia, and Asia, he worked through the nights as a humble cobbler, a significant fall from the heady days in Jerusalem.

AD 41: THE EXECUTION OF JAMES ZEBEDEE AND THE CAPTURE OF PETER

According to the book of Acts, the newly appointed king of Judea, Herod Agrippa I, "laid violent hands on some who belonged to the church" (Acts 12:1). Among those he imprisoned were James Zebedee, whom he executed by the sword (i.e., for political crimes), and Peter, who later escaped.

Peter and James were, respectively, the first-most and third-most senior of the leaders of the church in Jerusalem. In other words, Herod Agrippa's action was calculatedly directed at the current leadership of the Christian movement in the Holy City. After his escape, Peter fled from Judea, although his place of escape is not stated (Galilee?).

The point to be made here is that the king's actions were probably done in concert with the high priest, who was at that time Matthias, fourth son of Annas. It is well known that Agrippa was at heart a gentile, and friend of the profligate Caligula, and of the future Caesar Claudius. When Claudius appointed Herod Agrippa king of Judea in 41, he made a show of piety for the people

---

8. Since the book of Acts makes no reference to this, it is reasonably assumed to have occurred in Paul's so-called unknown years in Syria and Cilicia before he launched into his westward missions.

of the Holy City. Josephus commented enthusiastically: "[Agrippa] liked to dwell in Jerusalem, and that continuously; he observed the traditions of the forefathers without blemish; he adhered to all the rites of purification and did not let a day pass without assisting at the sacrifice prescribed by the Law."[9]

It is reasonable to assume that Agrippa's newfound adherence to the law and his residence in Jerusalem brought him into close contact with the high priest, Matthias. There is little doubt that Matthias agreed with, or indeed may well have been the inspiration for, violent action against the most senior and third-most senior leaders of the Christians in Jerusalem. Thus, the king and the high priest acted together to destroy the leadership of the Jesus movement in Jerusalem.

It is significant that the assault on the leaders of the church occurred during Passover, to remind believers of the occasion of the execution of their leader, Jesus. Moreover, that season brought the greatest number of pilgrims to the Holy City.

After the fall of Matthias son of Annas, the rival house of Boethus regained the high priesthood.

AD 62: ANNAS'S EXECUTION OF JAMES, BROTHER OF THE LORD

The fifth of Annas's sons, also named Annas, was responsible for the death of James, brother of the Lord, leader of the church in Jerusalem. Josephus, our sole source for this event, is no supporter of this younger Annas, referring to him as "a bold man in his temper, and very insolent; he was also of the sect of the Sadducees, who are very rigid in judging offenders, above all the rest of the Jews."[10] It is also likely that the assault of Annas II on the brother of Jesus was also an example (the last) of the vendetta against Jesus and his followers that began at Passover 33.

In 62 Nero Caesar had dispatched Albinus as procurator of Judea to replace Festus, who had died in Caesarea while still in office. During the interregnum, King Herod Agrippa II, king of Chalcis, grandson of Herod the "Great,"[11] dismissed Joseph the incumbent high priest and appointed Annas II. We are left to guess the king's motives. Did Annas bribe him, or was the king also an enemy of the followers of Jesus?

9. Josephus, *Jewish Antiquities* 18.143.
10. Josephus, *Jewish Antiquities* 20.199.
11. Chalcis was a small kingdom in Asia Minor, not part of the Holy Land. Nevertheless, as descendant of Herod the Great, he enjoyed continuing powers.

Whatever Agrippa's motives, the new high priest seized the moment and arraigned James, "brother of Jesus who is called Christ," before the Sanhedrin.[12] Annas charged James and some companions with breaking the law and delivered them over to be stoned. The accusation, more specifically, must have been that James's support of Jesus was blasphemous.

The most likely explanation for Annas's motive is that James presided over a considerable community of Christians in the Holy City and represented a threat to the leadership of the high priest and Sanhedrin. The Acts reference to Paul's meeting with James five years earlier supports this understanding. Luke quotes James's companions to say to Paul, "You see, brother, how *many thousands* there are among the Jews of those who have believed. They are all zealous for the law" (Acts 21:20). The large community of believers in Jerusalem would have been a threat to Annas's hegemony, especially since these followers of Jesus were "zealous for the law."

Josephus further reports that leading citizens in Jerusalem rebuked the king for what had happened and sent representative to Albinus, still in transit in Alexandria, informing him that Annas had broken Roman imperial practice by assembling the Sanhedrin without the governor's consent. Albinus wrote to Annas threatening punishment, whereupon King Herod Agrippa II stripped Annas of his office as high priest. He had been high priest for only three months.

THE ANNAS DYNASTY, AD 7–62

The dismissal of Annas II in 62 marked the end of a dynasty of high priests that began in 7 with the appointment of Annas I. Throughout the years 7–62 Annas I, his son-in-law Caiaphas, and five of Annas's sons held the office as high priest and president of the Sanhedrin. At every point where we catch a glimpse of them, the members of this powerful dynasty opposed Jesus and his followers.

Annas effectively forced Pilate to have Jesus condemned and crucified; he condemned Stephen to be stoned for blasphemy; through the agency of the Pharisee Saul, he effectively drove the believers from Jerusalem and then sought to arrest and extradite believers from Damascus. In circa 41, in concert with Herod Agrippa I, the high priest Matthias, son of Annas, arrested Peter (who escaped) and James Zebedee (whom they executed). In 62, Annas II illegally convened the Sanhedrin, where James, brother of Jesus, who is called Christ, was stoned for blasphemy.

12. Josephus, *Jewish Antiquities* 20.200.

Persecutions of the House of Annas

AD	High Priest	Persecution
33	Annas + Caiaphas	Prosecution of Jesus
34	Annas + Caiaphas	Imprisonment of Peter and John (Acts 3:1–4:22)
34	High Priest (? Annas)	Trial of Peter and the apostles (Acts 5:12–42)
34	Annas → Saul's citywide persecution Paul's journey to Damascus	Trial and stoning of Stephen
42	Matthias, son of Annas	Arrest of Peter, beheading of James
62	Annas II	Execution of James, brother of the Lord

CONCLUSION

The execution of Jesus of Nazareth followed the trial dominated by high priests Annas and son-in-law Caiaphas. Their hatred of Jesus was inspired by the threat he posed to them by his expulsion of traders and money changers from the Court of the Gentiles. Unexpectedly, the crucifixion of Jesus did not mean the end of his movement, but rather its very significant growth. These leaders took great interest in the activities of the believers in Jerusalem and arrested their leaders when they bore witness in public. They were quick to rid themselves of the charismatic Stephen. Saul, the young Pharisee scholar, commended himself as a hatchet-weapon to destroy the movement in Jerusalem, but also its fugitive members in Damascus. The new king Agrippa I and most likely Matthias son of Annas imprisoned Peter and executed James Zebedee. Years later the younger Annas opportunistically but foolishly arrested and stoned James, brother of the Lord.

Meanwhile, through Saul's astonishing volte-face, he broke from, or was excluded from, the patronage of Annas and Caiaphas and took his life in a completely new direction.

25

THE PASSING OF THE JUDGES

One of the ironies of history is that those who condemned Jesus to death in 33 were themselves to die, or be removed from their position of power, soon afterward.

36   High Priest Caiaphas died
     Pontius Pilate sent to Rome for trial
37   Tiberius Caesar died
39   Herod Antipas exiled
40   High Priest Annas died

Meanwhile, the history of Judea ran its predictable, tragic course following the conversion of Judea from a Herodian ethnarchy to a Roman province. The census followed by the imposition of tribute tax payable directly to Caesar provoked the uprising of 6 led by Judas and Saddok, founders of the so-called Fourth Philosophy.[1]

THE FOURTH PHILOSOPHY, 6–66

In Josephus's mind, this new "philosophy" repeatedly expressed itself in violent acts in subsequent years and ultimately necessitated the Roman invasion

1. Most likely as named by Josephus.

in 66, whose climax was the destruction of the temple four years later. In the *Jewish Antiquities*, his account of the violence in 6 was to signal prospectively the miseries that were to follow, culminating with the final tragedies, the loss of the land.[2]

In his *Jewish War*, however, he refers retrospectively to the succession of insurgents whose futile violence anticipated the blood and fire that engulfed Israel in 66.

If we combine details of insurgents identified in *Antiquities* and *War*, we are left with the impression that the years 6–66 consisted of a succession of "sign" prophets and leader-led uprisings:

6–60		Acts	Jewish War	Jewish Antiquities
6	Judas the Galilean	5:37	2.433	18.1–10
44–46	Theudas[3]	5:36		20.98–99
ca. 54	The Sicarii ("assassins")		2.254–257[4]	20.186, 204, 208; 21:38
46–48	James, Simon, Men-achem (sons of Judas)			20.102
ca. 57	The Egyptian prophet	21:38	2.261–262	20.169–171
60s	Bands of brigands		2.264	
66–70				
66	Eleazar ben Deinaeus		2.235–623, 253; 20.121, 161	
66	John of Gischala		5.275 +	
66+	Simon bar Gioras		2.521 +	
66+	Eleazar ben Simon		2.564–565 +	
66+	Eleazar ben Yair		2.447; 7.253	
	the Idumeans		17.254	
	the Zealots[5]		2.651 +	

2. Josephus, *Jewish Antiquities* 18.1–10.

3. Luke, or more probably his source, wrongly located Theudas before Judas.

4. For further references to the Sicarii in *Jewish War*, see 2.425; 4.400–405, 516; 7.253, 254–262, 275, 297, 311, 410–419, 437, 444.

5. Josephus, *Jewish War* 7.252–274.

According to Josephus, "the Zealots" (note the definite article) were a discrete faction, composed of priests who staged a final desperate attempt to defend the temple from the Romans. There is no evidence in Josephus for the Zealots as an organized faction prior to the siege of Jerusalem. Rather, the terms "zeal" and "zealot" were applied to extremist *individuals*, although not by Josephus.[6]

When these leaders were killed, either by the Romans or by fellow insurgents, the movement died very soon after. The protagonists would return to their homes and their former trades, perhaps awaiting the rise of another leader with whom they could enlist.

One exception was the Galilee-based dynasty of Judas, son of the warlord Ezekias, who rebelled against Varus in 4 BC. This Judas, known as the Galilean (aka Gaulanite), also took part in his father's revolt. Judas reappeared in 6 as coleader with Saddok in the rebellion against the Roman census and the imposition of tax payable to Caesar. His death did not spell the end of this rebel dynasty. In 46 his sons James and Simon led a revolt against the procurator Tiberius Alexander, an aristocratic but lapsed Jew. Judas's son or grandson Menachem was a leader of the Sicarii faction in 66.[7] It is possible that the members of the dynasty had pretentions of royalty. W. R. Farmer argued that this family were in fact of Maccabean descent.[8]

THE YEARS 6–66: THE LANGUAGE OF "ZEAL"

Josephus was the historian on whom we mostly depend for Jewish history from the time of Herod (40 BC) to the destruction of the temple in 70. However, his *Jewish War*, written soon after the war, is thinly veiled propaganda written to dissuade Jews from further wars against the Romans. This was the message of King Herod Agrippa II in his long speech in Jerusalem in the face of the outbreak of war.[9] In *Jewish War*, written immediately after their disastrous defeat, Josephus employed the king's speech to dissuade the Jews from the futility of waging war against the invincible might of the Roman legions.

6. For example, Luke 6:15; Gal. 1:14.

7. J. S. Kennard, "Judas of Galilee and His Clan," *Jewish Quarterly Review* 36 (1945): 281–86.

8. W. R. Farmer, "Judas, Simon and Athronges," *New Testament Studies* 4 (1957–1958): 150–52.

9. Josephus, *Jewish War* 2.344–407; 2.418, 421, 426, 429, 481, 483.

The narratives of both the *War* and the *Antiquities* are dotted with references to acts of violence that would be precursors of the final, climactic tragedy, the ferocious Roman onslaught on the besieged people of Jerusalem and the torrents of blood and fire that were unleashed. As noted, Josephus does not use the language of "zeal" for Judas in 6, or for those insurrectionists listed above.

The "zealot" phenomenon that periodically arose when the Lord's covenant with his people was threatened was probably inspired by the "zeal" of Mattathias in 167–165 BC. In the era of Jesus and the early church, it was not so much a movement or faction but a deeply religious attitude in some individuals that was triggered into action when the honor of the Lord and his law was under attack. What marked the "zealot" off from other Jews was the specific "zeal" for the Lord that inspired direct action regardless of the cost.

The language of "zeal" appears within the New Testament, but it doesn't refer to an organized faction (as would appear during the war years, 66–70), but rather to a violent mind-set.[10]

One of Jesus's disciples was named "Simon the Cananaean" in Mark 3:18 (followed in Matt. 10:4). Luke clarified the Aramaic word "Cananaean" by referring to "Simon who was called *the Zealot*" (Luke 6:15; Acts 1:13). Was there a faction named "the Zealots" or was this a nickname for a person who held extreme and violent views? The latter is the more likely.

The apostle Paul, reflecting many years later regarding his pre-Damascus values, wrote: "as to *zeal*, a persecutor of the church" (Phil. 3:6; cf. Acts 22:3). Again, Paul was not saying he belonged to a sect of the zealots, but rather to having a "zealous" temperament.

THE BIRTH OF THE CHURCH: LUKE-ACTS AND WORLD HISTORY

The following table relates to the early years of the church. Cited are linkages that Luke makes connecting events and people in his narrative with known people and events in the wider world.

---

10. Martin Hengel, *The Zealots* (Edinburgh: T&T Clark, 1989), contended that the various insurrections were examples of "zeal." For the classical rebuttal of Hengel, see Morton Smith, "Zealots and Sicarii, Their Origin and Relation," *Harvard Theological Review* 64, no. 1 (1971): 1–19.

Date	New Testament Event	Independent Cross-Reference
28/29	In the fifteenth year of the reign of *Tiberius* Caesar, Pontius *Pilate* being governor of *Judea*, and Herod being tetrarch of *Galilee*, and his brother Philip tetrarch of the region of *Ituraea and Trachonitis* . . . during the high priesthood of Annas and Caiaphas, the word of God came to John. (Luke 3:1–2)	. . . the nation was divided into three provinces under the *sons of Herod*. (Tacitus, *History* 5.9) *Pilate*, being sent by *Tiberius* as procurator to Judea. (Josephus, *Jewish War* 2.169) *Herod [Antipas]* put *John the Baptist* to death though he was a good man. (Josephus, *Jewish Antiquities* 18.113–117)
33	*Pilate* asked [Jesus], "Are you *King of the Jews*?" (Luke 23:3)	Christus . . . suffered the *extreme penalty* . . . at the hands of Pontius *Pilate*. (Tacitus, *Annals* 15.44)
34	For before these days *Theudas* rose up, claiming to be somebody, and a number of men, about four hundred, joined him. He was killed, and all who followed him were dispersed and came to nothing. After him *Judas* the Galilean rose up[11] in the days of the census and drew away some of the people after him. He too perished, and all who followed him were scattered. (Acts 5:36–37)	. . . when Fadus was procurator of Judea [44–46], a certain imposter named *Theudas* persuaded the majority of the masses to take up their possessions and follow him to the Jordan. He stated that he was prophet and that at his command the river would be parted. . . . With this talk he persuaded many . . . Theudas himself was captured, whereupon they cut off his head and brought it to Jerusalem. (Josephus, *Jewish Antiquities* 20.97–99) In 6, 7 a Galilean . . . Judas incited his countrymen to revolt [over] paying tribute to the Romans. (Josephus, *Jewish War* 2.118)

11. Luke, or more probably his source, located Theudas before Judas.

Date	New Testament Event	Independent Cross-Reference
44	On an appointed day *Herod* [*Agrippa I*] put on his royal robes, took his seat upon the throne, and delivered an oration to them. And the people were shouting, "The voice of a god, and not of a man!" Immediately an angel of the Lord struck him down, because he did not give God the glory, and he was eaten by worms and breathed his last. (Acts 12:21–23)	Clad in a garment woven completely of silver . . . he [*King Herod Agrippa I*] entered the theatre at daybreak . . . his flatterers addressed him as a god . . . the king did not rebuke them . . . felt a stab in his heart . . . after five days he departed this life. (Josephus, *Jewish Antiquities* 19.344–349)
44–45	Agabus . . . foretold . . . a great *famine* over all the world (this took place in the days of Claudius). (Acts 11:28)	It was in the administration of Tiberius Alexander [AD 46–48] that the great *famine* occurred in Judea. (Josephus, *Jewish Antiquities* 20.101)

Luke's two-volume work covered almost seventy years, from the birth of John the Baptist to Paul's two-year imprisonment in Rome. From the above table it is evident that there are many linkages from Luke's history of Christianity to the complex world history of the earliest years of Christianity.

These cross-references, when read alongside related texts from the New Testament (mostly Luke-Acts), contribute to providing a more complete historical picture. Furthermore, and of great importance, the cross-references from Josephus and Tacitus quietly draw attention to the birth and earliest years of the church.

CONCLUSION

Our historical sources, Christian and non-Christian, point to a new movement that entered the stream of history from circa 33. The death of its founder would have expected the death of the movement soon after, something that usually happened. We are right to assume that *the judges of Jesus*—Annas, Caiaphas, Pilate, Herod Antipas—believed that the death of the man they condemned would have spelled the end of his so-called kingdom. What they could not have predicted was that their condemnation of Jesus, followed by his execution, would have ignited a movement that rapidly grew and became an ever more powerful force.

By the midnineties in Rome, the great chronicler-propagandist Flavius Josephus observed that "on the third day [Jesus] appeared to them restored to life, for the prophets of God had prophesied these and countless other marvellous things about him. And the tribe of Christians, so called after him, has still to this day not disappeared."[12]

12. Josephus, *Jewish Antiquities* 18.63–64.

26

ANTINOMY

Joseph's words to his brothers are expressed in an antinomy, a two-part statement where each part is true, where each is the opposite of the other, yet when read together, they are not contradictory but meaningful: "As for you, you meant evil against me, but God meant it for good" (Gen. 50:20).

The narratives of the Gospels and those of Josephus and Tacitus indicate that the arrest, trials, and execution of Jesus are historically imaginable and can be credibly explained. His actions in Jerusalem inspired the deadly hatred of the all-powerful high priests, who secured his conviction and execution despite the misgivings of the Roman governor.

At the same time, however, Jesus came to Jerusalem aware that his death was to achieve a universal, God-given redemptive act, one that would establish the kingdom of God in human hearts, destroy the power of Satan, and liberate his captives (Mark 3:27; 10:45).

The intentions of Jesus, on the one hand, and those of the political authorities, on the other, are polar opposites. Each is coherent, and each, taken together, represents one coherent, believable narrative.

THE ARREST, TRIALS, AND EXECUTION OF JESUS UNDERSTOOD HISTORICALLY

There were many reasons the temple authorities wanted to be free of Jesus of Nazareth. Chief among them, however, was their reaction to his ejection of sacrifice merchants and money changers from the Court of the Gentiles. Jesus's action was an indirect but real assault on the flow of money into the coffers of the high priests Annas and Caiaphas. It was, in effect, a potent assault on the temple and the entire edifice of the Sanhedrin as led by high priests Annas and Caiaphas.

Their challenge to Jesus to explain his "authority" for these actions issued in his parable of wicked tenants and his citation against them of Psalm 118:22–23— "The stone that the builders rejected. . . ." Jesus portrayed himself as the Lord's "beloved Son" and as the rejected "stone" destined by God to become the foundation stone of the new Israel. Furthermore, Jesus's prophecy of the temple's destruction would have come to their attention (Mark 14:58).[1] Clearly, this Jesus was the enemy of the holy place, which was the base of their power.

Judas's betrayal of Jesus enabled the authorities to locate him and bring him in chains first to Annas for a private interrogation, and then to an ad hoc council trial presided over by Caiaphas, who handed him over to Pontius Pilate.

The high priests through their associates then acted as de facto prosecutors at the Roman trial. Pilate had a bad reputation as a harsh governor, yet he was unconvinced that Jesus was a would-be "king of the Jews." He demonstrated no warlike manner, and, importantly, he had gathered no army.

Pilate saw no reason to indict and crucify his prisoner and asked the gathered assembly for their goodwill to release him. Stirred on by the chief priests, the crowds demanded the crucifixion of Jesus.

The Praetorian prefect Sejanus, Pilate's initial Rome-based patron, who was now dead (October 31), had been posthumously dishonored by the Senate's decree, *damnatio memoriae*, that he was now to be regarded "of damned memory." All public memory of Sejanus was to be expunged.

Pilate was now entirely dependent on Tiberius, which he understood, and which the high priests also understood. Their voices, spoken through their colleagues, tellingly said to Pilate, "If you release this man, you are not Caesar's friend. Everyone who makes himself a king opposes Caesar" (John 19:12). To be a "friend" meant conforming to the conventions of absolute loyalty expected of a client to a patron (*amicitia*), a bond Pilate would breach with Tiberius if he failed to execute "a king of the Jews."

The military governor of Judea was at the mercy of the high priests and the temple authorities. The story is too well known to bear repeating. Under Pilate's instruction the execution squad crucified Jesus and, later that day, Friday, he was found to be dead. So ends the narrative of the young prophet-rabbi at

---

1. However, Jesus's alleged claim to rebuild the temple after three days seems to echo John's version of Jesus's words at the beginning of Jesus's ministry (John 2:19) rather than Mark's account from the very recent past (Mark 13:1–37).

the Passover in Jerusalem in 33. The high priests' plans had been fulfilled. In disposing of Jesus, they had reigned supreme, even to the extent of bending the military governor to their will.

The four "trials" of Jesus, and their respective outcomes, are credible and imaginable: powerful religious leaders blackmailed a vulnerable governor to remove a charismatic prophet from Galilee, a hotbed of insurgents.

The Gospels' various accounts of the involvement of Annas, Caiaphas, Herod Antipas, and Pilate make good historical sense. There is no need to accuse the gospel writers of slanting their narratives for apologetic purposes, for example, to exculpate Pilate and the Romans and to inculpate the high priests and the Jews.

But there is more to this story than the bare accounts of Jesus in Matthew, Mark, Luke, John, Josephus, and Tacitus. Jesus had anticipated exactly what was to happen. Within and through the events of that fateful night, the Almighty One was achieving a cosmic act of redemption for the whole of humanity, the inauguration of the kingdom of God.

What is before us, then, is an antinomy: two seemingly discrete events, each of which nonetheless is "true," and the whole statement of which is meaningful, profoundly so.

THE ARREST, TRIALS, AND EXECUTION OF JESUS UNDERSTOOD REDEMPTIVELY

Throughout his several years in Galilee, Jesus was foreshadowing a great and unique event.

From the moment of his baptism, Jesus was continually traveling. Mark gives an almost bewildering account of Jesus's movements: first his mission in Galilee (including crisscrossing the lake), then in the north and east escaping from Herod's Galilee, finally to fulfill his God-given vocation, traveling from Caesarea Philippi to Jerusalem.

The voice from heaven spoken to Jesus in the Jordan identified him as "my beloved Son," fit for whatever service the Father intended. The immediately following testing of Jesus in the wilderness confirmed his readiness for the supernatural, demonic-inspired conflict that lay ahead.

The arrest of John the Baptist was the signal for Jesus to step out from under his shadow. In the manner of a prophet, he immediately began to announce the nearness of the approaching kingdom—the rule—of God.

Mark captures the sense of the inexorable movement toward a future, great apocalyptic event. Jesus's numerous healings point toward a coming restoration of ultimate health. Likewise, the castings out of unclean spirits indicate the future binding of Satan and the spiritual liberation of his captives throughout the world.

Early in his narrative, Mark signals Jesus's impending sense of death. In his parable of the bridegroom Jesus states, "The days will come when the bridegroom is taken away from them" (Mark 2:20). Jesus understood himself to be the heaven-sent bridegroom to his bride, God's elect people. Nevertheless, he will be "taken away," unable yet to complete the marriage.

Mark also notes that the Pharisees and Herodians[2]—unlikely partners— conspired against Jesus, to destroy him (Mark 3:6).

Likewise, early in his gospel we see Jesus's gathering of the twelve disciples, his instruction of them, and his dispatch of them to call the people to repent (which implies that they first proclaimed the approaching kingdom of God).[3]

Jesus's call of and training of his disciples is of singular importance. In the second part of his gospel Mark portrays Jesus instructing them for their mission following his death. It was to become their calling to proclaim to the world the meaning and application of the death and resurrection of their leader in the Holy City.

However, Mark delays explaining his future and theirs until the last months of their third year together. At the previous Passover Jesus had addressed and miraculously fed a large, gathered multitude on the eastern side of the lake. So moved were they that the multitude attempted to impose the kingship of Galilee on him (John 6:15). This forced Jesus to lead his disciples on a long trek to the north and east, beyond the reach of Herod Antipas, tetrarch of Galilee-Perea.

Eventually, Jesus and the Twelve came to Caesarea Philippi, capital of the tetrarchy of Iturea and Trachonitis, a largely gentile region, which signaled that Jesus would be welcomed by the gentiles but not by the Jews. A momentous conversation occurred here between Jesus and the disciples. He asked, "Who do you say I am?" Whereupon Peter replied, "You are the Christ," that is, the long-awaited son of David, who was to deliver Israel from her enemies and set up a theocratic state, governed by the law and focused on the temple.

Later, in Jerusalem, when asked by the high priest if he was the Christ, Jesus didn't deny it (Mark 14:61). Nor did he deny it earlier at Caesarea Philippi.

---

2. The Herodians were a faction (military leaders, courtiers, estate owners) loyal to Herod Antipas, tetrarch of Galilee-Perea, for whom they sought recognition as "king" (as in Herod's fifth will).

3. See Mark 1:15 where Jesus's announcement of the approaching kingdom of God is accompanied by his call for them to "repent."

Rather, he referred to himself as "the Son of Man who must suffer many things." Here Jesus was radically redefining the Christ in terms of the celestial figure prophesied by the prophet Daniel (7:13–14), but who was to suffer and be killed at the hands of the temple authorities, but after three days rise again.

Twice more on the way to Jerusalem Jesus repeated his words about rejection, death, and resurrection, to the mystified astonishment of the Twelve. He strode out ahead while they straggled querulously behind.

One thing they did understand, although wrongly, was that the kingdom Jesus had announced meant "power," as exercised by the Roman Caesar. In his corrective response, Jesus revealed what was at the heart of his mission: "the Son of Man came . . . to serve . . . to give his life *a ransom* for many" (Mark 10:45).

Jesus's final and most complete revelation of his mission occurred on the night he was "handed over." When he broke bread and poured wine, he portrayed his crushed body and shed blood, which physically displayed how human redemption was to be achieved.

His agonized prayer at Gethsemane is a window into the infinite dimensions of suffering that awaited him, and from which he recoiled. It revealed his understanding of the ransom price he must pay: painful torture and crucifixion and indescribable suffering as bearer of the world's sin.

CONCLUSION

In the four Gospels we have mystery, a paradox, and, as I understand it, an antinomy. Through the Gospels, but also through Josephus, we have a credible and understandable account of the hostile high priests wielding their power over the vulnerable governor to secure the removal of a troublesome Galilean prophet.

On the other hand, however, beneath their narratives the Gospels portray the anointed and "beloved" Son proclaiming God's impending kingdom, which would be the outcome of the unspeakable ransom price he was to pay for the liberation of Satan's captives. The Gospels—Mark's in particular—relate Jesus's journey from Caesarea Philippi to Jerusalem, where the betrayal, desertion, denials, the mistrials, beatings, and excruciating death fulfilled his redemptive mission.

27

THE BIRTH OF THE CHURCH

The birth of the church occurred soon after the trials of Jesus and his execution, the evidence for which is found in both hostile and sympathetic sources.

HOSTILE SOURCES

The earliest hostile reference to Christianity is in 49. Suetonius stated that Claudius Caesar expelled the Jews from Rome because they "constantly made disturbances at the instigation of Chrestus."[1] This probably related to the preaching of Christ in the synagogues in Rome that brought division to the wider Jewish community. The book of Acts provides tangential confirmation: "Claudius had commanded all the Jews to leave Rome" (Acts 18:2). Among them were Aquila and Priscilla, who had gone to Corinth, and who we know were Christians because Paul immediately joined them.

It is not known by whom or when (between 33 and 49) Christian Jews came to Rome. The reference to "disturbances" suggests the recent arrival of outspoken believers who created the serious divisions that prompted Claudius's drastic action. Whatever the date was, Suetonius's observation is consistent with evidence from the Acts of the Apostles.

---

1. Suetonius, *Claudius* 5.4. *Chrestus* was usually understood as an innocent misspelling of *Christus*. However, *chrēstus*, meaning "good" (as in Ps. 34:8 LXX), may have been an intentional wordplay.

Paul's letter to the Romans, written in 57, addresses several Jews among his readers, suggesting that Claudius's death in 54 had opened the way for them to reside again in Rome.[2] Paul wrote the letter to prepare for his own impending visit to the Eternal City. By 64 Tacitus observed that following the great fire "vast numbers of [Christians] were convicted . . . of hatred of the human race."[3]

Suetonius and Tacitus attest the presence of Christians in Rome, in 49 and 64, respectively, indirectly and independently confirming the testimony of the early Christian texts regarding the birth of Christianity in Jerusalem in 33.

CHRISTIAN SOURCES

There are numerous early Christian sources that attest the birth of the church that followed immediately after the trials and execution of Jesus, and his resurrection. There was no hiatus between this cluster of events of the Passover of 33 and the birth of the church at the Feast of Pentecost fifty days later.

I am directing our attention to two sources, Paul's letter to the Galatians and the Gospel of John.

PAUL'S LETTER TO THE GALATIANS

Paul's letter to the Galatians, written circa 48, is of great importance: it was his earliest written letter, and the earliest written Christian text.[4]

From Galatians we can establish a chronology[5] of Paul's movements from the time of his persecutions of the church in Jerusalem (in 34) until the present moment in Antioch when he wrote the letter (in 48).

2. "Greet Prisca and Aquila . . . Andronicus and Junia, my kinsmen . . . my kinsman Herodion" (Rom. 16:3, 7, 11).

3. Tacitus, *Annals of Imperial Rome* 14 (Loeb Classical Library).

4. Those who hold the "North Galatians" theory of Paul's later missions to central and northern Galatia argue that 1 Thessalonians, written circa 51, is Paul's earliest surviving letter. This is not the view held here, based on the absence of evidence of or opportunity for Paul's missions to northern Galatia in the 50s.

5. This chronology is based on data from Luke's writings, his Gospel, and the Acts of the Apostles. From Luke 3:1–2 we learn that John the Baptist began preaching in the fifteenth year of Tiberius Caesar, that is, circa 28 or 29, which suggests the span of Jesus's ministry circa 30–33. From Acts 18:1–2 and Suetonius, *Claudius* 5.4, we calculate that Paul arrived in Corinth circa 50. The chronology noted above is based on the seventeen years between the first Easter (33) and Paul's arrival in Corinth (50). Paul

Galatians

This letter opens a window into a critical decade and a half of earliest Christianity that touches on Paul's relationships with the church of God (Jerusalem); the apostles Cephas, James, and John; also Barnabas, Titus, "false brothers" (in Jerusalem), the church in Antioch, and the churches of Galatia. These are the words of a contemporary to the events and people he narrates. They are the more valuable since they are written in Paul's self-defense and are accidentally and not intentionally historical.

Paul's attempt to destroy the church of God is clear evidence of its existence circa 34 that presupposed its birth in the previous two years. "For you have heard of my former life in Judaism, how I persecuted the church of God violently and tried to destroy it" (Gal. 1:13).

After Paul's famous volte-face outside Damascus, he writes, "[I did not] go up to Jerusalem to those who were apostles before me, but I went away into Arabia, and returned again to Damascus. Then after three years I went up to Jerusalem to visit Cephas and remained with him fifteen days. But I saw none of the other apostles except James the Lord's brother" (Gal. 1:17–19).

From this compressed statement we learn of Paul's travels throughout three years, from Damascus to Arabia, to Damascus, to Jerusalem. In Jerusalem he lodged with Cephas and "saw" James, the Lord's brother. Cephas and James were leaders of the church of God.

Based on Paul's statements, whose accuracy is not to be doubted, we have firsthand evidence of the church of God in the year 34 when Paul attempted to destroy it, which is confirmed by reference to the year 36 when Paul engaged with its leaders. I conclude, therefore, that the church began (was born) between the death of Jesus in 33 and Paul's attempt to destroy it in 34.

There is more to be said. Paul attempted not only to destroy the church of God but also its "faith." "The churches of Judea that are in Christ . . . were

---

spent fourteen of those years between the Damascus "revelation" and his second return to Jerusalem (i.e., from Syria and Cilicia). Two or so of the remaining years would have been spent in his mission to Cyprus and southern Galatia and his return to Antioch. Of those seventeen years, only one remains, the date Paul traveled to Damascus, which would have been circa 34.

hearing it said (in Syria and Cilicia), 'He who used to persecute us is now preaching *the faith* he once tried to destroy'" (Gal. 1:22–23).

Thanks to Paul's care in addressing the Galatians, we have a statement that probably resembled or was that "faith."

> But when the fullness of time had come,
> *God* sent forth *his Son*,
> born of woman,
> born under the law,
> to redeem those who were under the law,
> so that we might receive adoption as sons.
> And because you are sons,
> God has sent *the Spirit of his Son* into our hearts,
> crying, "*Abba! Father!*" (Gal. 4:4–6)

This creedal-like statement embedded in Galatians may have been the "faith" of the "church of God," or perhaps Paul's adaptation of it. We note "eschatological fulfillment," an extended statement about the Son (born of a woman, born under the law, to redeem, for adoption), expressed as triune: Abba Father, his Son, the Spirit of his Son. The "Abba" reflects the memory of Peter, James, and John of Jesus's heartfelt prayer in Gethsemane (Mark 14:36).

Historically speaking, Paul's letter to the Galatians is arguably the most important documentary evidence for earliest Christianity. Alongside this letter we are justified in adding the two great "traditions"—the Last Supper "tradition" and the resurrection "tradition." These are both cited in Paul's first letter to the Corinthians (1 Cor. 11:23–27; 15:3–7) and were probably "delivered" to Paul by Cephas and James in Jerusalem circa 36.

THE GOSPEL OF THE BELOVED DISCIPLE

The other evidence chosen for the birth of the church is the Fourth Gospel. We could have chosen other texts, for instance, the Gospel of Mark or other the sources for the Synoptic Gospels, "Q," "L," or "M."

The Identity of the Author

At the conclusion of this gospel an anonymous voice in an affidavit identified the author as "the disciple whom Jesus loved" (John 21:20, 24). Earlier that disciple declared himself to have witnessed the miracle "signs" of Jesus (20:30), to have been present at his crucifixion, and to have gone with Peter to the empty tomb (20:4–5).[6] The same disciple, without identifying himself, implied that he had been a disciple of John the Baptist and, based on John's testimony about Jesus as the "lamb of God," had become his follower (1:35–39).

Two other pieces of information contribute to identifying this disciple. One is that he was a friend of Simon Peter (13:23–24; 20:2–10; 21:20). The other is that he was one of seven disciples to go fishing on the Sea of Tiberias (21:1–3). Three are named (Simon Peter, Thomas, Nathanael), two are unnamed, and the two remaining are the sons of Zebedee (i.e., James and John). It is unlikely that the author is one of the two unnamed disciples, but likely that it was either James or John Zebedee. On balance, the author of this gospel was identifying himself as John Zebedee; James Zebedee was killed in 41 (Acts 12:2).

This was confirmed by Irenaeus, an early church leader, writing circa 170: "John the disciple of the Lord who reclined on his breast issued a gospel while he was living in Ephesus."[7] Irenaeus was well qualified to make this important statement. He was a pupil of Polycarp, bishop of Smyrna, who had been a pupil of John the apostle.[8]

Some claim that not John Zebedee but "the (unidentified) elder," author of John's second and third letters, was the true writer of this gospel. It is more likely, however, that "elder" was merely John's alternative way of referring to himself; he was, after all, a venerable figure in early Christianity, especially in the East.

Credible Early Detail

The Gospel of John is so theologically powerful that we easily pass over its many geographical, cultural, and political details.

The author effortlessly reveals an awareness of the "ups" and "downs" of the topography of the land (e.g., John 2:13; 4:47, 49, 51). He knows that the lake was about five miles wide (6:17, 19, 23), and he knows the names of vil-

---

6. For argument that the witness and the evangelist are one and the same person, see D. A. Carson, *The Gospel according to John* (Grand Rapids: Eerdmans, 1992), 625–26.

7. Irenaeus, *Against the Heresies* 3.1.1.

8. Irenaeus, *Against the Heresies* 3.3.4.

lages and their distinguishing qualifiers (e.g., Bethany "across the Jordan," 1:28; 10:40; Cana "in Galilee," 2:1; 4:46; Aenon "near Salim," 3:23); he is aware of the geographical conjunction of Sychar, Joseph's field, Jacob's well, and Mount Gerizim (4:4–6, 20).

Among the many cultural issues, John confidently mentions in passing that Jews refuse to share drinking vessels with Samaritans based on mutual enmity (4:9),[9] and that they insisted on using stone vessels for purifying (2:6),[10] and the credible conjunction of a place of shelter (Solomon's Porch) and winter (a cold season) that occurs at the Feast of Dedication (Hanukkah, John 10:22).

He notes that the Roman governor mounted his *bēma* formally to pass judgment on the accused at a place called *lithostrōtos*, in Hebrew "Gabbatha" (19:13).

Very striking is the political setting of the Roman trial of Jesus. As C. H. Dodd pointed out, "John's trial narrative belongs authentically and distinctively to the pre-66 period, when the Roman governor ruled the province of Judea as surrogate of the distant Caesar in an uneasy partnership with the high priest."[11] This was to change forever *after* the Roman invasion in the years 66–70, when there would be no more temple and no more high priests.

No longer would the Romans govern Judea through intermediary "client" kings or by a high priest–led Sanhedrin. Roman rule now would be direct and unmediated in a "full" military province renamed Colonia Prima Flavia Augusta Caesariensis.

There were many changes following the invasion of the Romans, 66–70, and their assault on the landscape.[12] The hillsides surrounding Jerusalem were denuded of vegetation by its use for the siege of the city. According to Josephus, "those who visited the city could not believe it had ever been inhabited."[13] Other cities and towns throughout Israel were also ruined.

---

9. J. P. Meier, "The Historical Jesus and the Historical Samaritans," *Biblica* 81, no. 2 (2000): 229.

10. J. Charlesworth, "The Dead Sea Scrolls and the Gospel according to John," in *Exploring the Gospel of John*, ed. R. A. Culpepper and C. Clifton Black (Louisville: Westminster John Knox, 1996), 68. See further m. Sukkah 4:9–5:4.

11. C. H. Dodd, *Historical Tradition in the Fourth Gospel* (Cambridge: Cambridge University Press, 1963), 120.

12. See E. Schürer, *The History of the Jewish People in the Age of Jesus Christ*, rev. and ed. G. Vermes and F. Millar (Edinburgh: T&T Clark, 1973), 1:514–28.

13. Josephus, *Jewish War* 7.3.

The point is that in relation to geography, culture, and politics, the Gospel of John portrays an earlier and different time. While memory can recapture things as they were, with the passage of time it is increasingly difficult to do so, especially in an age before photography, daily newspapers, and accessible archives. This author only had his memory.

The Dating of This Gospel

These numerous geographical, religious, and political details locate the writing of the gospel close to the events it narrates. Furthermore, the Gospel of John reflects an early struggle between the new community of believers in Jerusalem and the established Judaism.

This emerges subtly in Jesus's dialogue with Nicodemus, who at one point is cast in the role of a representative Jew. Jesus said to him, "Do not marvel that I said to you, 'You must be born again.'" Modern English translations mask the importance of the original pronouns, "Do not marvel that I said to thee (Greek singular, *soi*), 'You (Greek plural, *humas*) must be born again.'" Jesus was informing Nicodemus that the whole religious nation must be reborn.

Furthermore, John's portrayal of Jesus fulfilling the theology of the temple and the great feasts (John 2:19–22, 29; 3:16; 6:35; 12:32), especially the Passover, but also Tabernacles and Hanukkah, subtly declares that Jesus has superseded these great festivals that have now been replaced by the Son of God crucified, resurrected, and the giver of God's Spirit.

John's Gospel conveys a sense of hostility in the immediate postresurrection period between the members of the early church (as associated with the leadership of John) and the temple-based, high priest–led religious community.

On that basis, we can envisage John writing his gospel within the years 33–50. Among other things, this early dating explains the sheer volume of geographical, topographical, cultural, and political detail that occurs within this gospel.

Evidence from Ephesus

Notwithstanding the weighty evidence of earliness, it is widely held that the Gospel of John was written later than the Synoptic Gospels, that is, in 85 or later. This is consistent with comments from the church fathers. Irenaeus's verdict that John "issued a gospel while he was living in Ephesus" points to a late rather than early date of authorship. Likewise influential has been the statement of Clement of Alexandria (reported by Eusebius): "But that John, last of all, conscious that the outward facts had been set forth in the Gospels, was urged on by his disciples, and, divinely moved by the Spirit composed a spiritual Gospel."[14]

Clement implied that the "outward facts" (i.e., historical, geographical, and cultural details) had been "set forth" in the Synoptic Gospels and that John "last of all . . . composed a spiritual Gospel." By "spiritual Gospel" Clement was probably referring to its unquestionably profound theology, deemed to be deeper in this regard than the Synoptics.[15]

In part influenced by Clement, many modern authorities find details in John best explained by a theory of late dating. One example is the threefold reference to "synagogue exclusion" (*aposynagōgos*, 9:22; 12:42; 16:2).[16] Since Benediction 12 at the Council of Jamnia circa 90 declared a curse on "the Nazarenes" (i.e., Christians), some have therefore dated the writing of the Gospel of John to the last years of the first century. However, exclusion from the synagogue was practiced from at least the time of the Qumran community from the first century.[17]

Perhaps, though, John has passing references that were not needed if in fact John wrote his gospel in Palestine within two decades of Jesus. Why, for example, does he need to explain to Jewish readers that "Rabbi" means Teacher, that "Messiah" means Christ, or that "Cephas" means Peter (or rock) (John 1:38, 41, 42)? The fact is that John's Palestine-based audiences knew the meaning of these words but that Greek-speaking readers of the revised draft in Ephesus depended on these explanatory glosses.

John: An Early Palestinian Gospel

So, the important question is: Was John written early and from Palestine, close to the events it narrates, or much later, from Ephesus, where he had come to

---

14. Eusebius, *History of the Church* 6.14.7.

15. Clement is incorrect when he implies that the Synoptics provided the "outward facts" for John to supply the theological insights. John provides more details than the Synoptic Gospels combined, while being deeply "spiritual."

16. Notably, J. L. Martyn, *History and Theology in the Fourth Gospel* (Louisville: Westminster John Knox, 2003).

17. For the practice of synagogue exclusion, see Schürer, *History of the Jewish People*, 2:431–33.

live? A credible response is that John wrote an initial version of his gospel in Jerusalem by the fifties but rewrote it in Ephesus after the 70s.

The famous verdict of B. F. Westcott still stands. "The Author of the Fourth Gospel was a Jew of Palestine of the first century. . . . It is inconceivable that a Gentile, living at a distance from the scene of religious and political controversy which he paints, could have realised, as the evangelist has done, with vivid and unerring accuracy the relationship of parties and interests which ceased to exist after the fall of Jerusalem."[18]

Earliness of writing this gospel matters because it strongly implies the early existence of the church, which in turn points to the earliness of the birth of the church, that is, soon after the trials, crucifixion, and resurrection of Jesus. In turn, this indicates that between Jesus's call to follow him and his death three years later, he had imparted to them a full measure of his teaching so that they were immediately prepared to begin preaching Jesus's gospel wherever they were and under whatever their circumstances.

The Problem of John's "High" Christology

It is universally recognized that the Gospel of John has a distinctive, high Christology. For many this will be seen as evidence of John's lateness of authorship and theological distance from the Synoptic Gospels and from the historical Jesus. In short, for many this is evidence that John is not historically based, but an ingenious theological construct.

Consider this example: "So Jesus said to them, "Truly, truly, I say to you, the Son can do nothing of his own accord, but only what he sees the Father doing. For whatever the Father does, that the Son does likewise. For the Father loves the Son and shows him all that he himself is doing" (John 5:19–20; also 6:44; 10:38).

However, there are equally "high" christological passages to be found in Matthew and Luke, each dependent on their common "Q" source, notably: "All things have been handed over to me by my Father, and no one knows who the Son is except the Father, or who the Father is except the Son and anyone to whom the Son chooses to reveal him" (Luke 10:22 / Matt. 11:27)

It is evident that Matthew and Luke, by quoting this text, believe in its integrity and subscribe to its high Christology.

18. B. F. Westcott, *The Gospel according to St. John* (London: John Murray, 1903), x.

Likewise, we find a "high" Christology in the Gospel of Mark, the early gospel that predates Matthew and Luke. This is indicated by the title, "The beginning of the gospel of Jesus Christ, the Son of God," which is confirmed by the heavenly voice at Jesus's baptism ("You are my beloved Son, in you I am well pleased") and restated at the transfiguration ("This is my beloved Son, listen to him"). At Jesus's dispute with the temple authorities, he declared that his "authority" to clear the sacred place was because he was God's "beloved Son." At his crucifixion the Roman centurion confessed him to be "truly . . . the Son of God" (Mark 15:39). From first to last, this very early gospel is focused on Jesus as Son of God.

Furthermore, Mark captures the centrality of Jesus's identity as "Son of Man," as prophesied by Daniel:

> "I saw in the night visions,
>> and behold, with the clouds of heaven
>>> there came one like a son of man,
>> and he came to the Ancient of Days
>>> and was presented before him.
> And to him was given dominion
>> and glory and a kingdom,
> that all peoples, nations, and languages
>> should serve him;
> his dominion is an everlasting dominion,
>> which shall not pass away,
> and his kingdom one
>> that shall not be destroyed." (Dan. 7:13–14)

Jesus referred to himself from the beginning of Mark's Gospel, but intensively so at and after Caesarea Philippi. At the trial before Caiaphas, Jesus stated unasked that he was the returning Son of Man, in response to which the high priest declared Jesus guilty of the blasphemy of claiming deity. Jesus was forthwith taken to Pontius Pilate. For Caiaphas the "Son of Man" statement of Jesus was outrageous, blasphemous, and demanding death.

The Gospel of Mark, the "Q" and "M" texts, and the Gospel of John shared a common but independently high view of Jesus. He is uniquely the Son of the Father, obedient to do his will, the celestial and divine Son of Man. This is what believers from the worlds of these authors believed.

The heartrending paradox is that the eternal but now incarnate *Logos*, the Son of the Father, is "the Lamb of God who takes away the sin of the world" (John 1:29). We rightly look to chapter 3 verse 16 for John's own explanation of Jesus's death: "For God so loved the world, that he gave his only Son, that whoever believes in him should not perish but have eternal life."

God's love was and is expressed to the world that is in revolt against him, a revolt painfully soon to be evident in the leading Jews' hatred of the heaven-sent Messiah that issued in their demand for his crucifixion, but also in the cowardly Roman acquiescence to their demands. John's words directed to "whoever" signify God's love for every and any person, great or small; they invite "belief" in God's crucified "only Son" and promise "eternal life" instead of "perishing."

John wrote these famous words as one who was present with the crucified, dying Christ. Through the horrors of his friend's crucifixion, he discerned the love of God toward him, a love that permeates his writings and those of others in the canonical texts. Writing from Rome in the 90s, Josephus refers to the enduring love of Jesus's followers toward their Lord.[19] Indeed, the whole New Testament is permeated by love—God's love for us, ours for him, and ours for one another.

A lifetime of reflection and study would not be enough to more than superficially understand this remarkable text. It is and will remain an unsolved mystery how a fisherman who was also a fish merchant could write such profound words.

PAUL AND JOHN

Paul's exalted words about Jesus in Galatians were written retrospectively, but within fifteen years of Jesus's trials, crucifixion, and resurrection. He was dependent for his understanding on his amazing, God-given volte-face outside Damascus, and various teachings he received at his baptism there, and from Cephas and James in Jerusalem three years later. His testimony that he had attempted to destroy both the church of God and its faith is proof positive of the prior existence of both entities.

John's words were also written retrospectively of Jesus but were based on three years of mostly private exposure to Jesus's teaching and miracle "signs."

---

19. Josephus, *Jewish Antiquities* 18.64.

John had probably been a disciple of John the Baptist who, following the Baptist's testimony to Jesus, transferred his discipleship to him. John Zebedee heard Jesus's teaching and saw and understood his miracle "signs," entered the empty tomb, and saw the risen Christ on at least three occasions. Thus, even before the trials, crucifixion, and resurrection of Jesus, he was, in a sense, already a believer. The birth of the church was already a prospective reality in him.

In Galatians Paul wrote retrospectively of Jesus, based in part on the apocalyptic vision and on the human testimony of the leading apostles. In his gospel, John writes what he had already come to know, prior to that fateful visit to Jerusalem, that his master and friend was "the Christ, the Son of God."

THE RESURRECTION OF JESUS AND THE BIRTH OF THE CHURCH

The resurrection of Jesus was the event without which the birth of the church would not have occurred. As noted throughout, the deaths of leaders spelled the end of their movements.

The Gospels report that the crucified Jesus died, his body taken down from the cross, and laid in the tomb. If that really had been the end of Jesus, the disciples, family members, and friends would have remained in Jerusalem for some days but then drifted back to Galilee to return to their trades. Soon enough, Jesus, his deeds, and his teaching would begin to fade from memory.

Josephus devoted several paragraphs to John the Baptist but little to his continuing influence, apart from brief popular resentment against his murderer, Herod Antipas. Regarding Jesus, however, Josephus notes the continuing reality of the Jesus movement in Rome sixty years later.

Historically speaking, the early existence of the church in Jerusalem, as attested by Paul in his letter to the Galatians, is best explained by the resurrection of Jesus. The nonexistence of the church would point to the absolute finality of Jesus through death. But the reverse holds true: the sure, post-Easter reality of the church in Jerusalem is a credible pointer to the resurrected Jesus.

OTHER GOSPELS

The four canonical Gospels were written and in circulation by the end of the first century. From the second century, other gospels began to appear, usually written in the name of one of the leading disciples. Their intention was to fill out the felt shortcomings of the earlier gospels. Those gospels left unanswered many details, for example, what happened to the nails used in the crucifixion? and why wasn't the resurrected Jesus a physically greater figure?

An anonymous Christian from the second century wrote the Gospel of Peter, indeed narrating the removal of the nails and speculating that the disciples hiding in the temple had attempted to destroy it by fire. These "explanations" are minor, however, compared to the huge, resurrected figure of Jesus, whose head reached the skies, and who is followed by the cross who talks.

How different are the four Gospels that were written by his disciples (Matthew and John), or by Mark (an associate of Peter) or by Luke (dependent on the original disciples of Jesus). Their details are plentiful but understated and credible. We sense that their accounts are true to the facts and soberly written. Not least important, they point to the historically early birth of the church, that is, soon after the trials of Jesus led by Annas, Caiaphas, Pontius Pilate, and Herod Antipas.

CONCLUSION

Non-Christian and Christian sources combine to attest to the birth of the church soon after the trials, crucifixion, and resurrection of Jesus. The letter of Paul to the Galatians, written circa 48, is the earliest written Christian text, which presents a remarkably "high" view of Jesus. There is every reason to believe, however, that Paul's views echoed those of the earliest apostles who formulated the "traditions" of the Last Supper and the resurrection appearances.

This is consistent with the view that the church that was born following Jesus's trials and crucifixion was actually "conceived" three years earlier when Jesus called the Twelve to be "with" him. His instruction of them in private effectively precreated the church and the body of belief that was born at the Passover, in 33, and proclaimed immediately in the Holy City.

REFLECTIONS

REFLECTION 1. On that fateful Thursday night, Jesus foretold his impending death in words and actions with a loaf of bread and a cup of wine. Later he would be arrested and brought before Annas, Caiaphas, the Sanhedrin, Herod Antipas, and Pontius Pilate, who handed him over to the soldiers who crucified him midday under the caption (*titulus*) "king of the Jews." By late afternoon Jesus of Nazareth was dead.

The four men who engaged with Jesus during that night and their soldiers would have expected that his death would mean the end of his movement.

Fifty days later, however, the public preaching of Peter in Jerusalem signaled the birth of the church.

REFLECTION 2. Reading the Gospels easily gives the impression that their narrative picks up where the later book of Kings ends. In fact, more than four hundred years elapsed in between. During those years the Jewish people came under the rule of the Persians, followed by the Greeks—first from Egypt, then from Syria—whereupon the Maccabean dynasty seized the land and unified its constituent parts.

Powerful members of the neighboring Idumeans progressively gained control of the Holy Land, culminating in 37 BC with the appointment of Herod as king of Israel. To that point (40–37 BC) Herod had been dependent on the support of Mark Antony. In 31 BC Octavian (later Augustus) defeated Mark Antony at the Battle of Actium. Herod traveled immediately to Rhodes, where Augustus appointed him "friend and ally of Rome" and confirmed him as his "client" king of Israel.

Israel under Herod became increasingly "Roman," signified by the names of great Romans applied to the king's many buildings, most notably the great seaport Caesarea. At the same time, Herod was no less a Hellenist, evident in the appointment of the court historian Nicholaus of Damascus, and the creation of theaters and venues for Olympic-style games.

REFLECTION 3. Despite Herod's passion for his kingdom to remain intact and undivided, at his death in 4 BC it was necessary to divide it into three parts: Judea, Galilee-Perea, and Iturea-Trachonitis. In AD 6 Augustus dispensed with Archelaus as ethnarch of Judea and made it a Roman military province. The capital would now be Caesarea Maritima, residence of the prefect and garrison city for the Roman troops.

REFLECTION 4. One major consequence of annexation was that tax was to be paid directly to Caesar. This innovation provoked an uprising led by Judas the Galilean (or Gaulanite) and Saddok, a Pharisee. Josephus called their movement the "Fourth Philosophy." He doesn't use the language of "zeal," despite its importance since 165 BC when the Maccabees revolted against their Greco-Syrian master in Antioch. According to Josephus, the "Fourth Philosophy" inspired the series of nationalist and prophet-led uprisings that finally necessitated the Roman invasion in 66 and its inevitable outcome four years later, the sacking of Jerusalem and destruction of the holy place.

REFLECTION 5. Another development following annexation was the increased power of the high priest and his seventy-one-man council (the Sanhedrin). It seems that the high priest's powers extended beyond Jerusalem to the wider province of Judea.

REFLECTION 6. In the year 6, Quirinius (legate of Syria) and Coponius (prefect of Judea) appointed as high priest Annas, who held that position until 15. In 18 the prefect Gratus appointed Annas's son-in-law Caiaphas to the pontificate, the office he held until his death in 36. No fewer than five of Annas's sons were high priests from 16 to 62. Annas was renowned for his great wealth (from merchants and money changers in the temple), and it is likely that these riches enabled him to secure these appointments by bribing the Roman governors.

REFLECTION 7. Pontius Pilate was appointed prefect of Judea in 26, most likely by the Praetorian prefect, Sejanus. Tiberius Caesar was by then living in semi-retirement on the island of Capri (offshore from Naples). It seems that Sejanus and Pilate were both anti-Semitic. This would help explain the series of hostile actions against the Jews by Pilate soon after his arrival.

REFLECTION 8. Although governor of Judea, Pilate's sphere of interest would have included neighboring jurisdictions, the tetrarchies of Herod's sons, Herod Antipas and Philip. Soon after arriving, Pilate would have heard of the remarkable influence of John the Baptist in Perea, followed by his martyr's death in Machaerus on the border of Perea and Nabatea.

Even before the removal of John, another prophet arose, Jesus of Nazareth, whose influence was greater than John's, reaching beyond Galilee to the west, north, and east. It is likely that Pilate knew of this prophet's followers, who were traveling throughout Galilee preaching their leader's "kingdom" message. Moreover, Pilate would have been concerned by news of the five thousand Galileans gathered in what appeared to be a military formation to hear the prophet.

REFLECTION 9. The Jerusalem-based scribal authorities had been so concerned about the influence of this prophet in Galilee that they sent leading scholars to deal with his teachings on exorcism, the Sabbath, and purity laws (Mark 2:23–24; 3:22; 7:1). Furthermore, Galilee's two leading cities, Sepphoris and Tiberias, were significantly un-Jewish.

Accordingly, when Jesus traveled to Jerusalem for Passover in 33, he would have been well known as "the Galilean" to the prefect, the scribal authorities, and the high priests.

REFLECTION 10. It is of fundamental importance to recognize that Jesus fulfilled the dual roles as "prophet" and "rabbi." In public, Jesus was a prophet who announced the imminent advent of the kingdom of God. Likewise, he engaged in debate with the Pharisees, both from Galilee and from Jerusalem. At the same time and for three years he was a rabbi/teacher in private with his disciples. This meant that by the time of Passover 33, his disciples had been carefully instructed in what would be the theology that came to be the basis of the New Testament.

This helps explain how the disciples were immediately able to preach the Jesus message following his trials, death, and resurrection. Significantly, it explains the immediate birth of the church after his arrest, trials, crucifixion, and resurrection.

REFLECTION 11. It was the high priests Annas and Caiaphas who secured the arrest, trials, and death of Jesus. He arrived mounted in Jerusalem, he provocatively cursed the fig tree, and he cleared the merchants and money changers from the Court of the Gentiles. He was known to prophesy the end of the temple. Worst of all, when asked to identify his "authority" for these actions, he claimed to be the "beloved Son of God" and pointed to a prophetic psalm that declared the Jewish authorities' end as God's foundation stone.

REFLECTION 12. Inevitably, these explanations issued in his arrest on the eve of Passover, whereupon he was interrogated by Annas and Caiaphas and accused of blasphemy in an ad hoc meeting of the Sanhedrin. Significantly, he was handed over to Pilate, not for the charge of blasphemy, for which he would have been stoned, but for claiming to be "king of the Jews," for which he would have been crucified.

REFLECTION 13. The Jewish authorities did not want Jesus stoned for blasphemy, for which they would have been blamed. Jesus, like the martyred John, was highly regarded. Rather, they demanded that Jesus be crucified, heaping the blame on the hated Roman occupiers.

Furthermore, it is assumed that in their understanding the crucifixion of Jesus would have immediately meant the dissolution of his movement. These fishermen and peasants would go back to Galilee, never to be heard of again.

REFLECTION 14. The priestly authorities were able to bully the vulnerable prefect. Sejanus had been executed on October 31 and declared to be of "damned memory." Tiberius had seized the reins of power and sent messages throughout the empire that the Jewish peoples were to be cared for. Pilate knew that he simply could not release a "king of the Jews" despite knowing that Jesus made no such claims. In any case, Jesus had no army, proof positive he was no pretender-king. To ridicule the high priest and his fellows, Pilate insisted on crucifying Jesus as "king of the Jews." How ironic: a crucified, utterly demeaned, helpless man who was "king of the Jews"!

REFLECTION 15. It is noteworthy that the Gospels devote so much of their narratives to the trials of Jesus and so little to their outcome, his crucifixion. The reason is obvious: each of the trials reveals the innocence of Jesus and the culpability of his judges. This points to the innocence of the one able to pay the price of the redemption that Jesus foresaw. Furthermore, it portrays the faith in God of the innocent sufferer, as many slaves and poor people were in a fundamentally unjust society.

REFLECTION 16. The Gospels operate at two levels. According to the surface narratives, we see Jesus traveling, prophesying, debating, betrayed, deserted, arrested, subject to trials, beaten, crucified, resurrected. It's a sequence that comes to an end.

There is another reading, below the surface, with Jesus in private with the Twelve, of which we catch only fleeting images. But it is this private world of rabbi-to-disciple that is in parallel with the surface accounts. The impact and revelation of what had transpired in private begin to be seen and heard once Jesus is killed. What comes out on this side is the now-born church, which had been formed and forged beyond our sight during those previous three years. Evidence for the birth of the church fifty days after that Passover is irrefutable.

REFLECTION 17. Meanwhile members of the Annas dynasty were determined to wipe out the church. Having failed to lock Jesus into the silence of death, it became necessary to employ Paul to remove Stephen, to drive believers from Jerusalem, and, furthermore, to destroy the movement in Damascus. In the early days of King Agrippa I (in 41), Matthias son of Annas secured the imprisonment of Peter and the death of James Zebedee. In 62 Annas II had James, brother of the Lord, stoned for blasphemy. It was nothing short of an Annas vendetta.

REFLECTION 18. The early writings by followers of Jesus point to the birth of the church soon after his trials, crucifixion, and death. Evidence in Paul's letter to the Galatians and in the Gospel of John demonstrate that the birth of the church followed soon after the trials of Jesus.

REFLECTION 19. With Jesus's redemption of the world, his sacrifice did not have a religious setting. There was no temple, no priests, no slain animals. That setting was secular and political, and Jesus was executed unjustly and with cruelty.

The sacrifice of Jesus was noncultic but was the outcome of political jealousy.

The hours of Jesus's crucifixion were climaxed by his death midafternoon Friday. Jerusalem experienced hours of darkness signifying a cosmic redemption. They were preceded by the evils of the previous night when the lonely Jesus faced a series of corruptly conducted trials and beatings.

At every point the events of that night and of the day following were unjust and brutal, a wicked misuse of power. Completely absent was any sense of a duty of care. Meanwhile, Jesus was abandoned by followers and friends, apart from the women and the Beloved Disciple.

INDEX OF AUTHORS

INDEX OF SUBJECTS

Praetorium, 59–60, 148
priests. *See* high priests
Ptolemies, 2, 20–23, 34
Ptolemy I Soter, 21
purity rules, 96, 127

Quirinius, procurator of Syria, 76, 99

resurrection, of Jesus, 201
Roman trials: comparison of Synoptic accounts, 141–46; before Herod
Antipas, 145, 153; John's account,
148–52; Josephus's account, 155–60;
before Pilate, pardoning, 142–43,
144–45, 150–51; before Pilate, questioning, 7, 8, 87, 88, 118, 141–42, 144,
149–51; political charges, 98, 107, 118,
141–42, 144; Praetorium as setting
for, 59–60; standard procedure, 7
Rome: control of Palestine and Judea,
3–4, 34–41, 54–55, 75, 76–78, 109,
195; revolts against, 3, 8–9, 34, 38,
45, 65, 77, 86–87, 115–16, 135, 178–80.
See also specific rulers and officials
Rufus, prefect of Judea, 79, 109

Sabinus, procurator of Syria, 71, 73
Saddok, Pharisee, 3, 45, 65, 77, 135,
180
Sadducees, 77, 80, 99, 175
Salome, 44, 53, 58, 66, 73
Samaias, Pharisee, 65
Samaria, political history, 3, 31
Samaritans, 31, 117, 119–20
Sanhedrin: authority of, 3, 78, 105;
earlier meeting of, against Jesus, 97,
103–4, 151; and Herod, 56; James's
trial before, 176; Jesus's trial before,

135–37; as Ptolemaic *Gerousia*, 21–
22; relationship with high priest, 80;
scribes in, 128; Stephen's trial before,
171; trial procedures, 6, 134, 135
scribes: and Hasideans, 17; Jesus's
debates with, 96–97, 127–28
Sejanus, Praetorian prefect, 4, 110, 111,
112, 117, 118, 143, 146
Seleucids, 2, 20, 23–25, 26, 29, 34
Sepphoris, 123, 125–26
Simon, apostle, 89
Simon, high priest, 79
Simon, Maccabean leader, 29
Simon, rebel leader, slave, 71–72, 87,
123, 135
Simon, rebel leader, son of Judas, 180
Simon the Cananaean/Zealot, 181
Simon Peter, apostle, 61, 62, 89, 91,
94, 169–70, 174, 194
"Son of Man" designation, 72–73,
91–92, 98, 106, 136–37, 139–40, 163,
189, 198–99
Stephen, 106, 108, 134, 170–72
stoning, death by, 97, 98, 104, 106,
140, 151, 171–72
Syllaeus, Nabatean leader, 44, 58

taxation and tolls, 3, 34, 38, 63–64, 72,
76–77, 126–27
temple of Jerusalem: corrupt practices
in, 97–98, 100, 101–3, 105; Jesus's
clearing of, 97–98, 102–3, 105, 136;
rebuilding of, 15, 17, 58–59; Roman
destruction of, 3, 34, 37, 38, 59, 104;
Seleucid control of, 24
Testimonium Flavianum (Josephus),
155–60

INDEX OF SCRIPTURE AND OTHER ANCIENT SOURCES